Smuggling

Exploring World History

Series Editors
John McNeill, Georgetown University
Jerry Bentley, University of Hawai`i

As the world grows ever more closely linked, students and general readers alike are appreciating the need to become internationally aware. World history offers the crucial connection to understanding past global links and how they influence the present. The series will expand that awareness by offering clear, concise supplemental texts for the undergraduate classroom as well as trade books that advance world history scholarship.

The series will be open to books taking a thematic approach—exploring commodities such as sugar, cotton, and petroleum; technologies; diseases and the like; or regional—for example, Islam in Southeast Asia or east Africa, the Indian Ocean, or the Ottoman Empire. The series sees regions not simply as fixed geographical entities but as evolving spatial frameworks that have reflected and shaped the movement of people, ideas, goods, capital, institutions, and information. Thus, regional books would move beyond traditional borders to consider the flows that have characterized the global system.

Edited by two of the leading historians in the field, this series will work to synthesize world history for students, engage general readers, and expand the boundaries for scholars.

Books in This Series

Smuggling: Contraband and Corruption in World History
    by Alan L. Karras

The First World War: A Concise Global History
    by William Kelleher Storey

Insatiable Appetite: The United States and the Ecological Degradation of the Tropical World
    by Richard P. Tucker

Smuggling

Contraband and Corruption in World History

Alan L. Karras

ROWMAN & LITTLEFIELD PUBLISHERS, INC.
Lanham • Boulder • New York • Toronto • Plymouth, UK

Published by Rowman & Littlefield Publishers, Inc.
A wholly owned subsidiary of The Rowman & Littlefield Publishing Group, Inc.
4501 Forbes Boulevard, Suite 200, Lanham, Maryland 20706
http://www.rowmanlittlefield.com

Estover Road, Plymouth PL6 7PY, United Kingdom

Copyright © 2010 by Alan L. Karras

All rights reserved. No part of this book may be reproduced in any form or by any electronic or mechanical means, including information storage and retrieval systems, without written permission from the publisher, except by a reviewer who may quote passages in a review.

British Library Cataloguing in Publication Information Available

Library of Congress Cataloging-in-Publication Data
Karras, Alan L.
 Smuggling : contraband and corruption in world history / Alan L. Karras.
  p. cm. — (Exploring world history)
 Includes bibliographical references and index.
 ISBN 978-0-7425-5315-6 (cloth : alk. paper) — ISBN 978-0-7425-6732-0
(electronic : alk. paper)
 1. Smuggling. I. Title.
 HJ6619.K37 2010
 364.1'33609—dc22

                                                                    2009019439

♾ ™ The paper used in this publication meets the minimum requirements of American National Standard for Information Sciences—Permanence of Paper for Printed Library Materials, ANSI/NISO Z39.48-1992

Printed in the United States of America

Contents

Preface

This book has spent a long time in gestation; this is not entirely, or even mostly, a result of unrealistic authorial ambition. Indeed, because the topic itself required original research, the concept of delay inevitably became built into it. Contraband commerce, by its very nature, is a subject that resides in the historical shadows; as a result, even the most dedicated archivist would find using contemporary databases, indices, and search engines somewhat frustrating. With less than a handful of notable exceptions, most smugglers, like other kinds of criminals, did not keep meticulous records of their illegal activities. This is not an accident. Those who participated in such enterprises wished themselves and their activities to remain anonymous as much as they possibly could. To judge from the existing historical record, most were successful at that goal.[1]

Official legal records, where they do still exist, are scattered in various archives and repositories around the globe; gaining access is not as easy as walking in and asking to see them. Because most of them are not indexed as collections of smuggling documents, many of them are only now beginning to become accessible through computer database searches using keywords such as "smuggling" and "contraband." In the majority of cases, at least in my experience, relevant documents are buried in much larger, generally uncatalogued, collections of state and private papers. As if overcoming such a document dispersal problem were not sufficiently challenging, another problem soon manifested itself. In order to evaluate both historical and contemporary manifestations of smuggling, it became essential to understand the legal systems—or regimes—of more than one place.[2] All of this is meant to explain at the outset why this book's appearance has taken longer than expected. Though its conceptualization took place longer ago than I care to admit, the idea of always wanting to find additional information, even with the knowledge that such information remains widely scattered and deeply buried, made it nearly impossible to collect it especially efficiently or with any kind of economy of scale. Every story was interesting to me, as was its relationship to cases that I had earlier uncovered or encountered in other scholars' works.

My time has also been in much shorter supply than I anticipated when I began to explore the social history and, later, the political economy of smuggling over a decade ago. I managed to do far more *thinking* and talking about the subject with my students and colleagues than I ever managed to carve out the time to get those thoughts systematically down on paper. Nevertheless, over the last few years, various parts of the evidence and argument that appear in this book have been published elsewhere in article form.[3] But a fuller articulation of my argument, along with many new illustrative examples, appears for the first time in this book. I hope that readers will find it to be both clear and persuasive. The case studies that are used to support the argument are meant to be illustrative of larger patterns and processes rather than a demonstration of exhaustive archival research; nevertheless, each case has been chosen because on some level it represents a larger pattern that is observable across both time and space.

When I began the project, I imagined that it would be a study of eighteenth-century Caribbean history, albeit one that was conceptually linked to the rest of the Atlantic World. The bulk of my archival research, for years, dealt with intraregional smuggling around the Caribbean. Many of the case studies that appear in the following pages have been drawn from that set of data. I also began with an assumption: this book would be my opportunity to write a different kind of Atlantic history, one that was not so closely centered in the British North Atlantic. But, as I began to contemplate smuggling in the Atlantic World, I realized that what I observed in this geographical region might well have taken place in other parts of the world, especially those where geographic and legal boundaries were in such close proximity to each other. Moreover, I began to sense that where the political and legal boundaries of states and empires (or imperial states, such as China) were being established, contested, or otherwise changing, evidence of smuggling and contraband would likely be available.

Armed with this small epiphany, I slowly began to mine various European archives to collect historical smuggling data from some non-Atlantic regions.[4] In doing so, it quickly became clear to me that several world regions were engaged in intraregional contraband in much the same way that the Caribbean and the Atlantic World were. Moreover, in some cases, several systems of illegal trade converged across these wide geographic spaces—making the Caribbean a decent jumping-off point for a broader, more global, exploration of interregional smuggling as well. To be sure, there are parts of the planet, such as South America, whose smuggling activities remain largely undiscussed in these pages.[5] Nevertheless, this book will address the role that smuggling has played, and continues to play, in world history. It will argue that individuals, whether smugglers or consumers of those smuggled products, have forced the development and coordination of laws and regulations, even as they have found ways to avoid these very same policies.

Finally, the longer that I worked on this book, and the more time I spent teaching the classical theory of political economy, the more I realized that an argument could be developed about the uses that smuggling has played in political economy. The examples in this book that are drawn from periods outside the eighteenth century and outside the Caribbean support this general approach. It will, nevertheless, remain essential for scholars who are more versed in these far-flung regions, especially those with knowledge of Asian languages, to test the argument that emerged in my research and carry it forward. I am confident that this will prove interesting work indeed.

Acknowledgments

In the undergraduate senior honors seminar course that I teach each year, students present weekly submissions of their works in progress. I noticed a few years back that each student, in advance of discussing his or her paper, would provide what came to be known as the "apologia." This was an apology for bad punctuation, or poor proofreading, or a glaring omission that the rest of the class would already have caught as they read the work. Or sometimes it was for just turning it in late and expecting that other participants would have time to read it and digest it before class discussion. Such introductory remarks have now become ritualized; students are allowed to begin with an apologia that can take no more than a minute or two. I have come to like the concept.

So here's my own apologia. I have worked on this project, in one incarnation or another, for a very long time. As a result, I have accrued debts of gratitude to many people in many places. No brief acknowledgments could hope to recompense all of those who have helped, but I can do nothing else. Though enumerating each individual's contribution would make me happy, it would not necessarily make for enjoyable reading. I'll go even farther: despite terrific help over the years from many people in many places, any errors and omissions in this book are entirely my fault.

The research for this project received funding through fellowships from the Newberry Library in Chicago and the John Carter Brown Library in Providence, as well as, in its very earliest incarnation, from a Fulbright Award to the Bahamas. The University of California at Berkeley has also provided financial support through the IAS Dean's Fellowship Fund as well as from the Professional Development Fund. Over the last several years, this has proven to be a terrific benefit as I have pushed to wrap up the archival hunting and gathering.

I have received extremely helpful advice and generous criticism about various ideas in these pages from Richie Abrams, Dee Andrews, Liza Bakewell, Jerry Bentley, Laurie Benton, Sharon Cohen, Warren Cohen, Bob Fogarty, Richard Godbeer, Rick Halpern, Shan Holt, Fred Hoxie, Bob Marks, John McNeill, Ken Mills, Andrew O'Shaughnessy, Ann Plane, Karen Sawislak, Patti Seleski, Mike Stevenson, Bill Taylor, Nancy Tucker, Merry Wiesner-Hanks, and Mike Zuckerman.

I have, as well, benefited on my many research and writing trips to Britain and France from the personal largesse and critical engagement of Andy Bell and Angela Frain, Alan Clements and Kirsty Wark, Justine Frain, Allan Little, Mary Loftus, Kevin Traynor, and Alistair Whyte and Jan Spencer-Whyte.

Over the years, I received various amounts of (unpaid) research assistance from Vanessa Chan, Noah Cline-Cohen, and Anthony Wise, all of whom have moved on to do other things but whose research has significantly informed this book to one degree or another.

Moreover, I'm truly delighted that this book is part of a World History Series edited by Jerry Bentley and John McNeill, both of whose work has been critically important to my own. The manuscript also benefited greatly from an extremely careful and thoughtful review by Laurie Benton, whose views about how to reshape the final product have proven very wise. Susan McEachern at Rowman and Littlefield seems to know everyone I know, and then some. There's a reason, of course. Her advice has proven invaluable.

Parts of several chapters have appeared in other articles that I have written. I am grateful to the University of Hawaii Press for permission to revise and reprint some small sections of my essays that appeared in the *Interactions: Transregional Perspectives on World History* and *Seascapes: Maritime Histories, Littoral Cultures, and Transoceanic Changes* volumes. I am similarly grateful to the editors of *Pennsylvania History* for permission to revise and reprint part of an essay that appeared in a special supplement to that journal in 1997.

And no acknowledgments could ever be complete without a nod to the people without whose love and support this enterprise would have been simply impossible. I'm grateful to my mother for her curiosity and I'm indebted to David Schulz, without whose energy, tireless support, and enthusiasm, this project would never have come to fruition. He pushed at the end of the day, when I wanted to do nothing more than collapse.

Central America and the Caribbean. University of Texas at Austin, Perry-Castañeda Library Map Collection

Southeast Asia. University of Texas at Austin, Perry-Castañeda Library Map Collection

CHAPTER ONE

—ᴍᴍ—

Smuggling in Regional and Global Perspective
"Truck, Barter, and Exchange"

As the modern world (generally considered to be after 1500) developed, states expanded their territory and consolidated their control over the people who lived in those territories. Such activities simultaneously required more revenue, even as they generated new sources of wealth. These new and expanding states asserted themselves by levying taxes in a variety of forms. In some cases it was a head tax, in others an income or production tax, and in others still consumption taxes on imports and exports. Governments that increased taxes or levied new ones found it essential to secure the support of their populations, at least if they did not want to risk their power, authority, and legitimacy. From the perspective of taxpayers, however, the choice of whether to pay or evade certain kinds of levies in large part depended on whether or not they would personally benefit in any demonstrable way.

Tax evasion has historically taken place in many forms, and this book is concerned with one of them—smuggling. It will demonstrate not only that smuggling has played a role in the construction of states in the modern world, but also that the same people who regulated smuggling often benefited from it. Moreover, it will assert that though states preached free trade, they simultaneously restricted it; those who broke the trading restrictions were rarely punished, which allowed their legal regimes to continue to exist, even to thrive. Those who refused to comply with the trading restrictions—smugglers and their customers—constituted a wide segment of most of the colonies and empires considered in this book. And though these people regularly transgressed statutes, they did not often resort to violence, or feel the need

1

to resort to violence as criminals stereotypically do. In short, their crimes were an essential part of state building, even though refusing to pay taxes directly undermined the state that most of them thought was essential to their protection.

This book's argument will be presented in several parts. Moreover, the book's argument will draw upon examples from across a wide variety of time periods in the modern world, in an effort to show that the same sets of issues appeared at various places and at various times, so that a traditional historical approach that considers change over time to be the main driver of the historical narrative does not work so cleanly here.

Complaints about contraband—or other illegal economic activities—are fairly widespread, if deeply buried across the historical record of many societies after 1700.[1] It is absolutely impossible to claim with any accuracy that illegal trade amounted to 10, 20, 30, or even 50 percent of any given country's total commercial exchange at any particular historical moment; nevertheless many of those who are interested in the subject of smuggling regularly want those of us who study it to hypothesize about the problem's scale and its scope.[2]

I will refuse to make any assertions about the economic scale of global patterns of smuggling in these pages, since I am neither capable of, nor interested in, producing economic models to project what happened in the past; indeed, it would be foolhardy to do so—since any numbers created could easily be proven wrong with the discovery of new evidence. So, while understanding *what* was smuggled and *why* smuggling took place is a fairly straightforward enterprise, discovering *how much* smuggling took place is simply impossible to do with available historical archives. As one early-twentieth-century Indian customs official sagely claimed:

> [t]o hold strong opinions on the subject of *ganja* smuggling is easy. To support these opinions by plausible arguments is also easy. But to adduce anything like proof of these opinions is practically impossible. Statistics are proverbially treacherous, and in the case of *ganja* they are often positively misleading. Arguments based on figures have therefore been avoided as far as possible.[3]

Because no country's bureaucratic or political institutions systematically recorded the quantity of products that its citizens or subjects illegally carried across international borders, any effort to quantify the value, or the scale of, prohibited or extralegal commerce would, by definition, lead to an inaccurate claim that could never be substantiated with enough evidence to prove it convincingly. As a result, this quantitative approach strikes me as precisely the wrong one. Governments simply could not know, and did not know, exactly how much material, of any kind, crossed their porous frontiers; the same could be said of most countries today. Record keeping was imperfect, because record keepers were either willfully or woefully ignorant of activities taking place directly under their noses. Geographic separation between several parts of a single state or empire, like that between metropoles and their colonies, because it was often oceanic, made physical inspection and verification difficult—at least at a reasonable cost. I initially came to this conclusion by considering the Caribbean and the Atlantic World in the eighteenth and nineteenth centuries, but the same could just as easily be said about most states outside of the Atlantic basin, especially those that were engaged across the various parts of the Indian Ocean in the nineteenth and twentieth centuries.[4]

It is therefore much more useful to claim that though smuggling was certainly practiced on a large historical scale, which it almost certainly was, it is ultimately more important to consider smuggling's roles and meanings as devices used in the construction of states, or empires in so much as they behaved like states, in the modern world. By examining specific illustrations that have survived in the historical record and then determining what patterns they formed across an increasingly interconnected globe, it then becomes possible to glean important information about the constantly evolving relationship between these developing polities and those who lived under their authority.[5] Though spotty, the historical records come in various forms, are located in various kinds of record groups, and are readily mined for case studies that can be used to construct arguments and further analysis. Most of the records that have been used in this enterprise are qualitative, but a few provide some small quantitative basis for the book to make a claim or two about smuggling's scale in a particular place.[6]

As indicated, the stories and fragments of stories in these pages nevertheless can help to identify some interesting patterns at the same time that they inform what I hope will be some compelling arguments about the changing relationships between states and empires and those who lived under their rule. For example, this book asserts that studying smuggling allows readers to understand the ways in which those who lived under a particular government, whether individually or collectively, understood that regime's role in their daily lives. A population's flagrant violations of laws, statutes, and edicts could, and indeed should, be seen as a way of telling those in authority that their activities in a particular area, such as collecting imposts and duties, were at the least unwelcome and, at the most, unnecessary or even undesirable.[7] Through their actions, which included legal transgressions, populations chose their own terms for engaging with the state.

An increase in the number of reported cases of smuggling should not necessarily be used to infer that smuggling was on the increase, just as a rise in the number of people who might be arrested or accused of shoplifting should not imply that more people overall are shoplifting. In the case of rising complaints about smuggling, it could simply mean, at least for present purposes, that more people got caught breaking the law or even that government exercised its powers of enforcement as a way to gain control over those who lived under its authority at a particular moment in time because it needed to do so for other reasons. Indeed, there were many reasons for a government to increase legal compliance. It might have needed to assert itself in order to gain legitimacy in the eyes of its population.[8] Or it might have needed to do so simply in order to raise revenue. Even so, by looking at patterns of the enforcement against smuggling over a sustained period of time, it is possible to discern the roles that cycles of peace and war played as states decided whether or not to act against their own subjects, as well as against those from other states, for participating in contraband commerce.[9]

At least in the modern world, it becomes possible to assert that governments expanded their previously acknowledged powers to wage war.[10] Individuals increasingly expected that government would protect their growing amounts of property, which they had frequently accumulated through widening commercial networks of exchange.[11] These expanding webs of engagement, which increasingly crossed oceans and continents, meant the individual and collective acquisition of more property, in more diverse forms. Ships at once transported people, commodities, and luxury goods across regional frontiers. In order to protect this transfer of resources, the European states that increasingly controlled the high seas pushed their own territorial boundaries farther, beyond the purely physical and geographic, and established global legal regimes.[12] The transference (or diffusion) of European legal systems, designed purely for the convenience of those in the metropole, would eventually supplant existing indigenous policies and practices, most of which had fully developed in response to local circumstances and internal momentum long before Europeans arrived and colonized their territories. When we talk about colonization, or imperialism, we must also remain cognizant that the spread of European commercial and legal views around the world profoundly transformed pre-existing local understandings of merchants and commerce.[13]

The new legal regimes at once restricted commercial and acquisitive opportunities for local and native populations, while simultaneously guaranteeing protected markets—and, not coincidentally, rising opportunity for European merchants to profit and accumulate. Given these facts, one might expect to see widespread smuggling by local and native people against their European colonial rulers. To be sure, there was no shortage of that.[14] But this is by no means the entire story. Indeed, as I will argue here, smuggling was practiced by all ranks of people in all societies, including the very merchants whose trade was being protected by statutes that maximized their abilities to generate profits while minimizing their competition.[15] Thus, laws that had been designed to ensure European supremacy in commercial matters by protecting national traders were regularly violated by the very people who were supposed to benefit from them and who, incidentally, had been among their most vocal proponents. But the problem was more widespread than merchants simply wanting things both ways. In the words of one nineteenth-century historian:

> We have not yet done, however, with all the ramifications of this vast and magnificent league [of smuggling], for it extended itself . . . to almost every class of society. Each tradesman smuggled or dealt in smuggled goods; each public-house was supported by smugglers, and gave them in return every facility possible; each country gentleman . . . dabbled a little in the interesting traffic; almost every magistrate shared in the proceeds or partook of the commodities.[16]

The author, in asserting a unanimity of class (or socioeconomic) interests, even suggests that magistrates, who were charged with enforcing the law, could be corrupted by the temptations of cheaper goods or a cut of the profits gained from cheating the government treasury. Moreover, as earlier stated, those who asserted a need for commercial protections and regulations also violated the same rules that they had a hand in creating.[17] In this fashion, for example, eighteenth-century merchants undermined the very states whose authority they invoked to protect their businesses. It thus would appear that Adam Smith's described human propensity to "truck, barter, and exchange one thing for another" trumped the very clear need for government protection of "life, liberty, and property."[18]

In short, smuggling became the way for local populations—of every ilk—to act locally and think globally (or internationally)—in fact, much more globally than their governments had been thinking. The laws, and the legal regimes that both generated and supported them, were located thousands of miles away. Though the technology of transportation improved as time progressed, which brought distances closer together, at least in terms of travel time, the separation between physical spaces expanded with further colonization; in turn, such expansion provided to individuals in every geographic location a rather wide latitude to determine which laws to accept and which to ignore.[19] *Understanding* the laws as written in any particular place, regardless of whether it was a colony, a state, or an empire, in no way guaranteed that the statutes in the books would be followed or even engaged.[20] Indeed, understanding the law is insufficient to determining anything about its enforcement patterns. As United States Attorney General Michael B. Mukasey asserted on 12 August 2008, "Not every wrong, or even every violation of the law, is a crime."[21] Such an argument flies in the face of what most legislators believe, but is much more in keeping with historical facts. Mukasey basically claimed that crimes needed to be charged and prosecuted to be crimes.

We must therefore begin to explore commercial legal restrictions, especially those that differentiated any legal system from its rivals. Though all legal regimes had commercial restrictions in the modern world, they looked different from one place to the next. At the same time, it is essential to consider *plans* to transgress these laws and policies, as well as any *actions* and *negotiations* that resulted from those plans. In this way, patterns will begin to emerge; these patterns reveal a dynamic understanding of the state's relationship with its constituents or the empire's connection to its far-flung subjects.

In order to engage more fully with the ramifications of violating commercial restrictions, and in order to make the argument less abstract for readers, it becomes essential to examine the examples of smuggling activities that I have gathered from archival sources. Using several illustrative cases, it then becomes possible to generate claims about the significance of the contraband exchanges (and/or planned exchanges that failed to come to fruition). By organizing the resulting assertions into patterns, and then showing how these patterns evolved or remained constant over time, it becomes possible to get a much better sense of what contraband commerce meant to its many participants. Though some of the tales that appear in these pages have an anecdotal quality about them, which I hope makes them enjoyable to read, they have all been selected both to make and to illustrate the book's larger arguments.[22] In this sense they are very clearly representative of the kinds of cases that are buried throughout the archival collections.

This book then examines governmental entities (or states, or empires), the commercial restrictions that existed within their geographic boundaries, along with the responses to these statutes taken by their subjects and citizens. Because the commercial statutes in most societies focus most of their attention on property, the ways in which it can be legally acquired, and its continued preservation after its accumulation, most of our attention will be on individuals and groups of individuals who pursued property in a legally proscribed way. Looking at the interactions between the law and those who violated it leads to an important conclusion: smugglers were (and are) the ultimate free traders.[23]

Smugglers and their customers regularly broke down national commercial and legal boundaries without regard to actions other than maximizing their own and others' consumption. Though smugglers were *free* traders—they were really doing nothing more than exchanging one thing for another—they were not perceived to be *fair* traders, who tried to make exchanges while adhering to legal requirements. Fair traders, thus, were not free traders, because they accepted the commercial restrictions placed upon them that also restricted their ability to "truck, barter, and exchange." Smugglers were referred to as the opposite of fair traders; they did not accept the commercial restrictions, at least if they had an opportunity to violate them. In other words, it is possible to claim that smugglers required the state in order to exist, since it was the act of violating the law that defined smugglers by assigning to them a criminal status. Without prohibitive laws, they would have been free traders. Fair traders also required the law to exist, for exactly the same reason—without the law, they would have been free traders as well.[24]

Smugglers of all kinds generally accomplished their goals without resorting to either the use or threat of violence, especially in comparison to the pirates who will appear in the next chapter. Just as many smugglers did everything in their power to escape detection by the authorities, pirates were generally more willing to challenge official authority directly. (This is, in fact, why pirates are much better known than smugglers, despite their smaller numbers and narrower geographic ranges.) In many cases, corrupt officials facilitated smuggling; this was especially true in colonies that were located far from metropolitan legal centers that were determined to enforce the letter of the law. The combination of evasive action and corrupt officials explains why it was only in rare circumstances that smugglers were actually identified, reprimanded, and/or prosecuted; their crimes were generally victimless (unless one counts the legal regime as a victim). G. P. R. James reminded his readers that across nineteenth-century Kent, in England:

> The magistrates and officers . . . were in general so deeply implicated in the trade themselves, that smuggling had a fairer chance than the law in any case that came before them, and never was a more hapless enterprise undertaken, in ordinary circumstances than that of convicting a smuggler, unless captured in flagrant delict.[25]

Though James focused his study on the English countryside, he could easily have been talking about anywhere in the world that regulated commercial exchange, so rarely were smugglers brought to court, let alone tried and convicted. Yet it was precisely the act of getting caught smuggling, or even of being publicly accused of being a smuggler, which allows us to learn anything about the ways in which smuggling took place, as well as the identities of those who participated in illegal trade and the consumption that at once both drove contraband commerce and resulted from it. Even so, a majority of those whom the legal authorities reprimanded, or those who they prosecuted, were generally not themselves involved in grand-scale actions or activities. Rather, the smugglers about whose activities we know anything simply happened to find themselves in the wrong place at the wrong time.[26] Most smuggling was successful in that its participants evaded detection; their actions will forever remain in the historical shadows.

Illuminating the Shadows: Smugglers and Violence, or the Lack Thereof

Even so, there are still plenty of occasions across time and space where legal officials detected smuggling activities of one kind or another. Looking at these instances reveals a few patterns, though none of them shed any light on the scale of smuggling in any particular society or region. Rather, what the instances of smuggling do reveal are a series of relatively straightforward questions about the identities of smugglers, the products they smuggled, and the government's responses. But what of those who got caught, in the words of G. P. R. James, "in flagrant delict"? Who were they and what repercussions did they face?

Getting caught, being identified as a smuggler, was often the last action that a smuggler took—since those who were caught were sometimes turned into cautionary examples for the rest of the population. At the very least, they were subjected to public exposure—in the press, in the courts, or both. At worst, they faced incarceration. Moreover, their property was likely to be confiscated. With these possibilities as potential outcomes, contraband traders who felt that they were trapped, either because they would lose too much property or could not bear a life without freedom of movement, sometimes reasoned that they had nothing to lose by resorting to violence as a last resort; violence came only when smugglers believed they had no other recourse. Such examples should not be treated as global representations of the ways that smugglers operated—since getting caught was in no way a normative experience. Though it is easy to imagine that every smuggler had a particular point beyond which he (or she) could not be pushed without resorting to violence, historians will never know what those points were. The paucity of smuggling prosecutions from the historical record, along with a generalized lack of violence within those cases that do appear in historical documents, do not really allow for a complete theorization, or predictive model, of precisely when a case would turn violent. Even so, the following three examples of smugglers turning violent can provide a rough sense, at least, of what drove smugglers to lash out at their prosecutors or, in their minds, persecutors.

In 1789, residents of Dominica—exactly which ones still remains murky—rowed out to a ship anchored in Roseau's harbor. Customs collectors had earlier impounded the vessel for having on board illegally obtained, or smuggled, goods; in this case, they were shingles from North America.[27] This direct confrontation between the residents of Dominica and the island's customs collector was not really the usual pattern for the residents of Dominica, who were generally attuned to challenging their government through somewhat more passive means. The island changed colonial governments several times after 1761, when it became British after having been settled by the French. France officially ceded the island to Britain in 1763, but again attacked it in 1778 during the American War for Independence, gaining control of the colony until 1783, when France returned the island to Britain, under whose jurisdiction it would remain until its independence late in the twentieth century.

Though they were mostly of French extraction, Dominica's white residents generally preferred British control, largely because of Britain's more "liberal" trading policies.[28] French sugar, much of which came from Dominica, Martinique, and Guadeloupe, was regularly passed to British ships that were loading in neighboring British colonies. It was, in other words, passed off as British produce, in order to fetch a higher price on the British market than it would likely obtain in the French markets.[29] So too did ethnically French residents of Dominica deem French consumable goods, which had to be clandestinely and illegally imported, superior to the legally imported British goods.[30] It was especially galling, then, for both the French and British residents of Dominica to learn that their government acted against its own residents' interests as it seized goods that were meant to be illegally imported and sugar that was meant to be illegally exported. The check on the free market practices of local Caribbean residents was simply unacceptable.[31] In this case, to Dominica's colonists, fair trade was, well, *unfair*.

The Dominica colonists found themselves embroiled in a direct jurisdictional conflict with those whom their metropolitan authorities had charged with enforcing imperial law in the colonies. The laws in question not only regulated commercial exchange, but they also restricted access to all kinds of goods and produce through state-protected monopolies that prevented free trade. In this small colony, far away from bigger island economies such as Jamaica, or more established colonies such as Barbados, one might have expected to see *less* governmental interference—since Dominica was not particularly central to Britain's (or France's) colonial enterprise.

But that was not the case in the 1780s. Dominica's British governor, John Orde, considered himself to be, and was widely considered by others to be, a stickler for details.[32] In the 1789 incident, Governor Orde and the customs collector ordered a party of enforcement officials to confiscate a ship because it contained shingles made in North America. Since the United States was now a sovereign country, it was no longer entitled to any sort of protected status within the British Empire. In cases like this one, the confiscated products would be sold at auction; the costs for the trial and commissions to the officers would be deducted from these receipts. Any remaining proceeds were divided into equal thirds, to be shared by the monarch, the governor, and those officials who made the seizure, or informed on the ship being seized.[33]

The island's residents—ordinary consumers who would have been most likely to purchase these illicitly imported goods had they not been seized—therefore stood to lose. In order to prevent such a loss, those who were involved in the smuggling acted against those who would try to stop such activities. Just as the customs collector was about to order the detained ship to be seized and its illegal cargo confiscated, he himself was captured:

> After some ill treatment and injurious language [the customs collector] was thrown into the Sea, where his Loaded Musket, which had been wrested from him in the Ship, was presented at him and twice snapped without Effect. Whilst he was swimming to the shore . . . afterwards the sloop in some hurry cut one of the Cables and went off to sea.[34]

In all probability, the ship crossed the channel to Martinique where, because it was French, it would have been safe. It would have been legally allowed into Dominica as a Free Port, but then it would have violated French law by returning to Martinique without paying hefty duty. In many cases, this kind of story would have ended here as it disappeared from the historical record; this one does not. About a week later, the customs collector positively recognized the ship that had thrown him overboard; it had returned to Dominica, perhaps bringing in French goods without paying any duty. The ship's captain could not provide a droghing book—a record of its voyages and cargoes that it was required to have on board—so the customs collector seized the vessel and its cargo. The judge of the Vice-Admiralty Court, a merchant by the name of Mr. Stewart, refused to condemn the ship and confiscate its cargo. Instead, he believed the captain's alibi, ignored the customs collector's testimony, and acquitted the ship.[35]

At first glance this story might seem unremarkable. It nevertheless illustrates a moment where those who would have been perfectly happy to flout the law by smuggling prohibited goods without calling attention to themselves felt that they had no other choice than to use violence in this very public act of humiliation directed at the customs officer. In short, Dominica's residents and neighbors punished the very same people who had been charged with protecting them. This was not just a typical response against an unpopular action; rather it was a premeditated act where violence was perceived to be the only action that remained to both the smugglers and their customers. Local residents no doubt felt that the legitimate opportunities to negotiate with authority had completely slipped away from them; there was simply no other attractive choice. John Orde's personality and policies, as well as those of lower-level officials who found success in his government, must also have contributed to the closing off of more typical evasive and nonconfrontational actions.

For the next few years, Governor Orde and Vice-Admiralty Judge Stewart feuded. As Stewart wrote,

> I know of no Lawful Authority that is vested in your Excellency [Orde] and Council to interfere with me in my Judicial Capacity as Judge of the Admiralty, consequently, I do not think it necessary to give my reasons in justification of any Sentences I may have pronounced, they will answer for themselves.[36]

And while Orde and Stewart feuded, mobs attacked customs house officers who had seized goods that, they believed, had been imported into Dominica without the proper payment of duty.[37] On 27 March 1790, for example, "the Public Peace and Civil Government of this colony was interrupted and broken in a most daring and outrageous manner." John Blair, an island resident, gave information to the customs collectors about goods being illegally imported. A mob responded and "in a manner most disgraceful to civil society stript the body of the said John Blair and covered the same with tar and feathers, beating, kicking, and dragging [him] as a public spectacle through the streets of Roseau."[38] It was only the military that prevented the mob from killing Blair. It seems fairly clear that Orde's efforts to eradicate smuggling were increasingly fraying the local population's nerves. This violent pattern would continue; the island was on a path to having a government that could not function with its local population.[39]

Orde's problems with the island's residents had multiplied because his London masters insisted that he get the Island's legislature to raise taxes in order to cover the cost of the colony's government and defense—which were expected to rise as Britain once again prepared to go to war with France in the 1790s. The colony's legislature repeatedly refused to comply, making Orde's already tenuous position all the more difficult. Had he not been so intent on eradicating smuggling, he might have met a less hostile, if not necessarily a positive, response to his request for increased taxes. Before he left his government in the middle of 1792 so that he could explain in London why things had become so difficult in Roseau, the island's capital, Orde accused the island's Assembly of "having an interest in illicit commerce." In fact, he mistakenly argued that because of their proclivities toward smuggling, the Assembly had "withheld from the Executive Power in this Island, authorities, which the Governors have in almost all the others, respecting the Approach of Vessels and the landing and Residence of Foreigners amongst us."[40] Lieutenant Governor James Bruce almost certainly dampened any ensuing jubilation at Orde's departure among those concerned in extralegal commerce. Within a few months of Orde's removal, Bruce suspended Orde's nemesis, Judge Stewart, and charged him with corruption. Stewart wasted no time in appealing to Britain for reinstatement. He knew that Dominica's residents depended upon smuggled products to satisfy their consumer demand.

If eighteenth-century Caribbean smugglers and their customers generally used violence only as a last resort, when all other options for negotiations had failed, the same could also be said of smugglers in other world regions and at other times. Consider the following example from China in 1827; in this story, unlike that in Dominica, British subjects did not attack officials of their own government for interfering with their smuggling. Rather they attacked officials of the legitimately empowered Chinese state, simply because they believed that local Chinese officials were about to put a stop to the demonstrably illegal importation of opium into their own country. In other words, one country's subjects attacked another state's government officials for arresting that state's own subjects for smuggling.

On 5 March 1827, near Lintin[41] Harbor, a small Chinese boat, which almost certainly belonged to some local Chinese merchants, headed for a commercial, yet nevertheless illegal, rendezvous with an American ship that was then anchored in the harbor. Another Chinese boat, belonging to "Chinese

Mandarins," intercepted the first Chinese craft, and took it to a third Chinese ship, a "Chinese War Vessel."[42] At first glance, the interception seemed to be in order; the Chinese government and its representatives appeared to be patrolling the harbor and came across some activity that they considered suspicious and likely illegal. On behalf of the Chinese government, they arrested the perpetrators.

Nevertheless, foreign ships in the harbor, including those belonging to the British East India Company, refused to recognize the Chinese government's sovereign and legitimate right to police its own territorial waters and "armed their boats" as a precaution against their own arrest and detention; they simply did not trust the Chinese to engage in trade in ways that the East India Company desired. European traders who had observed the capture of the Chinese boat surmised, incorrectly it turned out, that one of their own, a foreign trader, had been taken into custody by the Chinese and that the foreign trader needed to be liberated from the clutches of the local government. That no such capture had taken place was irrelevant. At this juncture, foreign merchants demanded that the first boat's captives be immediately turned over to them. When the Chinese responded that they had not detained any foreigners, "a volley of stones was thrown" at the Chinese warship until "the Chinese abandoned the war vessel" and the Chinese captives had been released—to the European traders.[43]

The British East India Company employed European traders. The company's ships, of course, had come to Lintin Harbor to trade opium. This was, then as now, prohibited commerce, much as importing French metropolitan goods or American shingles into British Caribbean territory was contravened.[44] In the "volley of stones" that followed European demands to free the nonexistent European captives, ten Chinese soldiers were wounded and another was killed. Though the British consul in Lintin considered the unprovoked attack on the Chinese ship an act of "unnecessary aggression" and though his view was widely held by other witnesses and participants, no Chinese retaliation against foreign trading ships took place.[45] Those who used violence did so in order to protect their part in the contraband commerce in opium. The British then were defending their Chinese trading partners.

The Chinese government did not make much of an issue out of this particular attack. Instead, the Chinese state claimed, in exactly the same way that European governments proclaimed in the Caribbean half a world away, that it possessed a legal right to stop smuggling anywhere within its territory. The British government did not dispute this point.

Indeed, the British government asserted that its subjects in China, East India Company employees, were not acting forcefully enough to prevent the same embarrassing situation from occurring again. Officials of the London government viewed the British East India Company's threat of "dismissal from employment" to any employees who were found to be involved as insufficient punishment. The smuggled opium came from East India Company controlled territory on the Indian Subcontinent and losing a right to live and work in that territory was too small a price to pay for destroying what the British government increasingly saw as its own national interest. The East India Company clearly felt the pressure when it wrote to its operatives in China:

> We much regret therefore that . . . you did not immediately communicate the particulars . . . including the names of the ships, officers etc. to the [British East India Company] governments by whom the several ships were licensed to trade with China. First, [in order] that if the Bonds or Licenses, under which they traded, contained any penalty for committing aggressions on the Chinese, such penalty might be enforced on the Owners of the ships. [A]nd secondly if the Bonds or Licenses did not contain any stipulation to that effect, in such case, the [British East] Indian governments might have been prepared to devise some regulation, by which a more effective check and control should be obtained over ships engaged in the Chinese trade, *in order that every means within the power of our Servants might be used to our important interests in China from the ill effects likely to result from conflicts between the Crews of vessels engaged in that Trade from India.*[46]

London's official position could not have been clearer; preventing smuggling was in everyone's best interests. Such a position was even codified in one of the treaties ending the Opium Wars.[47]

What ought by now to be clear from thinking about these two cases is that the British state remained concerned that individual entrepreneurs, who were pursuing their own property and profits, appeared willing to violate national laws in order to achieve individual financial benefit. Any violence that resulted from enforcing trading restrictions was simply not acceptable, as it potentially showed the state's weakness in its ability to turn off the open spigots of contraband commerce. Unlike the case in Dominica in 1789, those in Lintin who took the law into their own hands in 1827 may not have violated European law, but rather ran afoul of Chinese law, which, though not well understood by Europeans, was not altogether dissimilar from many European statutes.[48] (At this time, there were no international trade agreements.)

The events in China, which took place two generations after those in Roseau's harbor, bear some additional similarities, in addition to differences, with those in the Caribbean island. In China, two distinct legal systems, British and Chinese, each with its own set of priorities and assumptions, clashed;

in Dominica, it was two factions within a single legal regime. The conflict in China exposed important questions of sovereignty that would within a generation completely undermine the Chinese legal regime; those questions of sovereignty had long been present in the Atlantic empires. This particular Chinese story is not itself wholly concerned with consumable luxury manufactured goods in the sense that eighteenth-century Europeans, whether resident in the Caribbean or in Europe itself, understood them. Nevertheless, the illustration is centered upon a prohibited luxury product, opium, being imported into China a decade before the famous Opium Wars of the late 1830s and 1840s.[49] British government officials in London found themselves sufficiently concerned about the reported incident when they learned of it that they sought more information from their subjects who were then trading near Canton (now Guangzhou). When they received the information that they had requested, the British government quietly urged better communication between East India Company officials who effectively ran the trade—on their own accounts and without governmental sanction—from the Indian Subcontinent and British officials stationed in China. As in the Caribbean, the British government was concerned with ensuring the legitimacy of the local government. It did not wish to be seen as interfering to protect smuggling.

A third example that demonstrates the use of violence as an activity of last resort in smuggling ventures will, I hope, reinforce the point. I have already talked of eighteenth-century British customs officials in Dominica being beaten simply for upholding the law at the direction of the governor. So too have I described nineteenth-century Chinese officials being forced to flee under a volley of stones (or worse) ahead of foreign merchants who challenged the Chinese government's legitimate efforts to interdict the opium trade, well before the two countries would go to war over the opium trade. This effectively got the Chinese smugglers out of trouble with their own government; they were released to their European opium smuggling counterparts. Such phenomena continued on into the twentieth century, though in a slightly different manner. Violence once again can be identified as the action of last resort.

As the French government in Indochina (Indochine) increasingly brought Vietnamese territory under its control in the late nineteenth and twentieth centuries, French metropolitan officials hired local Vietnamese to serve as their representatives around the colony. In some of the more remote villages, places like Van Tuê, French law remained vaguely out of reach to local residents, unfamiliar at best or irrelevant at worst.[50] Here, the legal regimes were not much in contact with each other, except when it came time for the French state to raise revenue for its own support. The French colonial government, like others everywhere, attempted to raise revenue on another luxury product that also affected social well-being: alcohol. The Chinese attempted to ban opium; the French wanted merely to raise revenue by controlling another addictive substance. The colonial government imposed a tax on alcohol at different rates, depending on whether it was imported or produced locally.[51]

In early January 1940, about two hundred local villagers seized and beat two ethnically Vietnamese revenue officers whom the French state had employed to gather taxes from villages being brought under French control.[52] The two Vietnamese revenue officers, who had been offered and who had subsequently refused a bribe of five piastres, wrote up a citation for illegal alcohol production and left the village.[53] Though the townspeople had begged these officials to ignore the prohibited still in which several villagers manufactured contraband alcoholic beverages, their official responsibilities, not to mention a French salary, maybe even a real dedication to the rule of law, caused them to tell the residents of Van Tuê that they would be "written up" for their contraband activities.[54]

The two officials left the village and headed back toward Hanoi, from where they planned to issue their report. It is important to note here that they were wearing French government uniforms, and thus they might be said to have been visibly representing the French Republic.[55] The villagers sent emissaries to follow the officers; they had been tasked with getting the officials to return to Van Tuê. These local residents approached the French government's emissaries with a story. This tale was clearly designed to stave off any punitive action against them. Perhaps more importantly, the villagers surmised that if the officers did as they said they would, increased governmental attention to the village's activities would be generated. Even worse, they reasoned that they might well lose the village still, through which they evaded taxation. If that were not sufficiently frightening, a report against Van Tuê opened the door to the collection of back taxes on the locally produced alcohol.[56] The villagers who followed the customs collectors as they left the village to return to Hanoi approached their nemeses. The villagers then told the officials that the person whose illegal alcohol and still they observed, and whose alcohol they had just confiscated, had become suicidal.[57] Not wanting to have a suicide on their consciences, or having to add a description of one to their reports, the Vietnamese officers quickly returned to the village to see if they could intervene and prevent a suicide. As they entered Van Tuê, a mob of upset villagers immediately pounced upon them, beating them with bamboos.[58]

What caused these *contrabandistes* to act out so violently is exactly the same thing that caused customs collectors in Dominica and Lintin to face bodily harm: by virtue of their office, the customs collectors left the local populations without hope of escape. The smugglers would have much preferred to remain in the shadows. But they could not do so, because the state was about to act against them. All of their previous efforts to evade detection through covert action and bribery had failed to achieve the desired ends. And since they had already been exposed to the state, or in modern parlance "busted," there was nothing more for them to lose by showing officials, of whose laws they disapproved, that regulation had gone too far.

Even so, the violence, and the governmental responses to it, clearly revealed the state's weakness. In none of these three cases is there much evidence that the state officially responded to the threats made against it. We know about the Dominica incident not because there were cases brought in the legal system that established matters of law, but rather because it was widely reported in the local newspapers—and because a zealous government official told the story to his superiors. We know about the Chinese case, not because the Chinese and the British entered into diplomatic remonstration with each other about an inappropriate use of force, but rather because the British government used the incident as a way to assert more control over its own East India Company (which, incidentally, did not meet with particularly great success). Moreover, we can glean something important from the Vietnamese case; the violence against state officials here is what seems most notable, rather than the fact that a remote village produced its own alcoholic beverages in order to avoid French taxation.[59] In all three of these cases, it was the violence that was unusual, and which caused the contraband commerce to become exposed. The cases are, in effect, just the tip of an iceberg that remains wholly submerged. Nevertheless, viewing these incidents allows us to get a sense of how smugglers operated and how they sought to interact with those who would prevent their activities when left with no other options.

This has perhaps been a rather long-winded way of reminding readers that the vast majority of cases of smuggling went undetected and unreported, and that there was little that authorities could do to eliminate it, especially if wide swaths of the population were interested in participating in such activities. Indeed, participation in smuggling so transcended many other social divisions, and involved such wide swaths of the population, that it became a subject against which religious leaders would sometimes preach. In the words of Robert Hardy:

> Of all the occupations, I look upon Smuggling to be the most pernicious. It introduces habits of *Art*, and *Slyness*, and *Deception* and *Concealment*; it leads to the way of *Lying*, and *Cheating*, and *Pilfering*, and *Fraud*; it breaks up the course

of honest and useful labour; it excites a fondness for spirituous liquors and makes men sots and drunkards; it lays the foundation of bad health, of painful and fatal diseases, and of premature death.[60]

Though Reverend Hardy never claimed that smuggling might lead to violence, clearly it could—and did. Smugglers sought to avoid the limelight, to engage in commerce without impediment, legal or otherwise, and to gain access to goods that their governments, in their views, unwisely prevented them from acquiring. Pursuing such products risked a fall into moral decay, whether from the act of smuggling itself, which involved dishonesty and deception, or from consuming products to excess, whether sugar, alcohol, or opium. Moreover, as this chapter has argued, smugglers risked another moral issue: being driven to use violence against others either to cover up or continue their deception.

For that reason there remains an odd perception that smugglers were violent people, and were involved in vicious crimes against anyone who stood in their way. This chapter argues that this was generally not the case, and indeed asserts that smugglers, as Reverend Hardy claimed, sought to operate with "art" and "slyness" whenever possible. Indeed, it was only in rare cases where the smugglers were forced to resort to violence which was, by definition, a much more public act than that to which they were accustomed. The only violence that smugglers typically carried out was not so violent at all; rather, it was perpetrated against legal regimes, across the legal frontiers that permitted a wide variety of states and empires to regulate their subjects' commercial and consumption transactions. Physical violence, whether against people or property, was clearly an action of last resort.

The perception of smugglers as violent people, at least in my view, derives from a very real conflation between smugglers and pirates in the popular imagination. Moreover, the violence that smugglers understood, and occasionally practiced, was nothing compared to the public threats and uses of violence that were regularly perpetrated by pirates. Indeed, smugglers and pirates, for this reason, seem often to have been confused. The distinction between the two groups forms the subject of the next chapter. So too does it consider a few occasions where smugglers "turned pirate" and vice versa.

CHAPTER TWO

—⚬—

"It's Not Pirates!"

The typical response from students, friends, even colleagues, when I explained that this project required researching smuggling at various places and times in world history, has been the befuddled look. After thinking for a few seconds about how to respond to my research interest, the vast majority of them came up with the same few words: "Oh, you mean pirates?" Though admittedly based on anecdotal evidence, it seems easy enough to hypothesize that the confusion between these two discrete criminal activities—piracy and smuggling—is widespread. Even those who ought to be able to distinguish the two subjects from one another have difficulty doing so. And though I have explained the differences between pirates and smugglers whenever I have been provided an opportunity to do so, with good humor I hope, the established misperceptions about the two subjects remain difficult to eradicate. For many people, "pirate" and "smuggler" are destined to remain virtual synonyms. This is unfortunate, as the two words connote altogether different sorts of legal transgressions.

Pirates have captured the popular imagination in a way that smugglers never have and never will. The thought that a movie entitled *Smugglers in the Caribbean* would sell out the local multiplex is laughable; anyone seeing such a film would come away wondering where the action was and how such a film came to be made. Indeed, even as I have been working on finishing this book, modern-day Somali pirates are garnering front-page attention in newspapers around the world, not to mention attracting United Nations resolutions condemning them. At the same time, most cases involving smugglers, if they get reported at all, fail to provoke international outrage and are generally relegated to the columns at the back of the newspaper.[1] Smugglers, both historically and contemporarily, have received far less attention than have their pirate counterparts.[2] Given the nature of their crimes, this is not in any way surprising.

Piracy is a much bolder and more aggressive action than is smuggling; as such, it makes for better headlines. Piracy requires direct confrontation and, in many cases, the threat or use of violence; its victims can be identified and sometimes can even describe their attackers.[3] By contrast, smuggling is carried out clandestinely, always seeking to elude discovery. It rarely uses violence—except, as I argued in the last chapter, after all options, including corrupting enforcement officials, have been exhausted.

Moreover, consumers of smuggled products do not look or behave differently from consumers of other products, despite their complicity in criminal action. Smugglers and their customers therefore could be said to represent the entire social and economic spectrum.[4] Pirates largely came from the working classes—at least in the Atlantic World; they seemingly had a broader social base in the South China Sea in the eighteenth and nineteenth centuries.[5] While both smugglers and pirates hoped to gain access to goods that were otherwise prohibited to them, smugglers more often saw as their sole enemies unnecessary and unpopular laws. The legal regime that created such laws was therefore the victim when its policies and statutes were evaded. In the words of John Wesley:

> Open smugglers are worse than common highwaymen and private smugglers are worse than common pickpockets. For it is undoubtedly worse to rob our father than one we have no obligation to. And it is worse still, far worse, to rob a good father. . . . King George is the father of all his subjects and . . . he is a good father. . . . Be as exacting in giving the King what is due the King as in giving God what is due to God.[6]

Wesley identified the king as the wronged party in smuggling; in fact, he simply attached a person to a legal regime in order to express the point to his audience. By contrast, pirates could *always* identify a specific individual or group of individuals as their prey. Whether it was the king's treasure fleet or the owners of a ship's cargo, pirates were always aware, or soon became aware, of whom they attacked. Though pirates had themselves been outlawed by the state for much of the period under consideration here, many of them saw the economic system and its resulting social inequalities, rather than the legal regime, as the object of their attack.[7]

Expressed another way, smugglers did not want to overturn the existing socioeconomic order though they might challenge its operation. Pirates, by contrast, confronted this order and forcibly redistributed wealth from one group to another through their "depredations." As John Wesley reminded his audience in his anti-smuggling sermon, those who hurt the states' treasuries by participating in smuggling also hurt themselves. Pirates saw hurting the states' treasuries, we can surmise, as directly benefiting themselves. Smugglers, through their actions, often fared quite well under the socioeconomic order in which they found themselves; this was rarely the case for pirates in the Atlantic World after the 1720s, though this claim may well be less true elsewhere or at other times.[8] Piracy, though not nearly as widespread as smuggling, was, and indeed still is, far more visible and dramatic and even romantic. As a counterpoint, consider this description of smuggling in Plymouth, England:

> We met several females, whose appearance was so grotesque and extraordinary, that I could not imagine, in what manner they had contrived to alter their natural shapes so completely; till, upon enquiry, we found that they were smugglers of spirituous liquors; which they were at that time conveying from their Cutter to Plymouth, by means of bladders fastened under their petticoats; and, indeed they were so heavily laden, that it was with great apparent difficulty they waddled along.[9]

This effort by women to appear overly pregnant shows the length to which smugglers were willing to go in order to avoid detection. Compare that to piratical raids.

Though there is a sizable literature on piracy, historical scholarship on smuggling is smaller and much more diffused. Because this is a book on smuggling, moreover, it would be very easy just to ignore piracy and anything "piratical" altogether. This was, in fact, my initial inclination and preference. Yet upon further reflection about the responses I've gotten from colleagues and students for the past several years, it struck me as perhaps a worthwhile endeavor to explain directly to this book's readers who expected to see buccaneers swashbuckling across the pages why that will not be the case and, more importantly, why they should not be disappointed that there are so few pirates here. In order to achieve this, however, it became essential to consider the differences between piracy and smuggling and how those crimes affected (the same) legal regimes differently.

By the same token, it is also extremely useful to consider a few specific historical and contemporary examples in which the two groups—smugglers and pirates—have interacted with each other. This might help to clarify further the differences between these two crimes. Though the two activities generally remained as distinct as, in Wesley's words, "highway robbery" and "pickpocketing," a few individuals managed to straddle the boundary between the two, though never for long; their experiences bring into further relief the differences between piracy and smuggling.

A (Very) Brief History

Scholars of the early modern Atlantic World cannot avoid the argument that pirates, despite their creation of an alternate socioeconomic order for themselves, significantly influenced the creation of the Atlantic World for everyone else.[10] In other words, the expansionist state building enterprises that the European states undertook in the Americas could be both directly and indirectly tied to piracy. (The same was also true in Southeast Asia, as will be considered below.) Pirates from one European state happily harassed those from another; in some cases they combined to attack the richest state, usually Spain. Sometimes they even had licenses from their imperial authority, known as "letters of marque and reprisal," to attack foreign enemy shipping. Those with such licenses were known as privateers; those without them, who acted entirely in their own interests, were the pirates.[11] By contrast, smugglers appeared on the scene much later, well after the new colonial governments of the sixteenth and seventeenth centuries had established their economic principles and legal regimes (or had them established for them back in Europe). In the Americas, at least, the political economy of state building became embroiled with the legal transgressions that are associated with *both* piracy and smuggling.

Though Spain was the first European state into the Americas in the late fifteenth and early sixteenth centuries, the Spanish did not remain alone in the Western Hemisphere. Their economic activities across the region, but most especially the extraction of bullion, drew other European states to the Atlantic's western shores. Most of them hoped to compete with Spain by finding ways to acquire gold and silver from territory that the Spanish officially controlled but did not effectively occupy. If that was not possible, which was almost always the case, European competitors hoped to find ways to get bullion directly from the Spanish themselves. There were several ways in which this could be effected: the first involved producing something that the Spanish would buy with their newly acquired and rapidly accumulating treasure. The second involved attacking Spanish ships loaded with bullion as they returned from the Americas to Spain. By contributing a share of such bullion to the national treasury—theoretically allowing the state to perform its functions, if not actually expand them—pirates gained some credibility with their monarchs, who inevitably had to withstand diplomatic protests from the aggrieved Spanish government.[12]

Such piratical behavior, generally defined as robbery on the high seas, employed at least the *threat* of violence if not violence itself and eventually resulted in the settling of islands across the Caribbean region; without places to spend their stolen treasure, pirates would have been able to do little more than hoard it.[13] Providing opportunities for pirates to spend their cash further increased migration to places that pirates regularly frequented around the Caribbean, such as Port Royal, Jamaica. In turn, this saw the development of local economies, with laws regulating commerce—among other things—and therefore provided opportunities for legally evasive smuggling activities to develop.[14]

The geography of the Americas, especially the wind patterns in an age of sail, meant that there were really less than a handful of viable sea routes back to Europe from Veracruz, where the Spanish gathered their newly mined and minted treasure before shipping it in a convoy back to the Iberian peninsula.[15] When combined with the physical geography of islands around the region, would-be pirates had a relatively easy time picking out the best locations for establishing bases from which Spanish shipping could be attacked. It was for this reason that pirates gravitated to small islands in the southern Bahamas as well as off the northern and eastern coasts of Hispaniola; such bases also allowed them the opportunities to develop and participate in their own economies, as no European state initially operated in those regions.[16]

The emergence of piracy in the Americas proved to be a major nuisance for the Spanish government, as well as for most of the countries whose residents harassed Spanish colonial residents. The masses of correspondence between diplomats at the European courts reveal the Spanish state's great displeasure with the non-Spanish pirates; they viewed them as interlopers in their extractive enterprises, as well as in their colonizing and evangelizing missions. The non-Spanish pirates nevertheless served a tremendously important purpose in the settlement of the Western Hemisphere. Not only did the pirates' bases for raiding and plunder eventually lead to permanent settlements that would later become non-Spanish colonies, in places like Florida and Carolina, but the pirates' actions also led to a partial redistribution of the New World's wealth from Spain to more northerly European states, who competed with it in the mercantile system.[17] The increased flow of bullion into European treasuries other than the Spanish one in turn allowed the

European states to recognize the pirates for their financial contributions, even as they officially disowned them and their activities.[18]

The Spanish government repeatedly complained about the prevalence of non-Spanish pirates residing near its territories in the Americas and near the Philippines. Other European states, however, at least through the seventeenth century's Golden Age of Pirates, claimed that they could not control the actions of their subjects who happened to live outside of their own state's geographical boundaries or "beyond the line."[19] The territories in which these illegal actions took place were under Spanish control, the argument went, so the Spanish needed to police their own geographic space. If the Spanish government could not or would not do so, then the countries from where private individuals migrated to the Americas could hardly be held responsible.[20]

In such a fashion, northern European states used pirates to establish their own colonies in the Americas by subtly transforming the pirates' land bases to thriving refueling stops and then making those into larger towns that required a hinterland to support them.[21] These increased settlements were of course funded by direct attacks on the Spanish treasure fleet. In effect, Spain wound up paying for its enemies to attack it—and set up societies that would compete with the Spanish all across the Americas.[22]

Pirates therefore laid the foundation for many non-Spanish states in the Americas. But this is certainly not the way in which pirates are remembered, or romanticized, in the current popular imagination. Few people now think of pirates as social critics or political economists, or even state builders. Yet their activities addressed all of these areas.[23] It is indeed much more likely for pirates nowadays to be remembered as rebels, individuals, mostly male, who took a visible and strong stand against authority in order to create through their crimes a radically more egalitarian, if also a more violent, world. The appeal of piracy, at least in part, may well have been similar to that of Robin Hood: redistribution of wealth along utilitarian principles.[24] By moving wealth around, pirates also facilitated a more egalitarian global order in ways that might not otherwise have happened had direct state policies and actions been implemented exactly as they were written and intended.[25] Moreover, the world of the pirate ship, with which this book is not at all concerned, has been portrayed as a place where landed society's social hierarchies were replaced with a much more egalitarian system. Pirate ships provided their crews with an alternate reality to the grinding poverty and inequality that so characterized the early modern Atlantic, as well as other early modern societies around the globe.[26] Piracy therefore subverted existing states and their social orders even as it contributed to the building of new states and social orders.

There is, to be sure, also an image of pirates becoming fabulously wealthy, no doubt based on the example of Henry Morgan, who became Jamaica's governor in the seventeenth century. There can be no doubt that this picture developed as a result of pirates' particular fondness for vast consumer spending and debauchery, whenever there was a place for them on land to spend and become debauched. Such an image, however, might well be inaccurate, as many pirates ended their years in the same poverty in which so many of them began their lives. So, while an adventurous life at sea as a pirate may have gone some way toward improving quotidian living conditions for many of these men, it did not universally lead to the kind of independent living to which so many of them must have aspired.[27]

Consumer goods were not always in great supply in the Caribbean, nor were they uniformly present in other societies. As importantly, the pirates' risks of dying a violent death were more than inconsequential; those whom they sought to victimize frequently challenged their activities. For those at the top of the pirate hierarchy, the rewards could well have been great. But for those at the bottom, circumstances would almost certainly have been somewhat less appealing, especially over the long run, as the risks were not borne equally nor were the rewards. Still, pirates saw improvement of their lots in life to be achievable through their actions.

This ought not to be surprising to readers. Pirates lived hard, and found ways to create alternatives to the societies from which they had come, whether they were on board the pirate ship or in settlements that they began and ultimately controlled, such as English Jamaica in the seventeenth century— that is, until they lost control of them after governments decided that they needed to impose a greater sense of order in their expanding empires. In short, pirates generally lived on the edge of society, or just outside it, trying to remake society using the tactics of direct action as they frontally assaulted the rights and privileges that kept them in lower positions than they otherwise would have wished.[28] Smugglers, by contrast, lived everywhere in society—in the center as well as on the periphery.

Of course, the purpose of this chapter is to demonstrate that pirates were emphatically not the same as smugglers. Pirates were, as has already been discussed here, far more flamboyant in their actions. Smugglers had no plans to remake the social order, by contrast, nor did they have plans to establish model new states. Most of them wanted simply to exchange goods without paying more for those goods than was absolutely necessary. Smugglers were, and are, nothing more than free traders. Most of them saw their crimes as victimless, though as John Wesley reminded his audience, it was the state or empire that was denied revenue to which it was legally entitled that eventually assumed the victim's role. Just as *some* pirates earned the respect or admiration of *some* members of civil society for their activities—largely because of the wealth that they generated (even if it was at others' expense)—smugglers earned the respect of *most* members of the social order for *their* activities. But this really meant very little, since most, if not all, members of civil society were in some way complicit in smuggling activities, either as active smugglers or as passive consumers of smuggled products. Indeed, many active smugglers were prepared to go on the record to complain about the actions and depredations of pirates, whom they viewed as needlessly reckless.

From the consumers' perspective, whether in peacetime or wartime, "free trade" always needed to continue if it already existed or be made "freer" in those places where it did not exist. Because smugglers were the ultimate free traders, they sought to move goods to the market—or from one market to another—at prices that people would be willing to pay. Smugglers always sought to facilitate the free exchange of one commodity or product for another; in the nineteenth century, they would be called liberals. Though privateers, and pirates too, could be thought of as free traders, their frontal assault on the law actually made it more difficult for free trade to develop. Since many states, especially in the eighteenth century, wanted to stamp out piracy, they saw no reason to stop there and did not hesitate to legislate commercial restrictions—actually creating more of a space for smugglers to operate. Privateers had the state's permission to attack enemy ships, confiscate their cargoes, and allow those cargoes to enter the foreign marketplace. This happened during wartime, of course. But during peacetime, the demand for foreign products did not diminish. Privateering was not legal then, nor was piracy. Smugglers conveniently filled in the gap.[29]

Several illustrations of the ways in which pirates behaved and interacted with the state and, on occasion, with smugglers follow in the rest of this chapter. These examples generally demonstrate that completely different people with different goals, even if occasionally complementary ones, engaged in smuggling and piracy. Moreover, these case studies also do something else, which is perhaps of greater importance. Each story, by looking at groups of people who straddle the boundary between smuggling and piracy, illuminates clear lines between the two activities. The individuals were at one time smugglers and at another time pirates; their actions in each case diverged rather significantly. As a result, it becomes possible to discern the different responses that government provided to each of the groups. It will come as no surprise that contraband traders generally fared better than pirates. Histories of pirates indicated that the state tolerated smuggling. This history of smuggling will show that this was indeed the case.[30]

Once a Pirate, Never a Smuggler

On 26 November 1750, William Blackstock, a sailor, smuggler, and eventually a pirate, appeared for examination before Gilbert Fleming, the British Commander in Chief of the Leeward Islands. Blackstock's questioning took place on board "the Sloop Christian" while it was still at sea; William Blackstock's appearance was not a typical court date, nor was he accused of an average act of piracy.[31] Blackstock's first confession was that his real name was not Blackstock at all, but rather that he was named William Davidson, and that he had come from Dumfries, in southwestern Scotland. Davidson revealed that Blackstock was his pirate name, one that he claimed he was forced to accept, along with the accompanying actions that were the cause for his present interrogation. This defendant chose to portray himself to the British naval officials who had captured him as a rather unfortunate character, almost deserving of sympathy. Blackstock was charged with piracy, yet it was his smuggling activities that got him into the lamentable situation in which he found himself. Even under questioning, he steered the conversation away from his smuggling activities and chose to focus elsewhere. Typical evasive behavior for smugglers, it helped to demarcate the boundary between contraband traders and pirates.

In October 1750, just a month or so earlier, Blackstock commanded a merchant ship that traveled from Rhode Island to Ocracoke Island, just off the North Carolina coast. At Ocracoke, he *found* "a Spanish galleon[32] . . . unloading goods and putting them on board two sloops (the names of which he doth not know) to transport them to Virginia."[33] One of the ships was loaded and ready to sail north to Virginia, according to Blackstock, while the other was not. That he claimed not to know the name of the two ships illegally loading and unloading in British territory is most likely an effort to obfuscate his own smuggling activities. In any case, North Carolina's governor found out about these ships' illegal presence in Ocracoke, and ordered that they be hauled to "Newburgh,"[34] where the governor was then resident. Blackstock's account matter-of-factly discusses the presence of a Spanish ship being unloaded at a remote island, far from settlement, and its contents being transferred to local sloops for distribution. In such a fashion, Blackstock basically admitted that smuggling took place at Ocracoke, and that he observed it. He did not, however, confess to dealing in contraband. Instead, he left open the obvious question of why a Rhode Island coasting ship would be landing at remote Ocracoke in the first place.[35] He never claimed, as did other vessels that got caught smuggling, that his ship was there to take on fresh water.

Blackstock continued his confession. He described how he had met Owen Lloyd, another sailor at Ocracoke, who claimed that he had "rescued" the distressed Spanish galleon coming from the Caribbean; he claimed that it was without either a master or "rider."[36] The story sounds suspicious; most likely it was meant to cover up a Spanish smuggling mission to North America. Spanish subjects in the Americas frequently found willing participants to engage with them in trade that their own government had restricted. But, of course, no one admitted to smuggling. Instead, Blackstock reported that Lloyd told him he had assumed command of the distressed Spanish galleon while it was at sea and that it was Lloyd's idea to tow the ship into Ocracoke. The reason that the Spanish ship was in distress is never discussed; it is quite possible, even probable, that Owen Lloyd was a pirate who had captured a Spanish galleon and was looking for a place to dispose of his newly acquired treasure; it is also feasible that he simply salvaged a wrecked ship or saved one in distress, as he claimed was the case when Blackstock inquired of him. It is also possible that the Spanish ship was simply involved in a smuggling mission in North America, and was not there for any reason other than of its own volition.

Whatever the case, Owen Lloyd soon proposed that he and his brother John, along with William Blackstock, should steal the two American smuggling ships, which had already loaded aboard the Spanish goods from the Spanish galleon. Since the galleon itself was being hauled to New Bern at the governor's request, likely for trial and condemnation, these criminals must have thought that it would be easier to steal a boat during the authorities' preoccupation with the Spanish galleon. Blackstock would later claim that he initially considered this a joke of a plan, until the Spanish galleon and its remaining crew actually departed for New Bern with most of the North Carolina colony's officials accompanying them, leaving the smugglers alone at Ocracoke. It is at this point that Blackstock met a dozen other North American sailors; they collectively decided to "liberate" the smuggling ships that were then anchored at Ocracoke; their plan, such as it was, required them to sail south, into the Caribbean Sea. None of the North American sailor/smugglers, except for Owen Lloyd, claimed ever to have been to the West Indies; there is, however, no evidence either to support or disprove this claim. When they left North Carolina on 9 October, Lloyd and his newly assembled crew planned to sell the Spanish goods at St. Bart's—at least that is what Blackstock reported to Gilbert Fleming after he had been caught. Thus, the crew left their own anchored ships at the Outer Banks and made off with the two boats that had been illegally trading with the "distressed" Spanish ship. At this precise moment, the smugglers became pirates, as they openly stole property and committed robbery on the high seas. The search party of law enforcement officials who pursued them soon faded into the horizon.

William Blackstock continued his story by describing how he and his crew went to Norman Island, an uninhabited island near Tortola in the Virgin Islands. The crew of smugglers turned pirates anchored there, unloaded their stolen ship, and found "Fifty chests of dollars, and containing each three Baggs and each Bagg a thousand dollars."[37] The ship also contained wrought silver, 120 bales of cochineal (each weighing about 130 pounds), 17 bags of indigo, and 60 bags of tobacco. The pirate crew divided the treasure, with most members receiving four bags of treasure—more than a chest for each man.[38] These men appeared to be doing very well indeed, especially given that they had escaped being arrested for smuggling only a few days before.

The crew quickly buried their bags of coins and silver on uninhabited Norman Island. Or, rather, they buried most of it. Owen Lloyd and one of the other sailors each took one of their chests back on board the stolen ship, putting it back with the cochineal and some of the manufactured silver articles. Lloyd's crew discovered him attempting to hide his share on the stolen boat; the crew confronted him and demanded to know what he was doing. Lloyd pretended that he and his mate had "come to stop a leak."[39] As soon as the crew seemed satisfied, they stopped their questioning and left the ship. Lloyd immediately hoisted anchor and stole the previously stolen ship, effectively marooning his accomplices on Norman Island. He then sailed his boat to the Danish Island of St. Thomas. While there he took a share of his booty and "bought a sloop for himself" and then sailed the newly purchased sloop to St. Eustatius, a Dutch free port in the Caribbean. The British would later refer to this Dutch colony as " a nest of Smugglers, Adventurers, Betrayers of the Country, and Rebels to their King."[40] Owen Lloyd hoped to acquire consumer goods, which he could pay for with stolen Spanish gold, at St. Eustatius. He would either then have the option of consuming the goods himself or exporting them and smuggling them into other territories for an inflated price. Blackstock, whose deposition largely provides the story's details, was unclear about exactly what Lloyd planned to do. This was perhaps unsurprising, given that Blackstock recalled this information later, since he was still in the Virgin Islands. It is impossible to say with any certainty whether Owen Lloyd intended to work in the future as a smuggler, or as a pirate, or as some combination of the two. What is clear is that he used his piratically obtained booty to acquire property that could be consumed.

Meanwhile, William Blackstock, along with another of the smuggler-turned-pirate crewmembers, managed to make his way to nearby Tortola; the men did so in the hopes that they might be able to claim a reward—by alerting authorities to the treasure that they themselves had buried! Recall that these men claimed to be first-time pirates; the newbies reasoned that coming clean, or at least partially clean, would have allowed them to go back to the smuggling traffic with which they were more comfortable. When they reached Tortola, they went to see the island's president to tell him that a ship and its pirate crew had been to Norman Island and had put ashore twenty bags of cochineal, two bags of indigo, and a quantity of useless tobacco. They knew about this, they claimed, because they themselves had pulled these goods out of a wreck at North Carolina. In short, they revealed to Tortola's president the least valuable part of the treasure, without informing him of their own part in acquiring smuggled booty. The president went with them to Norman Island to verify their claims; unsurprisingly, the farfetched story checked out. William Blackstock and his partner in crime apparently seemed to be in the clear, or so they thought. They had helped to recover either a missing or stolen cargo to local officials; the government would thus get a hefty share of the proceeds after the goods could be sold, and so would they. They had therefore preserved for themselves part of what they had stolen.[41]

Things did not, however, work out the way that they had planned. Real problems with the law began as soon as Blackstock and his friend involved the local officials. Unbeknownst to Blackstock, by the time the president of Tortola met him, the robbery/piracy in Ocracoke had gotten some attention in the region and "[s]everal people who had discovered or heard of the dollars were busy looking for and seizing them" in Norman Island.[42] Blackstock later claimed that he did not know from where the locals gained their knowledge of buried treasure on an uninhabited island; it could even have come from leader Owen Lloyd who was off consuming with his ill-gotten gains. Though the regional residents were busy searching for buried treasure when Blackstock and the president of Tortola arrived back at Norman Island, Blackstock nevertheless managed to convince the local official to divide up the previously identified loot. Tortola's president naturally kept his share, he claimed, for governmental purposes. The plan then required Blackstock and the other pirates to return to Norman Island a bit later, so that they could dig up their own share of the buried treasure—they had not informed authorities about *all* of the buried loot. Blackstock must have thought, as his plan took shape, "all's well that ends well." This was perhaps an appropriate thought for a smuggler to have, but it was far from accurate, since the treasure had been acquired through piracy—a different sort of crime altogether. Smugglers used deception to good effect on a regular basis; this was yet another opportunity for them to have done so. For a variety of reasons, however, this time was exceptional. It just did not work out.

When Blackstock went back to Norman Island two days later in order to retrieve that part of the treasure that he had not revealed to the authorities, he soon discovered that his buried loot was gone. He later learned that the president of Tortola, along with his son and a few others of their acquaintance, returned to Norman Island after paying off Blackstock and his accomplice for their information. These local officials then clandestinely dug up the treasure—intending to keep it for themselves. In this case, official corruption had neatly trumped piracy. Blackstock had been outwitted, which does not seem an especially hard task to have accomplished. His next response was to leave the area, following a smuggler's oft-trod path of evasion. He took some of the stolen money that he had not buried, bought a sloop, and began to sail toward North Carolina, where he hoped he could evade arrest for his piratical actions, perhaps even resuming his old life as a coastal trader and contraband commerciant. He got as far as St. Eustatius, before learning that Owen Lloyd had been imprisoned for piracy; he then sailed toward Anguilla, where he himself was taken into custody. In his examination before the naval commander of the Leeward Islands, Gilbert Fleming, he omitted any details of violence that might have taken place along the way; this was to be completely expected.[43]

Just a few weeks later, in November 1750, Commander Fleming issued a proclamation demanding that all of the remaining pirates be arrested and turned over to him—from wherever they were found hiding. The fact was, however, that several of the happenstance pirates had already been captured; it is likely that Fleming knew this and made his public demand to show the local population that he would never tolerate those who committed piratical acts within his government. More importantly, Fleming demanded that the inhabitants of territories under his control "deliver up to me . . . all and every part of the said treasure come to their hands, possession, or power, upon pain of being prosecuted as Law directs, as Partys and Accessories to the same Piracy and Felony."[44]

Fleming ordered the lieutenant governors of the Leeward Islands to search and seize any of the treasure that the inhabitants of their islands might have taken. Several weeks later, in early December, he reissued the proclamation and indicated that he had received *some* of the treasure, and had allowed those from whom he received it to keep a third of it as their salvage fee. In short, he rewarded the thieves of previously stolen property by allowing them to keep a portion, in order to get a majority of it back. This was, in fact, what William Blackstock intended to do. Fleming offered that any other residents who might come forward, if they had not already done so, a deal in which they kept one-third of what they turned in as a salvage fee. In addition, he offered locals a share of any cash that they might otherwise "recover" as well as a reward for any information they might possess that would lead officials to the stolen dollars. These offers again indicate the importance of the desire to retrieve the stolen Spanish dollars; whenever piracy was involved, government almost certainly would have had to respond to diplomatic protests and demonstrate that it took efforts to restore what it could to its rightful owners.[45] The president of Tortola's clandestinely unearthed treasure still remains buried; it is however possible that he withheld a third part of it as a salvage fee and turned the rest in to Fleming. He would have done so for precisely the same reason that Blackstock went to him in the first place—as a way to avoid or deflect suspicion. In this way, his corruption or even complicity in other illegal activity such as smuggling would have eluded the authorities when they were actually vigilant.

What this story should clearly reveal to readers is the way in which piratical actions received different responses from those that smuggling cases generated. William Blackstock was arrested and imprisoned for his crimes, as was Owen Lloyd. It is not at all clear from those who dug up the treasure, effectively smuggling Spanish coin into the local island economies, were ever punished, even though they were "accessories to Piracy."[46] Indeed local officials provided their residents a way to legitimate their acquisition of stolen property by requiring them only to return two-thirds of what they had acquired. In this way, the state effectively negotiated with its populations, preserving its own authority and legitimacy in the process. For their part, local island consumers were able to keep some of what they should never have had. But it is certainly worth noting here this book's claim that if a foreign government had not been directly involved because of the acts of piracy, locals would have been able to keep even more of what had been smuggled into their midst.

The Pirates Did It! For Real!

Just a generation later, in 1771, the Caribbean merchant house of Hay and Kingsley wrote to the British government from its offices in Antigua. These merchants *claimed* that six weeks previous to their letter, they had sent one of their small boats, the *Betsey*, from Antigua to nearby St. Thomas, then under the control of the Danish government, "to collect some debts due to them there."[47] (Why there would have been debts due to a merchant house in British Antigua from residents in Danish St. Thomas is an interesting question in itself; it might well be that Hay and Kingsley were involved in some sort of smuggling activity, and hoped to pass beneath the Coast Guard's patrols or "radar.") Claiming that the *Betsey* was simply collecting legal debts would seem to legitimize the company boat's location in foreign territorial water. The origins of the debt, the merchants hoped, would not be called into question, even though they were complaining to government.[48] According to Hay and Kingsley, the debt was to be paid in hardwood posts, given the absence of currency around the region. This, too, was suspicious—why posts? Posts would almost certainly have come from British North America, so the question of how they got to the Danish island needs to be considered here. It certainly seems plausible that Hay and Kingsley had a plan to smuggle these posts from St. Thomas into Antigua or other neighboring islands. But that is not what makes this story so interesting.

As the ship's crew loaded the *Betsey*, they claimed to discover that the quantity of posts that they loaded did not actually fill their ship's cargo hold. It would then be logical for readers to wonder why such a big ship was sent to a neighboring island in the first place; debt owners knew the amount to which they were entitled, as well as prices current for any commodities in which they were dealing. Few of them, if any at all, would have been likely to send such a large vessel to collect such a small debt, *unless there was some other business to be had.*

The *Betsey's* crew, if the letter from their employers is taken at face value, then independently decided to visit nearby, and uninhabited, Crab Island. There the crew independently decided to cut down enough additional wood to fill their ship, before returning to Antigua.[49] While the crew was on shore, collecting wood, "[a]n armed sloop, belonging . . . to the Subjects of the King of Spain . . . attacked, boarded, and forcibly carried the said schooner to Porto Rico, with the Master and three men, who was all that were on board."[50]

Hay and Kingsley claimed that this was piracy, since the seizure was made during peacetime. But there could also have been another explanation. The crew could have been engaged in contraband commerce inside Spanish territorial waters. In their remonstrance to the British government, the merchant firm made an effort to frame the problem in such a way as to elicit a governmental response. Hay and Kingsley claimed to their government that their little debt-collecting schooner, like many others in the region, had to be armed in order to "prevent little piratical boats and other vessels from boarding and plundering them."[51] This corner of the Caribbean, they asserted, was generally believed to be home to pirates, as it lay in a decent place to attack passing ships. Moreover, the merchant company preemptively claimed that this seizure, this piracy, *might* have been justified *if* its ship was engaged in contraband commerce. It was as if the firm anticipated their government's likely response. But because Hay and Kingsley maintained that their employees were not smuggling, and were merely collecting debts and chopping trees down on a nearby uninhabited island, the merchants sought governmental intervention against the Spanish in the region. It did not matter that the crew did all of this without instructions from their employer, or so they claimed. Though contraband trade was "generally done amongst these islands with impunity," they reported, the piratical attack against the *Betsey* seemed to them an improper and unfair response to their wholly peaceful purposes. In short, they acknowledged patterns of illegal trade in the region, claimed not to be engaged in them, and then represented themselves as victims of pirates, of whom there were not actually very large numbers in the 1770s, at least in peacetime.

Hay and Kingsley felt it necessary to claim explicitly not to be involved in contraband trade. Their ship, "by sundry affidavits sent to the Lieutenant General was upon no such . . . contraband trade, nor had she the value of five shillings of goods, wares, or merchandise on board. . . . "[52] Whether or not it really was a victim of piracy, as they represented, or whether the "pirates" were nothing more than the Spanish *guarda costa* capturing the *Betsey* after it had illegally, or perhaps even inadvertently, traded in Spanish territorial waters, the Antiguan merchants demanded that they be made whole for their losses. They made their claims to the British government, with the hope that a diplomatic protest could get the Spanish government to release their boat; this was standard practice for dealing with acts of piracy. It was therefore extremely important to Hay and Kingsley to stress their legitimate and benign trading intentions again and again—precisely so that their government would have an easier time if it could be persuaded to seek restitution from the Spanish government. Of course, the Spanish would perhaps have an alternative view of the *Betsey's* capture.

In order to assert their aggrieved position, the merchants needed to show, as they attempted to do, that the Spanish ship that had captured their vessel (whose name, incidentally, they never provided) was clearly involved in an act of piracy. Had the Spanish ship not been a pirate ship, but rather a legitimately employed *guarda costa*, the odds of recovering the confiscated cargo would have dramatically declined. The Spanish could easily assert that the *Betsey* really was involved in smuggling and it was taken as part of a normal law enforcement action. Claiming and, if necessary, proving piracy provided Hay and Kingsley with a relatively straight and clear, if not always easy, path to recovering their timber cargo. Thus, in this way too were smuggling and piracy related. It was piracy's violence against the innocent that caught and galvanized both the attention of government and its subjects, especially when such piratical violence could be laid as a complaint before a royal court or its diplomats. Smuggling did not provoke nearly as strong a response; indeed, its actions tended to be minimized and even written off altogether because they were so elusive. It was always much harder to overlook piracy's visible seizures, threats, and uses of violence. Smugglers, in other words, used the idea of being victims of piracy in order to gain their government's help—even as they denied the government the revenue, through their smuggling activities, that it needed in order to help them.[53]

More of the Same

Across time and space, there was more continuity than change to the basic distinction that I am drawing in these pages between pirates and smugglers. For example, in April 1809, the Grand Jury of Prince of Wales Island (now known as Penang, Malaysia) wrote to the British East India Company's Court of Judicature. They complained to the company about the "deficiency in the police establishment."[54] The reason that the Grand Jury issued its complaint was that a "numerous band of pirates has lately infested these straits." The pirates were landing "with impunity in various parts of the island."[55] Of course, smugglers landed with the same impunity at Prince of Wales that they did in many other places and at many other times. But what provoked the Grand Jury at this moment in time, and what made pirates the object of their collective complaint and scorn, is precisely the same thing that differentiated smugglers from pirates—the threatened use of violence. The accused pirates used violence to achieve their goals or, in the words of the Grand Jury, they "continue daily to commit the most daring and atrocious outrages so much so that no less than eight boats with their crews have been seized within this harbour and carried off by these piratical robbers in the last ten days."[56]

The Grand Jury went on to express its very grave concern that these pirates were going to make life difficult for the island's colonial residents, natives, and Chinese migrants. Most especially, the Grand Jury claimed that if a stop was not put to piracy, "the whole petty commerce of the island will be annihilated, the lives of his majesty's subjects sacrificed and endangered and the supplies indispensably necessary for the subsistence of the inhabitants of the settlement entirely cut off."[57] Piracy, boldly and dramatically, interfered with the "petty commerce of the island," including, no doubt, whatever smuggling enterprises in which its residents were engaged.[58] In this way, the piratical actions could again be seen as at odds with those of the smugglers—or "free traders." Local leaders at Prince of Wales reasoned that without the maintenance of a viable police force, that is one that could stop piratical raids and their resulting theft and violence, the newly emerging colony would fail. In short, the Prince of Wales Grand Jury demanded that government officials provide more than a basic police function, even as residents of the territory were involved in all kinds of regional and interregional smuggling activities. Their plea to the East India Company, of course, failed to mention this important fact. The residents wanted protection from a state that they actually undermined when they engaged in their contraband activities.

In 1829, a generation after the Grand Jury's protestations in Penang, the British East India Company's acting secretary of government, G. W. Salmond, received a letter from a British naval officer. The letter claimed that on 12 April 1829, members of the Navy's crew observed five boats floating near the beach on a local island off the west coast of the Malay Peninsula. When they were spotted, four of these boats immediately hoisted their anchors and quickly made off toward Pulau Bunting, which was an uninhabited island. The boats' oarsmen rowed quickly, and they were soon "out of the range of our ship." This allowed the crew of the four boats to escape from the British naval forces, who, even though they pursued these small boats using small boats of their own, became concerned that they were getting too far from the rest of their own crew and the safety that it provided.[59] Such a story might lead readers to suspect the smaller boats of engaging in smuggling.

When the British crew returned to the area where the previous boats had been spotted, they discovered that the "boats which had made off were from very large Pirate prows, with from twenty to twenty five men in each."[60] These prows had captured a local trading boat that was engaged in "petty commerce." This boat was loaded with rice, tin, paper, *and other goods* from British-controlled Penang. When the British ship spied the activity, the pirates "were in the act of plundering her." Most likely the pirates had attacked a local coasting ship that, like the Hay and Kingsley example in the Caribbean, was itself engaged in petty commerce, if not smuggling.[61] The pirates made their escapes from the British officers; when they did, the British learned that they had taken with them all of the pepper and a third of the rice that had been on board the small boats. The pirate crew almost certainly intended either to consume these staples or possibly even to sell them. The British crew also found two severely injured men who had been held captive and two others nearby who had luckily escaped from the pirates. The survivors all indicated that they had fought for a long period of time before being "obliged to capitulate." The surviving crew also indicated that Tengku Kudin, a well-known pirate in Southeast Asia, coordinated the pirate raid on small-time commerciants.[62]

As can be seen from the above examples, pirates never hesitated to use force or at least threaten it against those who came between them and their desired cargoes. Moreover, pirates thrived in several places where intraregional shipping between territories was both common and regularly scheduled, places like the Caribbean and the Straits of Molucca. Pirates regularly found ways to prey upon ships, as well as people, who were either unsuspecting or unprepared as they passed through these areas—including smugglers themselves. Their goals differed dramatically from those of smugglers, as they could in no way represent themselves as either "free traders" or "fair traders." There was no trade for pirates; there was only theft.

More Recently: Understanding Somali Piracy

Contemporary piracy is actually not much different; that is, most of the characteristics of the distinction drawn here between smuggling and piracy remain the same even today. This ought to become apparent as a few contemporary examples of piracy are considered. In order to do so, however, it is important to say a few things about recent usage. Current news reports are regularly filled with stories about pirated goods, which are more accurately called copyright violation, intellectual property theft, or trademark and patent infringement. Such activities nearly always refer to making copies of luxury goods such as handbags, or duplicating songs, videos and/or films that are then distributed without the original manufacturer's, author's, or other copyright holder's permission. It is, like maritime piracy, theft, of course, and while it is not violent in the sense of plundering a boat or a village or swashbuckling across tropical archipelagos, it can be considered legal violence in that it deliberately and publicly flaunts the laws. It does not harm the state, however, in exactly the way that smuggling does; rather, it creates individual victims from those who own the legal protections of patent and copyright. In this regard, it also resembles maritime piracy.

For example, when I lived in Nassau, in the Bahamas, the video rental stores on the island illicitly obtained videotapes in order to rent them to their customers. The stores somehow obtained these films before they had been generally released; shop employees quickly made copies of them in the back of the store. Similarly, walking down the streets of almost any major city, one is barraged with "fake" luxury goods; in some cases they are identifiable as fakes, but in others the difference is not so easy to detect without looking at the price. When considering the production of such objects, it is certainly possible to discern *both* an intention to disobey the law and a challenge to the government that it enforce its own laws and statutes. Because the crime is against individuals, or companies that can be considered akin to individuals, it is much more difficult to interdict systematically.[63] The same could also be said about today's more traditional maritime pirates. They too have been able to find a way to negotiate with government, or rather other individuals, in order to avoid actually using violence. They do not, however, hesitate to threaten its use in order to achieve their aims, which, of course, clearly differentiates them from smugglers.

Over a period of years, piracy in the seas off the Somali coast has increased; the area is now known as a hotbed of pirates, as the Caribbean Sea, Barbary Coast, and Straits of Molucca once were. Pirates in this region are generally successful at capturing and boarding ships, making hostages out of their crews, and then ransoming both ship and crew back to their wealthy owners. The pirates are interested in maximizing their personal acquisition of wealth; attacking ships loaded with bullion and plundering supply ships are no longer viable possibilities, so they have resorted to the next best thing. Modern-day pirates pursue ships from those countries that have the greatest ability to pay to get their ships back. When the pirates receive their ransom, some of it can be actively invested in additional weapons, boats, and sophisticated tracking systems that will allow the pirates at once to identify their prey *and* avoid those who are set up to prevent them from doing exactly that.[64] These modern-day pirates have simply updated their arsenals of weapons over the years, but their actions continue as before.

There are generally believed to be about five main groups of pirates off the Somali coast. The weak Somali state claims that it is unable to stop them; others, however, believe that the government is complicit in their attacks and raids.[65] According to the British Broadcasting Corporation, pirates seized more than twenty-five ships in 2007. This makes the area around Somalia one of the most dangerous areas in the world for ships to traverse.[66] Even more recently, in the spring of 2008, a band of Somali pirates attacked a French yacht off the Somali coast, holding its thirty-person crew captive. This direct attack on a private ship and its crew clearly illustrates exactly the kind of maritime piracy that has been considered in this chapter. The pirates seized the French yacht's crew, publicly threatening them with violence, and demanded that the French company that owned the ship pay a ransom in order to get its ship and employees back.[67] If reporting on the subject was correct, the French owners paid a sum close to $2 million to get back their property.[68] Nevertheless, the ransom's payment did not completely finish this particular story, though it seemed to end like most other similar stories in the region.

According to reporters, "Gen. Jean-Louis Georgelin, chief of staff of France's armed forces, said the pirates had released the hostages after negotiations with the ship's owner. No weapons were fired, he said, and the hostages were taken to safety."[69] The mechanism of exactly how the hostages gained their release was never fully explained. The *New York Times*, moreover, said little about it except to note, "when the pirates went ashore, a French attack helicopter chased a vehicle carrying some of them. Local reports said eight people were killed, but the office of the French president, Nicolas Sarkozy, denied any pirates had died."[70] The difference between eight lives and no lives is not an insignificant one.

The French general claimed that six pirates were taken into custody and, as if to prove it, they arrived in Paris just over a week later to await trial.[71] This report does not markedly differ from an op-ed in the *New York Times* that argued that "French commandos went in with guns blazing and captured a gang of pirates who days earlier had hijacked a luxury cruise ship, the *Ponant*, and held the crew for ransom."[72] More recent reports have even suggested that the pirates whom the French will be bringing to trial are in some way related to the president of Somalia. If true, this would again indicate continuity with past piratical practices in that there was sometimes collusion between the state and/or its officials, both of which benefited from piratical income, and the pirates.[73] In other words, the Somali state, or perhaps its officials who claimed to represent it, sanctioned piracy especially as a way to enrich its own treasury. The general weakness of the Somali state lends further support to this idea. About $200,000 or 10 percent of the $2 million ransom was recovered with the captured pirates.[74] The 90 percent of the ransom that still remains at large ought to be considered to have been divided among the pirates and given, at least in part, to the otherwise weak Somali state—as a kind of payment not to intervene and as a way to acquire sorely needed foreign capital. It would have been consistent with actions of earlier pirates elsewhere in the world.

The following month, May 2008, another group of Somali pirates attacked a Jordanian ship en route to Mogadishu; the ship was loaded with sugar to be unloaded in the Somali port. The pirates seized the boat quite near its destination, and then began to navigate it away from the port. Ironically, the four thousand tons of sugar on board, which had come from India as an aid shipment, was intended to help alleviate Somali poverty by providing calories to its malnourished population. Of course, the pirates did not care about this; they were determined to get at the cargo solely as a way to get cash f or themselves, much like their earlier counterparts. This incident then became the latest in a series of piratical moments off the Somali coast, where pirate "mother ships" are known to lurk.

The usual way in which the pirates operate in this region, if news reports are accurate, is for the pirate crews to wait offshore until they are ready to attack, at which time they send speedboats full of armed men, who proceed to take over ships transiting the region, along with their crews and cargo. Their purpose is solely to ransom back the ships to their legal owners. These cash ransom payments effectively become the pirates' income. It could easily be spent as the pirates wish to spend it; this alone puts them in a different category than most of their countrymen who face high rates of poverty. Pirates acquire their incomes through direct confrontation, making demands, and threatening to use force and cause harm if those demands are not met.

Pirates in both the historical and recent past have been at once opportunistic and highly organized. Pirates were, and are, aware of what they have captured—and how best to dispose of their ill-gotten gains. Moreover they did, and still do, have plans to escape should the going get tough and their situations start to evolve in unanticipated ways. As importantly, pirates also generally divided the spoils among themselves; they still do. In almost all of these points, pirates diverge from smugglers. The more that smugglers can remain in the shadows and elude any kind of detection, the happier they will be; using violence, or even threatening it, is always a last resort. Though both groups plan contingencies in the event of detection, smugglers can simply pay a fine and walk away. Smugglers do not usually face capital punishment nor, as far as the evidence reveals, did they regularly face it in the past. That is simply not true of pirates, because the nature of their crime is so much more public. They therefore pose a more direct challenge to authority, which cannot easily be avoided.

According to news reports, Somali pirates are criminals. They also "are trained fighters linked to politically powerful clans that have carved the country into armed fiefdoms. Others are young thugs enlisted to do the dirty work for older, more powerful criminals, who turn a profit by taking a cut of the ransom money and selling the ship's cargo."[75]

This idea, that pirates are young thugs and criminals, also distinguishes modern-day pirates from smugglers, whose group and demographic characteristics are much more fluid and much less subject to easy characterization; certainly most smugglers would not be "trained fighters."[76] Smugglers, as we have seen, come from all walks of life and all levels of society, especially when consumers of smuggled products are included in the definition. According to Siyad, a Somali pirate who refused to provide his last name, the pirates are motivated by "money, so it is not our plan to harm the hostages we take. . . . We never agree to release the hostages or the ship before the ransom is paid in cash."[77] Smugglers could not withstand such pressure, any more than they could accept hostage taking, waiting, and public displays of misdeeds. Smuggling takes place in the shadows; its perpetrators want nothing more than to return there and avoid any spotlight on their activities—the very same spotlight that piracy requires in order to be successful.

In other areas too, modern-day pirates are not much changed from their earlier counterparts. "'I was giving away money to everyone I met,' said Siyad, a thirty-eight-year-old Somali pirate who claimed to make $90,000 hijacking ships this year. 'After two months, I had no money left. Can you believe it?'"[78] This certainly meshes with Marcus Rediker's description of seventeenth-century piratical communities generally being egalitarian, keeping track of plunder, and preventing anyone who tried to get more than his share from doing so—while at the same time going on wild spending sprees.[79] The difference, of course, is that the Somali pirates' largesse extends beyond their ships to friends and family who did not participate in their illegal enterprise; it is not clear that this was always historically accurate. Even so, as Rediker quotes a British governor in the Americas, "People are easily led to favour those Pests of Mankind when they have hopes of sharing in their ill-gotten Wealth."[80] In this, pirates and smugglers had something in common: they used the proceeds from their ventures to benefit themselves and those around them without regard for the morality of trafficking in goods that had not been legally acquired.

The long-term goals of modern-day pirates also remain eerily reminiscent of those who came before them. For example, Siyad planned to use his share of the booty to "escape the poverty and instability of Somalia. 'I want to go abroad using a safe route, using my money.'"[81] He referred to his share of the ransom as "my money," indicating that for him, at least, accumulation came from piratical depredation. His share, at least as it has been represented in the press, seems a bit high; $90,000 a year would put Siyad in the very upper echelons of Somali society, making his escape from poverty somewhat less necessary than others who earned significantly less. Other sources have suggested that pirates consistently earn between $10,000 and $30,000 annually, and that this is a large amount for Somalia.[82] Even so, Siyad's professed desire to escape echoed what past pirates had claimed. Pirates saw their occupation as a way out of the impoverished societies from which they came.

Taiwan's *China Post* simultaneously makes the appropriate reference to past pirates while reinforcing the point that pirates thrive in environments where states are weak:

> But who are these modern day buccaneers who ply the East African coast as well as waters in Southeast Asia? As with their historical ancestors flying the Jolly Roger, many are criminals of convenience, who are hijacking ships to gain ransom or plunder. While not supported by any of the local governments,

they easily take advantage of the regional chaos in Somalia, the lack of any lawful presence on the high seas, and use forced boarding to gain million dollar ransoms.[83]

The *China Post* did not see piracy supporting local populations as it did in earlier epochs; nevertheless it did recognize that pirates opportunistically take advantage of the lack of a strong local government (or state). In fact, this condition enabled earlier pirates at the same time that it empowered smuggling. As states grew stronger, piracy diminished. Smuggling, by contrast, adapted. Laws were not enforced, officials were corrupted, and populations acted to subterfuge authority that got in the way of individual accumulation.

Conclusion

What should by now be clear is that smugglers and pirates were different sorts of actors, with different agendas. While both thumbed their noses at legal authority, their mechanisms for doing so greatly diverged. Smugglers more often ended up as victims of pirate raids and attacks than they did making common cause with them, as the example from Prince of Wales Island in this chapter suggests. It was even more unusual for smugglers actually to become pirates. As has been shown earlier in this chapter with the discussion of William Blackstock's 1750 excursion from North Carolina to the Leeward Islands, smugglers did not make for very good pirates. They might have been skilled in the art of subterfuge, but they weren't especially good at responding to violence and double cross. They wanted to be free traders—not freebooters. Their hope was to evade the state, just as pirates were willing to confront it and its agents whenever possible. Even so, in all of the cases presented in this chapter, the state's role appears to have been limited. This may have been a function of colonial state building or it may have been caused by the weak personality of the officials in charge. Nevertheless, pirates and smugglers both took advantage of such limitations for their own ends. It must be noted, however, that the smugglers seem to have come out ahead, and not just because the state itself was victimized through their actions. There was no individual or group of individuals demanding restitution. Nor were there bounties on the heads of smugglers, at least not usually, because they served their customers well.

All of this suggests that while the state in all of these instances has been in the process of forming itself, or of being formed, different groups of individuals have sought ways to empower themselves at government's expense. Neither pirates nor smugglers ever did much of anything either to develop or to enrich state authority, though pirates contributed much more, at least early on, to the state's coffers. Oddly enough, this newfound revenue effectively allowed the state to pursue the eradication of piracy, rather than addressing the underlying inequalities that gave rise to it in the first place.

Smugglers too did everything that they could to prevent state revenue from increasing, for much the same reason. In order for a strong police force to exist, government needed money to pay for it. Once the force existed, it would turn its attentions to protecting government and the individuals who lived under its rule. Revenue needed to be increased as the state's boundaries grew larger and more globally diffused. Maximizing revenue meant enforcing the laws that were designed to do just that. As might be suspected, such activities did not sit especially well with smugglers, who, like pirates, thrived on a real lack of enforcement. They could, however, evade enforcement actions much more easily than pirates ever could.

The next chapter explores the problem that smuggling raised for the state. In particular, the chapter considers the ways in which smugglers and contraband traders manipulated the meaning of state policies toward their own actions. In addition, it examines the political economy of smuggling, as it developed across time and space.

CHAPTER THREE

—⚏—

The Political Economy of Smuggling

A Governor And . . .

In 1805, R. T. Farquhar, one of the British East India Company's employees, presented his employers with a plan. With the impending end of the Atlantic slave trade in 1807, he perceived that a labor shortage might easily develop in the Caribbean, especially since the slave population was not yet reproducing itself—a direct result of the appalling conditions that most slaves in the region faced.[1] R. T. Farquhar served the East India Company as its lieutenant governor at Prince of Wales Island, now Penang, Malaysia.[2] In this capacity, he began contemplating whether or not replacing imported slave labor with formally free, though very low paid, Asian workers would be profitable for Caribbean planters—and the British economy more broadly.

Farquhar suggested that the East India Company consider sending Chinese migrants, who had smuggled themselves out of China and into Prince of Wales Island, halfway around the world to Trinidad and other neighboring Caribbean islands. It is not at all clear that his plan ever gained any traction with the company's directors at the time that he made it, but what *is* clear is that his plan brought up political issues around the subject of smuggling. For example, the role of both Chinese and European state officials in preventing smuggling—whether people or goods—was raised, as were the ways in which contraband commerce directly challenged the wisdom of particular laws. If people failed to observe the statutes, this East India Company official implied that perhaps the reason for their transgression was that the laws were themselves flawed or that enforcement officials failed at their assignments:

If the emigration [from China] be absolutely contrary to the interest and orders of the Chinese Government, we must attribute the unlimited violation of this law to the want of an effective and pervading Legislation, or suppose that a systematic corruption governs the conduct of every public officer, from the highest to the lowest order.[3]

In the above passage, R. T. Farquhar observed that Chinese subjects violated their country's anti-emigration laws by flocking from China to the Malay Peninsula. "It is an indisputable fact," he claimed, "that many hundred thousands have already emigrated from China, and that many Thousands continue to emigrate annually."[4] They did so in direct contravention of the Chinese government's prohibition of such migration. Farquhar further claimed that though the Chinese government had clearly forbidden an activity, its police force (or others charged with enforcing the law) knowingly allowed Chinese subjects to evade the law. Even more importantly to Farquhar, tolerating such actions negated the enforcement officials' legal obligations to the state itself.

Why should this have been the case? Farquhar's initial answer, "excess population," seems somewhat simplistic, though it has been a frequent explanation for nearly every human migration. Chinese law officers would not likely enable a stream of prohibited out-migration simply because they perceived that there were too many people around or that the resources such people required were in short supply. How local legal officials and police officers would even have been aware of any overpopulation is difficult to imagine. What Farquhar meant, however, could easily be rephrased: the Chinese economy in many places did not produce enough to sustain a growing population. Even here, it could easily be argued that local Chinese officials would likely have had a difficult time observing such a widespread phenomenon. But, if they did detect it, there was little that they could do without more direct governmental assistance. Fewer still would have been able to identify the causes of a population exodus, particularly if that exodus was done surreptitiously or clandestinely, and obtain the resources required to stanch it. But even if they did, consistent state intervention across an area as big as China would have been virtually impossible.

Some members of the Chinese population, as a result of their perceptions—whether they derived from inadequate capital accumulation, hunger, or another reason—opened an escape valve for themselves. They emigrated from Chinese territory in search of increased economic opportunity or social standing. That their own government legally banned them from doing so is significant; this contravention put the subjects of a regime in the position of having to act against state laws in order to accomplish personal goals such as avoiding starvation or increasing wealth. The state therefore did not provide adequate care for its subjects.[5] Many Chinese migrants moved to Prince of Wales Island, drawn there by its growing economic connections to the rest of the world through European trading companies, as well as for a sense of possibility and prosperity.[6]

R. T. Farquhar nevertheless mused about what the Chinese migration to Prince of Wales actually meant. He considered what he saw as a paradox: "why a Government [China] so conspicuous for arbitrary Laws and usages, so severe and vigilant in its Police, and so summary in its punishments, should be so constantly disobeyed with impunity in so very important a branch of the Public œconomy."[7] He wondered aloud about what caused individuals to act out against their government, especially one with a lengthy statute book and a famously authoritarian police force. In short, Farquhar became concerned with the question of why people take risks in order to smuggle, whether people or goods. It is this question, which perhaps seems obvious, or at least less paradoxical today than it did in 1805, that this chapter considers on a theoretical level.

Before tackling such theoretical interpretations, however, it is worth considering *why* the lieutenant governor was even remotely interested in the question of Chinese emigration. Indeed, Farquhar's concern, like others in his position of authority at other times and in other places, was to gain economic advantage for his employer. In an attempt to find the East India Company a profitable use for this recently acquired and well-located island, Farquhar considered its available natural resources. What he found was a Chinese population that continued to grow through illegal Chinese emigration; the East India Company did not deport illegal emigrants to their native lands. He observed that, as he surmised was the case in China, the population had not yet achieved at Prince of Wales Island what would now be considered full employment.[8] The island's geographic location, however, made it a useful staging ground for commerce of all kinds—including human. Since the Chinese government had apparently closed its eyes to the movement of its people across its borders and outside its territory, Farquhar reasoned, China ought to have no objection if Chinese emigrants went even farther—from the Malay Peninsula to Britain's new Trinidad colony:

I can therefore see no material obstacle to be encountered whilst the Government of China continues to be administered as it is at present in persuading large bodies of those people to emigrate and establish themselves in our West India islands, if adequate advantages be held out in the first instance, and their confidence in us secured by the fulfillment of our agreements.[9]

The question that Farquhar raised next, however, was perhaps more revealing of his views on how individuals related to their governments. He attempted to understand the precise moment that a government wrote off those who lived under its authority or, phrased another way, when a legal regime separated itself from its subjects. In particular, Farquhar pondered whether or not the Chinese government should be made aware of any plans that the East India Company might develop to send Chinese subjects to the Caribbean as contracted laborers. Of course, the same question could also be asked of the migrants themselves, who after all had smuggled themselves out of China. Objecting to secrecy in principle, Farquhar nevertheless did not conclude that full disclosure would be helpful:

> I am persuaded that secrecy, or rather the attempt at secrecy, is likely to create that very jealousy in the Chinese government, and distrust in the Chinese Emigrants which His Majesty's Minister and the Secret Committee of the Court of Directors [of the East India Company] are anxious to guard against. . . . I do not mean to say that it would be prudent to publish at China or elsewhere that it is in the contemplation of the British Government to people the West India islands with Chinese in lieu of African slaves. This intimation would naturally excite sentiments of repugnance and alarm, and be inconsistent with a due circumspection.[10]

What becomes apparent, then, from reading this passage is that an agent of the East India Company, who was developing a plan to move people from one part of the world to another as a replacement labor force, did not want this information to be made public in China. He was fearful that it would create negative feelings among the Chinese populations both in China and at Prince of Wales Island. In fact, it was more than that. If the Chinese found out that the British East India Company contemplated using illegal Chinese emigrants, who had smuggled themselves out of China, as replacements for slave laborers in the Caribbean, the Chinese government might then begin to enforce its own laws against emigration, thereby closing off the British East India Company's potential to profit from illegal Chinese migration. The humiliation of such an action would almost certainly have been detrimental to the company's trade, which was actively pursuing greater connections with the Chinese.

The East India Company, in Farquhar's scheme, instead needed to rely upon the Chinese government's inability (or unwillingness) to enforce its laws vigorously, which effectively allowed the self-smuggling of people out of China. By becoming a supplier of cheap labor replacements in a global labor market, the East India Company itself could further expand. This relationship, between governments (or, in the case of the East India Company, quasi-governments) and the economy begs for some theoretical consideration. Such political economy, while not strictly and rigidly historical, ought to be seen as a history of ideas, or as a tool for understanding the ways in which individuals and governments understood the various actions that they took. Certainly the intellectual debates took place at the same time as the actions with which this book is concerned; it is useful then to contextualize the specific actions within the general ideas that were being discussed.

In this chapter, the ways in which smuggling intersects with the largely forgotten, but increasingly significant, discipline of political economy are considered. Doing so allows a discussion of smuggling not simply as a collection of anecdotes but also as an analysis and evaluation of the relationship that exists between the state (or government) and consumers who live under its authority.[11] As importantly, this chapter begins to provide insight into the *qualitative* meaning of smuggling across time and place. As earlier indicated, I believe that this becomes especially important because any *quantitative* evaluation of smuggling's scope across world history proves highly problematic.[12]

Smuggling, by definition, is a clear violation of trade, tax, and/or revenue laws, which happens to be carried out in a very particular way. Individuals import or export products, or even people (including themselves, as in the case of the Chinese migration into Prince of Wales Island) across a legal frontier. In many cases such frontiers can be identified by a physical or geographic boundary; this is one of the main appeals in studying islands. Goods and people may well be prohibited from either import or export or both, depending on the legal regime in existence on either side of the border. It therefore becomes important to contemplate the creation of both sets of laws, including their specific historical contexts and the goals behind their existence, in order to understand why people, whose governments after all passed such laws, resist them through disobedience.[13] Because a legal frontier has one set of laws on one side of it, and oftentimes a completely different set of laws on the other side of the boundary, smuggling may be a violation of only one set of statutes; likewise the act of contraband commerce could break two sets of regulations, depending on how the legal regimes were established and negotiated. What all of these transgressions have in common is that their perpetrators are seeking to avoid paying legally mandated taxes or interdictions on the movement of goods and commodities.

To look at every legal frontier across the totality of world history would be a Herculean task; it is perhaps more useful to look at a few such legal borders and, after determining whether or not there is an identifiable pattern, draw some conclusions about how statutory restrictions and prohibitions on trade came into existence. Once that task has been completed, it should become possible to theorize about the ways in which the state interacted with those who lived under its rule as commercial restrictions were put into place. Or, put another way, it becomes possible to identify and discuss patterns in, and ideologies about, the political economy of smuggling. The evidence generally shows that the state understood its enforcement of law, here defined as the prevention of smuggling or punishment of smugglers, to be a way of demonstrating state power and authority. At the same time, the state's residents believed that violating the law could be a fine way for them either to preserve or to gain control over their own lives, perhaps especially their patterns of consumption.[14] This sets the stage for a negotiation between state and subject.

That is, subjects and citizens *wanted* the state to think that it had authority over their lives and actions, but clearly understood that their own efforts to transgress the law effectively limited government's power in this regard. Similarly, the state *wanted* to be able to exert complete control over many aspects of its subjects' and citizens' lives, knowing full well that the government's power was much more limited in practice than it admitted in public. In short, smuggling transgressions everywhere effectively undermined, and sometimes severely limited, state authority. As importantly, the public— members of civil society—fooled themselves into believing that they exerted more control over their daily lives and actions than they actually did. Just because an individual or group of individuals could evade the law without punishment once, or twice, or three times, never meant that they would always be able to escape detection and penalty. Because the laws *were* on the books, even though they were only irregularly or selectively enforced, they *could* have been enforced at any time of the state's choosing on a regular and consistent basis. Indeed, some of them were enforced precisely because no one thought they would be.

. . . A Governor's Wife

Just as Farquhar planned an enterprise that involved Chinese subjects potentially increasing their illegal activity against their own government by continuing their exodus from China (and getting shipped to the West Indies), others had absolutely no fear of violating the law because so few, it seemed, ever got caught. This could explain why so many Chinese went to Prince of Wales Island. But it could also explain why more recent actors brazenly ignore laws designed to regulate trade, generate revenue for the state, and control consumption. Columba Bush, the wife of former governor of Florida Jeb Bush, found herself on the wrong end of the law nearly a decade ago.

On 17 June 1999, a customs inspector at Atlanta's airport impeded Mrs. Bush from returning to the United States from France. She was en route to Tallahassee, Florida's state capital, from Paris. While in Europe, Mrs. Bush spent $19,000 on clothing and jewelry. As anyone who has ever traveled on an international flight into the United States knows, the Customs Service (which, after 2001, was absorbed by the new Department of Homeland Security) requires every passenger to state a dollar value of all the goods that they acquired abroad. Mrs. Bush declared that she had made $500 worth of purchases in Paris. This was, of course, $18,500 less than the value of the merchandise that she carried with her. By writing this fictitious number down and trying to evade paying duty on her goods, Mrs. Bush committed a crime. She was, in fact, a smuggler.

In making a false declaration, she effectively lied to the U.S. government. Moreover, she did so more than once. When customs officials found some French receipts in her purse, they gave Mrs. Bush an opportunity to change her signed declaration. She refused to do so. Sticking to her story, she insisted that she was importing only $500 worth of new goods. The customs inspectors proceeded to search her bags, using her receipts as a guide. Florida's first lady then faced a fine of $4,100—three times the duty that she would have paid had she been honest with the government.[15]

U.S. Customs Service spokesman Patrick Jones clearly articulated the government's perspective: "Customs agents could have fined Mrs. Bush up to the full dollar amount of her purchases or confiscated the merchandise."[16] Because so many people daily fail to declare honestly their purchases, and therefore become smugglers, the Customs Service has resorted to a standard penalty to keep people moving through the ports of entry. Jones dubbed the fee "the-three-times-the-loss-of-revenue formula." The government designed the policy to "[g]et the [duty] revenue, get the penalty, and get these folks on their way."[17] Notwithstanding the incontestable fact that Mrs. Bush had violated commercial and customs law, the government's position toward her and others remained only mildly punitive. She was not arrested or imprisoned; indeed, paying the fine immediately freed her from customs authorities. Moreover, Jones's statement indicates that Mrs. Bush did not receive any different treatment than someone else who might be in the same situation. Government has made it a practice to negotiate with this particular kind of lawbreaker.[18]

The local media, while covering the story, generally misunderstood its significance. Although this example clearly illustrates how consumers ignore laws in their pursuit of rare or inexpensive goods, which is at least what *some* armed robberies are about, the media focused instead on Mrs. Bush's political and social position. She was married to a local official—who, at the time, just happened to be responsible for ensuring that the laws of a particular jurisdiction were consistently and fairly implemented. The problem, like so many the media portray, became a political issue rather than a moral or a legal one. According to the *St. Petersburg Times*, [Governor] Jeb Bush['s] . . . wife misled U.S. Customs Officials about $19,000 in new clothing and jewelry she brought into the Country *because she didn't want him to know how much she had spent on her five-day Paris shopping trip.*"[19]

Had reporters thought about this half-baked reasoning, it would have been clear that such a justification makes absolutely no sense. Only government officials in any airport's "sterile zone" can see the customs form, which travelers submit after landing and claiming their baggage. Because Jeb Bush was not present in the customs area, how would he have known how much his wife spent in Paris? Although it is true that Mrs. Bush had the store receipts with her, if she did not want her husband to know how much she paid to the French storekeepers, she could easily have discarded these pieces of paper in France, or on the plane, or at the Atlanta airport, or even somewhere in the state of Florida (that her husband was not likely to visit). Even if Jeb Bush were to find them, perhaps while checking the pockets before he did her laundry, his wife could then have told him that her total was 19,000 francs, and not 19,000 dollars (this was before the dollar–euro exchange rate would have increased the costs, because it was before the euro existed). Or that the exchange rate of francs to dollars was 10,000 to 1. In short, she had other options if she did not want her husband to know that she liked to splurge on clothes and jewels.

That being said, Jeb Bush could still have learned how much his wife spent in Paris simply by reading his monthly credit card and bank statements, assuming that the couple maintained a joint account. (And if they did not have a joint account, then why would the governor care about his wife's profligate spending at all?) In other words, smuggling goods and then lying to the government about it after getting caught is by no means required to hide expensive purchases from one's spouse, even if he happened to be a millionaire government official. Columba Bush's legal run-in was not, as the governor claimed and the media allowed, a private affair: "I love my wife more than life—she is my comfort and I am very proud of her. . . . What she does with our money is our business—she can deal with that with me."[20]

In fact, the money in question was not Bush family money at all. This was legal revenue to which the U.S. government was duly entitled, under "the rule of law," which can be found in Title 19 of the U.S. Code. Columba Bush was guilty of defrauding the U.S. treasury; she was a tax evader. But because cheating on import duties and customs declarations is so widespread, government officials adapted to the situation by levying fines on the spot and then getting "people on their way."[21]

Rather than treating incidents like Mrs. Bush's at Atlanta's Hartsfield-Jackson International Airport as yet another political embarrassment for elected officials, we ought to consider them as lenses through which we can view the problems of political economy. Columba Bush was unlucky enough to get caught, but many more people (no doubt including readers of this book) have routinely and successfully violated customs laws as they traversed national boundaries. The phenomenon is not peculiar to North America; the *India Tribune* published an editorial soon after Mrs. Bush's escapade that discussed the regularity with which the subcontinent's wealthy have evaded government tariffs.[22] The fact that government authorities have designed strategies to keep cheaters moving through airports suggests that they have entered into tacit negotiations with the public about the degree to which such criminal behavior can be tolerated. Indeed, this too is nothing new.

Both Farquhar, through his proposal, and Mrs. Bush, through her actions, were negotiating with the state. Farquhar's bargaining discussions were obvious, in that he wrote directly to his superiors in London. Indeed, he was part of a quasi-governmental organization when he wrote, seeking official approval to encourage the Chinese to continue violating their own country's law, in order that the scheme he championed could be implemented. Mrs. Bush, by contrast, claimed that her actions were private, and therefore unworthy of media attention. Without going too deeply into this last Bush claim, because it is largely a red herring, it nevertheless can be argued that she too had effectively negotiated with the state. Knowing full well that few returning citizens of the United States get arrested for smuggling, and fewer still are ever incarcerated, Columba Bush committed her crime with the hope that she would go undetected. Because she was caught, her story entered the public record—making it a significant illustration of smuggling. More importantly, the way in which the state, as represented by the United States Customs Service, treated her, by levying a fine and releasing her, indicates the degree to which individual smugglers can negotiate effectively with those who rule or at least those who have responsibility for legal enforcement. That her crime did not garner the maximum penalty allowable under law strongly suggests that crimes where the government becomes the victim remain less important than other sorts of crimes, where individual property owners are subjected to loss. In turn, this suggests that a certain view of political economy has achieved dominance, at least in much of today's globalizing world.

Smuggling's Peculiar Political Economy

After 1500, once the whole of the planet was, in some way or another, connected, legal frontiers emerged that mirrored the European states' expansion. As Europeans colonized territories, these new spaces were incorporated into European political, economic, and legal systems. Across the Atlantic, into the Indian Ocean basin, as well as in Europe itself, Europeans interacted with existing systems of political economy in order to achieve what would become the European position of dominance. In the process, these newly established legal frontiers began to be contested and transgressed.[23] Contraband commerce, or smuggling, is one of those transgressions that at once reveals both the strengths and weaknesses of an increasingly global system of trade.

There is perhaps no better place to begin a discussion of the political economy of contraband trade than by exploring the ways in which the legal frontiers across the Americas were established. These borders were all new and though some of them were rooted in defined geographic features, such as those of islands, most had been constructed out of expediency. They were based simply on which European power controlled a particular territory at any given moment in time. If a territory flipped control from one European state to another, so too did its legal regime change. There was, in other words, nothing at all organic about the laws that separated one place from another. Laws and policies changed depending on who was in control of the levers of government. The processes of incorporating new territories, which began with the Spanish in the Western Hemisphere, ought to prove instructive for contemplating future expansions, even when the Spanish were not themselves involved.

When Spain first arrived in the Americas at the close of the fifteenth century, it brought with it the European economic system. This effectively meant that European states endeavored to accumulate precious metals—gold and silver—faster than neighboring states. Because wealth was measured in terms of bullion, the size of Spain's treasury needed to increase for it to be considered a successful expansionist power.[24] These economic beliefs are easily seen in the Spanish colonizers' immediate request to see gold.[25] At the same time, individual subjects of the Spanish crown, whether in Europe or the Americas, themselves contributed to the Spanish colonizing enterprise by paying taxes and fees. Such payments were generally based upon the idea of consumption; virtually everything that was used could be taxed. Whether or not the Spanish tax collection paid for the colonizing mission is a subject of some debate.[26]

As the Spanish government proceeded with its American conquests, it discovered a few things along the way. First, the Americas *were* an excellent source of bullion—gold, but especially silver.[27] This satisfied the desires of the Spanish government and, for a time, allowed Spain to accumulate more bullion than other European states.[28] It also led, not coincidentally given contemporary European economic thinking, to the Spanish desire to monopolize the export of bullion from the Americas. To do so, the Spanish government collected its silver and held it until the ships could sail as a convoy or *flota* back to Europe. The logic in this, of course, was that the cargo was so valuable that it needed to be well guarded as it traversed the North Atlantic. In turn, this led to piracy, as the prevailing wind and water currents made it easy for other Europeans, whether or not they represented another government in competition for the bullion, to pick off ships in the convoy and abscond with their precious cargoes. Or, to frame it a different way, because the Spanish initially used the colonies to gain wealth for the state treasury, competition soon followed. Since the economic winners were based on bullion collection, other European states attempted to collect bullion by robbing the Spanish treasure fleet. Of course, these violent acts constituted piracy, robbery on the high seas, and not contraband commerce, as the last chapter demonstrated.

This narrative generally shows us the way in which the Spanish state managed its acquisition of bullion in the Atlantic economy. Though it is beyond this book's scope, it nevertheless becomes important to characterize the Spanish behavior, precisely in order to explain the *reactions* that other Europeans had to Spanish colonization in the Americas. Because the Spanish collected their extracted metals every year and sent these metals back to Spain, they enriched the royal treasury, as well as others involved in the Spanish court or government. In turn, these individuals themselves enriched the royal treasury because they paid a certain share of their wealth, in the form of taxes on commercial transactions or luxury goods, to government.[29] Those who had access to Spanish America's mineral wealth, in short, became expert consumers—and the Spanish treasury also benefited. It must be mentioned here that there was little attention paid to savings and investment, especially of the kind that Adam Smith would later advocate. The colonies therefore became a central part in an extractive economy, where those who enjoyed the richest results of those extractions generally did so from the Atlantic's eastern shores.

Spain's competitors on the European stage claimed territory of their own in the Americas in the sixteenth century, either as a way to replicate the Spanish extraction of bullion or, in the alternate, to find a way to part the Spanish from their colossal amounts of gold and silver. As indicated earlier, piracy became one of the byproducts of this activity, but it was not by any measure the only means to accumulate wealth in the Atlantic World. As other Europeans claimed territory, and Spain acquiesced because Spain itself did not want to pay for areas that did not produce much in the way of mineral wealth, the northern European colonizers began to use their territories for the production of luxury crops—that is, those that were rare in Europe, such as sugar and tobacco, and which the Spanish might purchase with their bullion.

The northern European hope was that Spanish consumers would willingly part with their wealth for objects that were both more useful and enjoyable to them; the risks of damage were far less than those associated with piracy. Other Europeans also set up governments to rule their territories, bringing over their own laws to assist in the colonial administrative process. Because Spain was first into the Americas, it effectively determined the pace. More importantly, because Spain prohibited its colonial residents from trading with anyone who was not a Spanish subject, or doing so with a ship that was not from Spain, it created a practice that other European states could easily emulate.[30] Many of them did so; England, France, and Portugal all set up a series of legal codes that prevented residents of their American colonies from trading with others who were resident in colonies that belonged to other European powers.[31] At the same time, European laws also restricted exports to their own national ships directly destined for the home country. They behaved exactly as Spain was doing, though they were not engaged in funneling bullion across the Atlantic.

The real effect of all of these prohibitions was to prevent the Spanish who lived in the Americas from directly trading with their French, English, Dutch, or Portuguese neighbors who happened to live under a different legal regime. They were, of course, retaliation for the Spanish creating a legal system that prevented these same Spanish (or, indeed, other European) subjects from a direct commerce with the European powers themselves, whether in Europe or the Americas. By the middle of the seventeenth century, the Americas had developed a series of legal frontiers that looked like mirror images of each other, with very similar prohibitions and policies on either side of the various borders.

All of these legal regimes ended up playing a very similar part in keeping Europe's new world divided among the European players, while simultaneously extending each European state's control over a particular geographic area. Spanish bullion was that much harder to come by for the northern Europeans, because the Spanish government attempted to limit consumers' ability to spend it. In short, by not sufficiently diversifying its American economy, the Spanish government failed to allow its consumers in either Europe or the Americas to consume locally produced products, because there were none. And by restricting trade to Spanish boats, the Spanish government refused to allow American produce from non-Spanish territory to be easily consumed. This meant that there was capital in the form of bullion around, though there was not enough opportunity to spend it easily within Spanish territories. Prices were, as well, higher than they would otherwise have been in a more liberal marketplace. As should by now be apparent, this kind of stilted trading system clearly led to the development of smuggling around the Atlantic.

The problem, of course, was that the division of the American hemisphere into imperial markets that operated on exclusive and monopolistic practices was utterly dysfunctional for the way that people lived in the real world; it was not in any way set up to facilitate consumerist behavior. Therefore, it did not work for the people who lived in the Americas. Colonial residents could not legally gain access to European products without going through the approved procedures and using approved vendors—even if some were available nearby at lower cost. The same could be said for European consumers, who paid higher prices than they otherwise might have done had competition on the trading routes been allowed. As Adam Smith put it, "the single advantage which the monopoly procures to a single order of men is in many different ways hurtful to the general interest of the country."[32]

It is instructive, for example, to consider that a resident of the French Caribbean colonies relied upon France to send over flour to make bread; even so, that flour arrived infrequently and when it did, it was often spoiled because of the length of its Atlantic crossing. Flour, however, was much more easily available in mainland North and South America, where wheat also grew, but the French did not control the flour-producing regions. As a result, in order to get flour at times when no French flour was available in the French Caribbean, island residents had to cross a legal frontier—and get it from an alternate, and therefore illegal, source. The Spanish residents of Cuba, in another example, might have wanted furniture at a time between the arrivals of the Spanish *flota* from the Iberian Peninsula. Cubans were legally proscribed from obtaining it from nearby British Jamaica, again leading

American residents to violate a legal frontier if they did not want to wait for the next legally permissible source of such goods to arrive at their territory. The same could also be said about slaves. In many cases, they were in short supply in one area, and plentiful in a neighboring island or colony that happened to belong to another country and its legal regime. Slaves, too, were no easier to acquire than any other property that had to cross a legal frontier.[33]

As time progressed, it became equally apparent that things were not really much better back in Europe. For example, European consumers relied upon their local merchants to make deals with their American correspondents to supply the market with luxury products such as sugar and tobacco from the Americas. The merchants were legally required only to engage with each other, and to make sure that the products were shipped in their country's boats. But the reality was that some products were perishable and could spoil if a ship did not arrive in time to ship them back to Europe. Or, by the same token, a shortage of one product from one island could not be overcome with the same product from a neighboring island, at least not legally. To avoid such eventualities, it would have made much more sense to allow any passing ships with space in their holds to carry products back to European consumers; in this way, eliminating shipping restrictions would have worked nicely. Of course, that would have required breaching a legal frontier, which most European states were not willing to do. A very pragmatic idea thus gave way to the legal reality and its rigidities. Consumers in both Europe and the Americas were therefore put in the position of having their personal interests as consumers put at odds with their own government's legal restrictions.

Of course, such a predicament is fraught with irony. Some of Europe's biggest proponents of government trade restrictions and other legal commercial protections were themselves traders. They sought protected markets in order to guarantee their own profitability and accumulation. Many of them did not understand, at least not well, that an expanded market or one freer of regulation might have benefited them by expanding and deepening their base of consumers. In an even greater display of irony, some of these very same merchants were also among the Atlantic World's biggest legal transgressors. They smuggled products across borders; they bribed officials to release captured cargoes. They also went to government for help, from time to time, if they were unable to achieve their desired ends. In short, they broke the law, even as they supported it and argued for its extension. As Dominica's Governor John Orde wrote, "The jealousy of an Assembly constituted principally of Merchants and Persons having an interest in illicit commerce has ever withheld from the Executive the authorities to act once and for all to eradicate smuggling."[34]

In order to understand the reasons why such a situation was allowed to develop over a period of centuries, it may be very useful to explore the questions of political economy that are raised by these transgressions of legal frontiers. For example, the relationship between governments and their subjects and/or citizens on the subject of consumption is pivotal to understanding smugglers' motivations. Moreover, evolving ideas about the very purpose of government itself, its raison d'être, is significant for understanding why governmental officials took some enforcement actions at particular moments but did not take either a similar or a different action at another time. It might also be useful to think about those who actually made the laws themselves. Though they created laws with a specific aim in mind, they also did so within a defined historical context, which limited the ways that the debate would have been framed. Circumstances could have changed from one period to another. Moreover, lawmakers were also consumers; they may well have made laws that did not always coincide with their own individual interests as consumers.[35] Even so, as consumers, they regularly failed to respect the laws they created if it was inconvenient to do so.

Government's interests in protectionist commercial policy were generally both financial and political. Controlling trade, whether in the form of guaranteeing the regular flow of bullion extracted from the American mines, ensuring ample supplies of manufactured consumer products, or, later, assuring that agricultural staples like sugar, coffee, and tobacco reached European markets, generated significant revenue to the state. At the same time, such actions theoretically prevented other states from achieving dominance through increasing wealth acquired from foreign commerce. Moreover, trading regulations served to define acceptable behavior by proscribing certain kinds of activities.

In order to ensure adherence to government's clearly stated policies, in order to advance compliance with the law, any government requires revenue—and those in the Americas (and, indeed, elsewhere) were no exception. Without a police force, or military officials who served the same functions, laws could not be enforced. In the past, as now, such a force demanded payment, which, of course, required revenue. In the past, as now, governments were loath to enact laws that increased government or public expenditure, such as that required by a police force, without figuring out a way to offset any increased costs with additional revenues. Though being "cost neutral" (meaning having expenditures equal revenues) may now be a generally laudable goal, this was not always the case in the Atlantic World—or anywhere else for that matter. This fit with mercantilist theory but perhaps more significantly, it also provided an opening to smugglers (as well as to other tax evaders) to avoid paying imposts and fees whenever possible.

It is, therefore, impossible to understand the development of smuggling in the Atlantic World and elsewhere without grasping the economic conditions of mercantilism and its successor economic systems. I cannot provide here a more extensive analysis of mercantilism than that which has already appeared in this chapter; suffice it to say that as countries encountered each other in an increasingly global world, a variety of laws appeared that had as their intent ensuring the security of national borders, regulating trade across those borders, restricting imports and exports, and protecting national shipping. In order to enforce these laws, the state needed revenue. It got this by charging duties (and levying other taxes) on imports and exports. The idea, as always, was to collect more in taxes than was spent on enforcement, as this would further increase the state's treasury. In many cases, this practice led the state to pay low wages to those charged with enforcement. Of course, this in turn led those who received such wages to seek additional payments when and where they could. Corruption and bribery became widespread, at least among those charged with enforcing revenue laws.[36]

More importantly, as had been planned, trading restrictions did lead to profits entering the state's treasury as well as to profits accruing to those involved in the protected trade, which was also anticipated by merchant advocates of such laws. As Adam Smith said,

> The interest of the dealers . . . in any particular branch of trade . . . is always in some respects different from, and even opposite to, that of the publick. . . . The proposal of any new law or regulation of commerce which comes from this order [merchants], ought always to be listened to with great precaution, and ought never to be adopted till after having been long and carefully examined, not only with the most scrupulous but with the most suspicious attention.[37]

As importantly, government's protectionist policies, which legally supported those who were involved in trade, also unintentionally undermined the very state authorities that they were designed to protect and ensure. Such protectionist actions effectively put consumers, who were attempting to accumulate property, at odds with their governments, which were charged with protecting whatever property had been acquired. In other words, government raised revenue in such a way that it effectively prevented its own citizens, subjects, and residents from further accumulating "stuff" through practicing individual consumer behavior as each member of civil society saw fit. In turn, the consumer's inability to act freely under existing law resulted in increasing illegal consumption, which further caused a decline in the efficacy of existing statutes. Mercantile governments therefore protected their own coffers from being reduced at the expense of their own consumers who, in turn, helped to undermine the state in a nonconfrontational way through illegal and extra-legal actions. As Adam Smith put it:

> Consumption is the sole end and purpose of all production; and the interest of the producer ought to be attended to, only so far as it may be necessary for promoting that of the consumer. The maxim is so perfectly self-evident that it would be absurd to attempt to prove it. But in the mercantile system, the interest of the consumer is almost constantly sacrificed to that of the producer; and it seems to consider production, and not consumption, as the ultimate end and object of all industry and commerce.[38]

With the passage of time, protectionist laws became more expensive to enforce, costing the state an ever-increasing share of the revenue that it gained through requiring that the laws be enforced. Having such statutes on the books thus became increasingly expensive. As a result, by the second half of the eighteenth century, Adam Smith had developed his powerful attack on the mercantile system that then permeated the Atlantic.

Before going more deeply into Smith's critique of eighteenth-century mercantilism, it is important to remember that as time progressed, the merchants, whose trade was protected from competition, became fierce advocates for one position over another. In general, those in Europe believed that such protection ought to be continued. (Those in the Americas did not concur, at least unless they directly benefited.) After all, they could fetch high prices in European marketplaces without regard to competition; it was as if a certain market share could be guaranteed.[39] Enlisting the government in this enterprise did not seem counterintuitive, most especially because merchants used their profits to support politicians. The economic growth in this early modern period in many places came from the profits generated from the protected colonial trade, at the expense of consumers:

> It cannot be very difficult to determine who have been the contrivers of this whole mercantile system; not the consumers . . . whose interest has been entirely neglected; but the producers whose interest has been so carefully attended to; and among this latter class our merchants and manufacturers have been by far the principal architects.[40]

Others, especially those in the Americas, who could identify only some small tangible benefits from European protectionist statutes, wanted to eliminate the laws and their enforcement mechanisms. Those in the colonies regularly saw their own consumer interests suffer, as the demands and needs of local residents could not always be met at a cost that they could afford. Prices for imported products were too high, they claimed; moreover, the prices that exports generally fetched in protected European markets were too low. To get around these conditions, at the very same time that they advocated for their removal, many "commercial people" turned to smuggling activities.

Indeed, it is the activities and combinations of merchants that Smith rails against in his *Wealth of Nations*:

> To widen the market and to narrow the competition is always the interest of the dealers. To widen the market may frequently be agreeable enough to the interest of the publick; but to narrow the competition must always be against it, and can serve only to enable the dealers, by raising their profits above what they would naturally be, to levy, for their own benefit, an absurd tax upon the rest of their fellow citizens. . . . [An attempt to negotiate with the government over the level of taxes] comes from an order of men, whose interest is never exactly the same with that of the publick, who have generally an interest to deceive and even to oppress the publick, and who accordingly have, upon many occasions, both deceived and oppressed it.[41]

Adam Smith believed that merchants were simply incapable of not combining to drive up prices, and with them their own profits. Since tariffs generally had the effect of increasing prices, merchants were sometimes fans of these taxes, so long as they did not have to reduce their prices to remain competitive. On the other hand, it is not insignificant that traders regularly argued against *raising* tariffs, since that could mean diminished profits for them, or increased prices for consumers, or, in all likelihood, some combination of the two. What is clear in all of this is that merchants wanted to protect their markets, which inevitably cost money, but they also wanted to keep out competition. So long as they could pass tax increases on to their customers, knowing that other merchants were going to have to do the same thing, they favored a protected market. If, on the other hand, increased tariffs meant traders had to lower their profits or raise prices, risking decreased consumption, the traders opposed the increases. This description in fact neatly suggests the divergence between those on either side of the Atlantic and, later, the divergence between those in Europe and those in the rest of the world.

For present purposes, the *Wealth of Nations* is best understood as a critique of the mercantile system as it operated in the mid- to late eighteenth century. I tell my students that Smith's critical assessment of mercantilism is one of the work's most profound points, and one that many readers will generally not contemplate because Adam Smith's poor organizational skills put the criticism far away from the solution to the problem that Smith proposes in his tome. Smith's critique of the eighteenth-century mercantilist economic system appears almost entirely in Book IV, yet many editions of the work now in publication exclude Book IV completely. Moreover, the first chapters of the work, in Book I, which *are* widely read, should be fundamentally seen as a solution to a problem that Smith has so nicely articulated in Book IV. Smith would have done well to present his argument in a different order, so that readers would be familiar with the critique as well as with the solution when they encounter the book for the first time. In its current form, the solution proposed in Book I to the problem identified in Book IV appears almost completely out of context—which has, not coincidentally, allowed people to appropriate Smith for their own political purposes, especially if they are inclined to argue for a complete lack of market regulation, regardless of context or circumstance.

In fact, Smith believed in some market regulation, just as he believed that government had several important purposes: defense, justice, public works, and providing some limited education.[42] Most significantly for the argument that I am making here, Adam Smith supported market regulation in one main area: the prevention of monopoly, whether private or governmental. Of course, this is exactly what the mercantile system had produced and exactly the cause of the problems he observed in eighteenth-century Britain. Monopolies hurt consumers by denying them choices, causing them to pay higher prices on necessary goods than they would have in an unprotected market. Government therefore hurt the interests of consumers. I use the term "necessary goods" quite deliberately here, since Smith did not believe that any single individual had an inherent right to consume "luxuries."[43] Policies that regulated luxury products as well, were also, therefore, generally acceptable to Smith.

The Atlantic economy that Smith observed, however, was not really commerce in necessary goods. Indeed, after bullion, its principal products included sugar, tobacco, coffee, and slaves. As Indian and Southeast Asian commerce became integrated with that of the Atlantic, tea and spices also became commercial commodities. When Smith wrote in the 1770s, none of these products was necessary; that changed with the passage of time, increased supplies, and their addictive nature.[44] Nor did Smith himself believe any of these consumer products was necessary; he saw them simply as luxuries. Once he observed that government had made a business of protecting this luxury trade, he developed his arguments against market regulation. Government had strayed from its basic functions by creating monopolies that limited choice and hurt consumers. This kind of trade ought to regulate itself, he asserted; practically, this required the removal of protectionist statutes and changes in pricing. Upward price pressure would have initially come from increased transportation costs, but that would soon have declined as new competition in the carrying trade created efficiencies and innovations that government could neither dictate nor itself provide. Moreover, the availability of products from foreign colonies in the European marketplaces would cause consumers to evaluate products in different ways, perhaps even increasing the pressure for improved colonial products, sparking competition within the colonial economies. This too might have effectively lowered prices as responses to the market permeated societies around the region. Free trade, then, had many benefits, across the Atlantic World and around the globe.

But what of smuggling, which really was the ultimate form of free trade? The removal of monopolistic protection, as Smith desired, would have meant that goods and people could easily cross legal frontiers. Nevertheless, the violation of legally installed monopolistic practices was in no way desirable. So while smugglers really could be described as free traders, they could also be described as immoral transgressors of a legitimately created, however flawed, legal regime. Because smugglers broke the law, even though the laws that they broke were bad laws, smuggling was reprehensible. The ends, in other words, could not justify the means.

Adam Smith's views were in line with much of the Enlightenment. First, in his mind, individuals needed to be "virtuous," and demonstrate "fellow-feeling."[45] Individuals and groups of individuals who violated the laws of the state that existed, in large measure, to protect life, property, and the right to accumulate additional property, demonstrated to Smith that those individuals held themselves apart from others; for him, legal transgressions of this kind represented a tear in the social fabric. This was not virtuous behavior, without which Smith's theoretically described economy could not succeed.[46] Whether buying or selling smuggled goods, or even acting as the smuggler, involvement in contraband commerce of any kind added to society's immorality.

In the late eighteenth century, as before, American products entering the European marketplace were often smuggled; this allowed for a broader market than might otherwise have been available given mercantile restrictions. Many of the luxury crops coming from the Americas had been produced with slave labor; slavery for Smith was problematic, as individuals who were slaves were unable to sell their labor power in a free market, in effect creating a monopoly on their labor by their owners.[47] Purchasing the produce of slave labor, he reasoned, increased demand for such products, which in turn encouraged additional slave production. The monopoly that owners had on slave labor allowed them either to avoid paying their slaves for the additional productive work or to increase the number of slaves who were used to cultivate and manufacture the desired products to satisfy consumer demand—or both. When combined with the legally mandated market and price protections for such staples, consumption of slave-produced goods maximized profits at the slave's expense.[48] There could be no morality in that.

Adam Smith's ideas about smuggling are firmly grounded in the intellectual tradition that John Locke began nearly a century earlier. For Locke, the primary purpose of government was to protect private property. Locke claimed that "the reason why Men enter into society, is the preservation of their Property; and the end why they chuse and authorize a legislature, is, that there may be Laws made, and Rules set as Guards and Fences to the Properties of all the Members of the Society."[49]

In order to accomplish this, as earlier indicated, government needed a revenue stream to pay for its required police force. Individuals would give up a certain amount of their private property in the form of taxes to ensure the protection of their remaining property, as well as that of their neighbors. The idea led to progressive taxation, as Locke, and later Smith, envisioned that those with the most amount of property would pay more for its protection than those with less.[50] As Adam Smith wrote, "The subjects of every state ought to contribute towards the support of the government, as nearly as possible, in proportion to their respective abilities; that is, in proportion to the revenue which they respectively enjoy under the protection of the state."[51] This last point is significant, because it locates the individual property owner within a larger community, or civil society, and recognizes the inherent connection between individuals as they interact with each other.

The problem with smuggling in this theoretical narrative is that smugglers and their customers avoided paying taxes on their property, regardless of whether it was property that they had consumed or property that they had produced. The net effect of this was that illicit trade effectively denied the state revenue, not just to which it was *legally entitled* but also which it *needed* in order to protect the property of everyone who lived under its rule, including the smugglers and their customers. As a result, individuals who involved themselves in smuggling activities enfeebled a state that they themselves needed for protection. In this sense, a single group of individuals—perhaps even a very large group of individuals—acted out of simple consumer self-interest, without regard to the rest of civil society. Though the individuals involved all had different backgrounds, and likely would not have identified themselves as a group that possessed a coherent identity, their self-interested actions put them at odds with their own collective interests as members of enlightened civil society.

Adam Smith and John Locke represent a particular strand of political economy, which in this case could be defined as one focused on the relationship between government and its obligation to protect individual property and guarantee every individual's right to accumulate such property. This came to be known in the nineteenth century as liberalism. Karl Marx, on the other hand, might be seen as representative of another strand of political economy. It is clear that Marx had no love for the merchant class for reasons similar to Smith's. Not only were they often among smuggling's biggest perpetrators, but they also controlled the means of production within the bourgeois industrial state about which Marx wrote.[52] He found it especially galling that even as the bourgeoisie argued for additional state protection, it violated with impunity some of its own laws and policies. In the words of the *Communist Manifesto*, "the executive of the modern state is but a committee for managing the common affairs of the whole of the bourgeoisie."[53] Later in his career, in discussing the role of the bourgeois state, Friedrich Engels described political parties as "great gangs of political speculators, who alternately take possession of the state power and exploit it by the most corrupt means and for the most corrupt ends—and the nation is powerless against these two great cartels of politicians, who are ostensibly its servants, but in reality dominate and plunder it."[54]

But what did Marx think about those who *consumed* smuggled products? On this, he was largely silent, but his clear ideology allows us to tease out an answer to this question. Apart from likely having been driven to contraband trade as a way to survive the bourgeoisie-controlled economy, Marx almost certainly would have focused on the momentary unanimity of class interests that smuggling helped to create; this was significant—and desirable. In this case, however, such unanimity of class interests was problematic—especially because it prolonged the inevitable march to class revolution. By participating in smuggling then, the bourgeoisie extended their own control over the levers of power.

Marx would surely have claimed that this corruption of a system by the very people who controlled it was nothing more than a bandage that allowed them to stanch the festering wounds of a failing system.[55] Because the merchants, in their role as consumers, engaged in smuggling activities, either by purveying or purchasing smuggled goods, they enabled otherwise failing regimes to prolong their lives, further immiserating the masses. Without smuggling, in other words, the economic and political system that the bourgeoisie supported would fail, because it could not provide for the needs of those who lived under its rule. Therefore, by both writing laws and tariffs and then evading these same laws and tariffs, or permitting others to do so, the ruling class remained in power. In this, both Marx and Smith could find common ground, despite coming from different ideological positions.

Eradicating smuggling then might actually harm the state—because it would effectively bottle up the economic pressures that contraband actions let flow. Without smuggling, the masses of consumers would have revolted in a general overthrow of the industrial capitalist order. Marx had therefore considered the same phenomenon that Smith observed, albeit a century later, and even understood it in similar ways. Smuggling, along with its corruption of the governing system, was useful in allowing the economic system to survive. But then the two diverged: Marx believed that the corrupt regimes needed to fail, and anything that hastened their demise was desirable. Though he did not say so directly, it is possible to imagine him as a strong proponent of the state's authority to curb smuggling wherever and whenever it could, believing that the further unhappiness of the masses would cause them to overthrow an oppressive regime. On the other hand, Adam Smith did not object to the state, so much as he objected to the lack of virtue demonstrated both by policy makers and by their merchant allies—as well as, to a lesser degree, by consumers of smuggled property. His solution to the problem of smuggling would have entailed cleaning up the regimes' corruption, eliminating policies that encouraged such corruption, and returning to the virtuous ideal of civil society.

By contrast, nineteenth-century utilitarian thinkers such as Jeremy Bentham and the Mills, James and John Stuart, would not necessarily have been so fast to condemn smuggling activities and their related legal violations. Though all of them were concerned with individual rights and safeguarding these liberties against government action, they also understood that any government action needed to ensure the principle of utility: "actions are right in proportion as they tend to promote happiness, wrong as they tend to produce the reverse of happiness."[56] In a practical sense, then, smuggling, because it allowed consumers to consume that which they desired freely and without governmental restriction, ought to be seen as beneficial. Smuggling actually benefited more people than did a strict societal adherence to protectionist laws. If Smith saw the laws as problematic but the violation of the laws as more problematic, the utilitarian thinkers would have asserted that the problematic laws deserved to be eradicated or, if not, violated.[57] In the words of Jeremy Bentham, the course of action seems clear. Government ought not to force "bad" actions, such as those that restricted consumption through improper market regulation, upon an unwilling population.

> It has been shown that the happiness of individuals of whom a community is composed, that is, their pleasures and their security, is the end *and the sole end* which the legislator ought to have in view; the sole standard, in conformity to which each individual ought, as far as depends upon the legislator, to be made to fashion his behavior. But . . . there is nothing by which a man can ultimately be made to do it, but either pain or pleasure.[58] (italics mine)

Jeremy Bentham is generally remembered for two things in world history: the idea of the prison as panopticon, which will not be discussed in this book, and the "felicific calculus," which is essential to putting the principle of utility into operation, at least in his view.[59] In order to understand the relationship between government restrictions upon private actions, which smuggling was, at least superficially, it is essential to consider the "costs" and "benefits" that are associated with smuggling across an entire society. Cheaper products would be a "benefit," for example, while diminished governmental revenue from tax evaders would be a net "cost." Governmental action, the utilitarians argued, could be justified when the benefits of that action outweighed the costs for the most number of people.

For example, the sum total of all of the individual benefits accrued from smuggling needed to be calculated. A savings of three pence or two francs or five dollars for every single person who smuggled a single lemon, or a bowl of sugar, or a slave, needed to be added up for each person and then multiplied by the total number of people who would gain from avoiding the required taxation. The sum total could then be properly called the total "benefit" to a collection of individuals. Against this accounting, lost revenues to the government, in terms of a diminished ability to enforce all of its laws and carry out other government functions, had to be weighed. Without revenue, government could not, as indicated, maintain as big a military or provide the rudimentary education that many governments provided.

This kind of a calculation seems impossible to make except in an extremely abstract way. As I indicated earlier, it is certainly not possible to know anything about the actual costs of smuggling, because it is impossible to know precisely who was smuggling, what they were smuggling, and when they were smuggling. Instead, to get a useful estimate of the costs of smuggling, we would need to think about the amount of money each state spent enforcing the antismuggling laws and what that money might have been used for elsewhere. This, too, proves difficult, as the costs of enforcing trade laws were often part of the military's responsibility; whether the military might have been able to use its budget for something other than smuggling enforcement is beyond the scope of this work.

By the same token, it might be possible to consider the amount of time that government officials spent enforcing tariff laws. Such a calculation might result in a very loose approximation of the net cost of this enforcement to government, when combined with the costs for dedicated customs and excise officers. Against these costs, however, the price that any confiscated goods would bring to the government would need to be weighed. So must any fees that informants might receive be considered; in many cases, those who reported smuggling themselves received a share of the confiscated goods, increasing their own benefit and decreasing the benefit to the state, which they were purportedly helping. All of this seems excessively complicated and difficult to quantify; it becomes easy for us to see how such quantitative utilitarian thinking results in imprecise arguments. Rather, given the framework of liberal political economy into which utilitarian thinking fits, it makes much more sense to think about the implications of smuggling for ideas of liberty and freedom.

Nevertheless, it is very hard to believe that these illegal traders, and those who became their customers, were attempting to make a statement about freedom and liberty. Rather, most were simply trying to improve upon the economic circumstances of their lives. The unintended consequence of this was a weakening of the very state whose support they depended upon for the protection of life and liberty. Smuggling, while not directly addressed in many philosophical political economy treatises, therefore stands at a critical crossroads and reveals that the costs to government can not only be considered in terms of economics and calculations, but also in terms of authority and legitimacy.[60]

More modern political theorists and sociologists, such as Jürgen Habermas, have written on the relationship between government and the governed. According to one scholar, "Habermas views the legitimacy crisis as an outcome of the evolving character of an economic system wherein demand outpaces supply and of the development of concomitant attitudes . . . of disaffection and alienation."[61] It is this idea that smuggling addresses—demand for consumer goods, or slaves, or labor, outpaces supply—at least through legally proscribed channels. It did not matter that the supply was kept artificially low through government taxation and regulation. Most states did not react more forcefully to suppress contraband trade because they understood that to have done so would have made the situation of government, and especially government of far flung places, more difficult by provoking a legitimacy crisis.[62]

Max Weber, who studied bureaucracy, recognized the contradiction of asking people who were charged with enforcing the law to do so when it hurt their own personal interests. This is, in many ways, why Weber supported the idea of a bureaucracy that could stand apart, and remain incorruptible. Such a bureaucracy would make the various utilitarian calculations that are too complicated to make here and then act according to utilitarian principles, putting laws on the statute books and making sure that they were fairly enforced. For Weber, then, the problems that Smith and Marx identified regarding the lawmakers' governmental interests being at odds with their consumer interests would have been fixed. Once a smuggling law was in place, impartial and incorruptible bureaucrats would have punished those who broke the law. The problem with this thinking, of course, is that it seems virtually impossible for bureaucrats in a real-world situation to ignore their own interests completely enough to be impartial arbiters and pure decision makers. Here is where the theory parts ways with the reality.

Theory Meets Reality: The Governor (Again)

To return now to the story with which this chapter began, the Chinese migrants passing through what is now Penang, Malaysia, disobeyed their own government by smuggling themselves across a legal frontier. And they were welcomed in British-controlled territory, not only because the British failed to prohibit such movement, but also because the East India Company representative in the region imagined a use for this human commodity. The Chinese likely believed their own government ineffective, perhaps even illegitimate, while the British East India Company's lieutenant governor puzzled over how to interpret the Chinese government's failure to enforce its own laws. One could reasonably assume that the lesson that the British took away was that the Chinese state was not always going to enforce its own laws.[63] Nevertheless, Farquhar's proposal to ship Chinese migrants to Trinidad calculated the degree to which the Chinese state should even be made aware of such a proposal. For Farquhar's plan to succeed, he reasoned, the Chinese government must not be made aware of it.

This is instructive, as it showed Farquhar's willingness to engage in a discussion of political economy, but only to a point. If it were adapted, the British East India Company's proposal would have had to stay on the right side of existing law at the same time that it remained concerned about fully disclosing the company's clear plans to use Chinese laborers in place of slaves. The idea that the Chinese could be used as field hands did not seem to trouble Farquhar; what bothered him was that the Chinese government might make an association between its subjects, even those who had illegally left, and the African slaves who would no longer be used in Caribbean agriculture. Farquhar wanted the commerce in people to remain legitimate under British law; disclosing this to the Chinese risked them enforcing their exit ban on Chinese subjects—thereby killing Farquhar's proposal.[64]

Though there is no evidence anywhere in the historical record to suggest that Farquhar himself engaged in smuggling activities, he nevertheless resembled many smugglers in his planning and plotting.[65] Many officials like Farquhar attempted to identify and then to exploit other countries' legal loopholes in order to achieve their desired results. Most never fully informed government and its officials of their private or "off the books" activities, though many clearly had them; they were, in other words, economical with the truth. Many, if not most, smugglers almost certainly understood that individuals who lived under any kind of governmental authority consistently found themselves negotiating with their own state and its officials about the degree to which toleration of illegal activity against other states could take place.

In the case of circumstances in 1805, the Chinese smuggled themselves out of China, breaking Chinese laws; at the same time, the Europeans welcomed them to the Malay Peninsula, where many found work. The negotiation between the Chinese state and its subjects might be described as a failure for both parties. The Chinese state failed to provide adequately for its subjects; they voted with their feet.

At the same time, British representatives like Farquhar wanted to investigate using these self-smuggled individuals in a different way than they might have envisioned for themselves. The East India Company, if it had decided to move forward with Farquhar's plan, would have needed to determine how much it could tell the Chinese government about the intended use of its lost "property." Providing too much information to China's government might have risked shutting down the impermissible migration across the legal frontier, eliminating the business before it even got started. Providing no information could well have meant that no challenges would ever have been made to the British proposal. But it could also have met a much fiercer attack on the East India Company itself, which of course concerned its employees.[66]

The calculation was complex, like Bentham's felicific calculus. It certainly revealed the ways in which smugglers' actions needed to be balanced against the state's right to raise revenue and protect its subjects, and therefore achieve the greatest good for the greatest number. Farquhar himself wanted to provide only enough information to the Chinese government to prevent arousing sufficient interest to protect its borders and eliminate its own willfully self-smuggled subjects. In this, he was like many other government officials in world history. So long as no one interfered with their ability to rule, they were prepared to look the other way when legal frontiers were transgressed. Of course, this led to inconsistency, the very kind of inconsistency that Max Weber thought a true bureaucracy should seek to avoid—and the very inconsistency on which smugglers generally thrived.

If smugglers thrived in an inconsistently enforced system of political economy, their own behavior was incredibly consistent from one society to the next and from one era to another. They moved goods across legal frontiers without declaring them to officials in the hopes that they could avoid paying taxes on them. This tax savings could then be passed on to consumers, enriching them at the expense of the state treasury. Moreover, the smuggling process and its implications was apparent even to theorists, who are usually thought to be immune from such observations. When talking about government, they understood, it was necessary to consider the revenue that was necessary to support it. And when considering that revenue, it became clear that smuggling played a part in its (non)collection. With that realization, governments ought to have been able to address the issues. They certainly tried, but without great effect. One reason for this was the changing nature of what was actually smuggled from one region to another, or at one time or another. The next chapter explores the kinds of goods that clandestinely crossed legal frontiers. Readers will quickly note the great variety of such products; surely the theorists were similarly aware. (They were, after all, also consumers themselves.) As a result, it is not an unreasonable claim to make that throughout modern world history it would have been a very rare product indeed that completely escaped the smuggler's attention.

CHAPTER FOUR

—ᛉ—

Smuggling

Patterns and Practices

People, Places, and Things

Considering what smuggling is—the clandestine and illegal movement of goods across a legal boundary in order to avoid paying tax—as well as what it is not—piracy—allows readers to contemplate the ways in which smuggling actually took place across the modern world as it developed over time. This chapter illustrates some of these paths and mechanisms; it is not meant to be exhaustive. Rather, it is intended to serve as a guide to understanding the ways in which populations found spaces to negotiate with their governments, as well as opportunities to improve the quality of their lives when such negotiations did not bear as much fruit as they might have wished. What should become clear to readers is that over the course of modern world history virtually no object has been exempt from the smuggler's attentions. So long as there were revenue laws and consumers, violations of those revenue laws took place.

Perhaps the most frequent question that I have been asked over the course of working on this project has been one of the most basic: "What did people smuggle?" This simple query has become virtually impossible to answer, embarrassingly enough, because it is so context specific. People smuggled sugar in eighteenth-century Dominica, tea in eighteenth-century Boston, slaves in nineteenth-century Cuba, opium in nineteenth-century Hong Kong, cocaine and heroin in twentieth-century Europe, and fashion in twenty-first-century America. This abbreviated list in no way should be considered anything approaching an exhaustive itemization of contraband consumables.

Rather, readers might do better to think of the products enumerated in this chapter as some of those that crossed illegal frontiers at some moments in time and in some places around the world. When faced with the very reasonable question of what attracted smugglers' interests, therefore, I learned that it became preferable to demur. A list of smuggled products in every time and place would not be particularly useful; an effort to create one would not provide much insight into *why* smugglers acted the way that they did and *how* it was that they made their determinations to act the way that they did.[1] This chapter argues that virtually nothing was exempt from the attentions of smugglers; it does so by using specific illustrations from specific times and places to demonstrate some of the ways smugglers operated across some of the many boundaries on the planet.

Nevertheless, historians are obligated to catalogue and categorize; if we failed to do so, the historical record could well be devoid of any analysis at all. It is, therefore, possible to find a number of commonalities, at least in terms of the basic categories of product that clandestinely crossed legal frontiers across wide swaths of time and space. For example, consumer goods of all sorts have always topped any list of smuggled items. Such products could range from either the latest in Parisian fashion, as Jeb Bush's wife Columba's experience at the Atlanta airport tells us, to fancy French linen covertly imported across *La Manche* into southern English towns and villages, to electronic goods of every shape and size.[2] Commodities of various kinds, such as tobacco, sugar, coffee, and tea, have also been regularly smuggled into distant territories—especially when import duties and protected markets raised a crop's price beyond what it might otherwise fetch in a completely free market.[3] This illegal commodity trade is, in many ways, the historical smuggling with which people already would be aware.

As importantly, depending on the region and timing, addictive and narcotic substances such as opium and its derivatives were also regularly smuggled out of one legal regime and into another. The whole of today's illicit drug trade could easily fit within this category.[4] Products that are naturally scarce can be quite expensive to procure; those whose scarcity was then exacerbated by prohibitive commercial regulations fetched even higher prices. Some scholars have even argued that such "manufactured" or legislated scarcity creates an even greater impetus to break the law in order to gain access to such products than otherwise might exist through following the simple principles that govern a market driven by consumer demand.

For example, the current debate over marijuana decriminalization (or legalization) in the U.S. and elsewhere can be seen as a version of individuals telling their governments, which are generally responsible to their citizens for their existence, that the restrictive actions that they take are simply unacceptable.[5] Regulating this kind of consumption is akin to an inappropriate or intolerable market intervention. Even as debates about which trade should and should not be prevented take place in the corridors of power around the world, most consumers usually have another choice. They can simply ignore the laws on the books and smuggle. They can, in other words, become free traders. Such contemporary debate is nothing new. Indeed, nineteenth-century opium addicts had a great deal in common with the individual who lived under the USA's prohibition on alcohol consumption, as well as having a great deal in common with today's crack and crystal meth(amphetamine) merchants. All participated in contravened activities. In addition to the public health issues such as addiction and its attendant problems which accompany and inform such substance prohibitions, there are also issues about individual liberties that enter into play here. In other words, banning addictive drugs may serve a public health purpose, but it also intervenes in an individual's choice about what best to consume and when. This reopens the concern that many individuals have with their personal liberties being violated by trading restrictions. Smuggling was one way to avoid a fuller confrontation with the state on this very subject. It allowed individuals to regain some control over their own economic lives.[6]

Adding to the list of smuggled products, of course, generally requires us to consider human beings as objects of smuggling, as well as agents in it. People have been, and still are, smuggled across a boundary from one legal regime into another. Scarcely a week goes by these days when there is not a press report about individuals being smuggled across an international border.[7] This typically happens as a result of an individual or group choice to make a better life, and generally follows the pattern of a resident from a low-wage society being smuggled into a higher-wage society in order to earn more money and, as a result, increase their individual or familial consumption. Sometimes they do this through remittances—sending earned cash to family members still at home—which could itself sometimes constitute yet another form of smuggling.[8] The view of such cheats, at least in the contemporary media, generally ignores the mechanisms in which smugglers easily cross the very boundaries that are designed to keep them out. The problem, of course, is that by focusing on the criminals, the crime and its meaning get ignored.

We might refer to such perpetrators, who are usually thought of as illegal migrants, as self-smugglers.[9] Sometimes, business networks developed among those who actually smuggled people across a frontier from one country to another. This, too, is most frequently considered to be a recent phenomenon, yet the historical past certainly had many versions of such enterprises.

Smugglers of coolie laborers and slaves are but two illustrations. In some cases, the smuggled individuals actively chose to be illegally transported across a legal boundary, but in many other cases the smuggled slaves had no choice at all about where to go.[10]

In 1792, with France in turmoil, an uprising against white colonial rule broke out in Saint Domingue. After 1792 and the commencement of hostilities, the trading laws became difficult at best to enforce.[11] The British Parliament, in 1792, was in the midst of a protracted and oftentimes heated disagreement about what to do with slavery. As usual, peace in the eighteenth century was short-lived. Jamaican colonists, at least on the north coast, took advantage of Europe's preoccupations to smuggle slaves from Saint Domingue into their own colony. Law enforcement officials in Jamaica believed that some of those slaves ended up on Zachary Bayly's plantation in St. Mary's parish.

The French colonists on Hispaniola were selling their slaves at a loss. In a desperate effort to control black access to revolutionary ideas, white residents of Saint Domingue exported the slaves whom they deemed irredeemable troublemakers. They hoped thus to prevent the contamination of the rest of their human property. In the crisis, however, they flaunted their own laws—rules designed to keep slave property within the colony by prohibiting its easy disposal outside of it. The illegal exportation of slaves exacerbated British fears; colonists did not want revolutionary ideas to spread to their own colonies. If, on the other hand, they acted to keep French slaves out of British territory, they might further destabilize Saint Domingue—the largest of the region's sugar economies—abetting a potentially catastrophic change to the international economic system.[12]

Sometime in mid- or late July 1792, a schooner carrying twenty-one slaves from Saint Domingue entered Port Maria, Jamaica, under the cloak of darkness. It quickly unloaded its cargo. All of the slaves on board went immediately to Zachary Bayly's local estates.[13] The ship's captain, several eyewitnesses agreed, then loaded Jamaican produce to be sold in Saint Domingue. Soon after, the ship sailed for Cap François, later Cap Haïtien, to dispose of its smuggled produce and take on more slaves for illegal export.[14]

In mid-August 1792, a special Court of Sessions convened in St. Mary's parish, Jamaica. The court learned that the ship had indeed returned to Saint Domingue. Its captain had there purchased about sixty more slaves. As he prepared to leave the French colony, "he was accidentally killed by the discharge of his own pistol, as he was ascending the companion ladder in coming out of the cabin."[15] This was, perhaps, a fitting way for a smuggler to die—by his own carelessness while on an illegal mission.

In order to prevent this second venture from failing (indicating the success of the first trip), one Captain Howell, a Charleston-based seaman, in Saint Domingue to trade a cargo from Charleston, perhaps of rice, agreed to bring the illegally exported slaves to Jamaica. When he got there, the slaves again found their way to Zachary Bayly's plantations. The Africans never passed through customs in Jamaica, thereby violating both local and imperial regulations. Captain Howell claimed to those who observed him unloading his cargo that he had simply come from Kingston, where he had cleared his slaves. He produced a droghing pass to prove it. He lied, knowing that few of those whom he encountered would bother to make the sixty-mile journey to the other side of the island to verify his story.

His ruse nearly worked. Any would-be critics were quieted until several witnesses overheard "the negroes speak the same broken French as our negroes speak broken English."[16] A Jamaican plantation owner accosted one of the slaves using French. The slaves responded properly, with all due respect—in French. Sensing that he had been exposed—it would have been near impossible to find legally obtained French-speaking slaves in Kingston—Howell admitted his activities. Within twenty-four hours, well before local officials got around to arresting him, he fled the island. Before leaving, however, members of his crew explained that "negroes are dog-cheap at the Cape (François), the prison ships quite full, and provisions very dear."[17] All of this information ought to be an explanation for why smuggling took place. The French in Saint Domingue were willing to exchange problematic slaves for food, even if it meant breaking their own laws. The English in Jamaica were willing to import illegally such problematic slaves as a way of increasing their own profits, since these smuggled slaves would have cost less than those who were imported legally. Of course, the law took no action against Zachary Bayly in this case. He was after all investing in the growth of the island's economy, even by resorting to immoral and illegal activities.

It also ought to go without saying that these kinds of transborder movements required capital, and much of such capital was never reported to tax or customs authorities. In some cases, people paid their smugglers for their services; it does not seem likely that such capital would have been reported to taxing authorities as earned income. The same could be said for those who spent their money to smuggle themselves; they likely would not have withheld any wage taxes that might have been due to their home government. Money, which was in any event easier to keep track of when it was in the form of precious metals, also could frequently become an object of smuggling. In some cases, it was even done surreptitiously by changing the weight of standard coins, a process that contemporaries generally referred to as "coin clipping."[18]

What this effectively meant is that people who smuggled themselves over a border created a problematic situation for the state; it needed to respond more directly and, perhaps, forcefully than it did when only goods were being smuggled.[19] Perhaps the worst situation of all was when slaves were smuggled, or smuggled themselves. This provoked among the harshest attacks that have been observed in the historical record.

Just as it has proven feasible generally to group smuggled goods into a few broad categories, as above, it is similarly possible to identify patterns of smuggling over time and place, or across otherwise divergent societies. As previously discussed, areas that restricted access to goods through imposing taxes such as import duties or export tariffs often found their residents circumventing those laws in order to acquire and accumulate goods at a better price and under better circumstances than their own governments permitted them to do. There was in fact little difference in *consumer* behavior from one society to the next, whether the contraband goods were a favorite food, a luxurious spice, harmless frocks, or (potentially) harmful addictive substances. But there *was* a difference from one smuggling case to another in the *mechanisms* used in legal enforcement, as well as in the actual frequency of such actions. Indeed, certain kinds of contraband commercial activities garnered the authorities' attention and intervention much more frequently during wartime than at any other time; this was usually a result of a greater police presence. Other kinds of activities, such as slave smuggling, nearly *always* elicited an official reaction, usually a strong effort to interdict such clandestine trade, regardless of whether or not a war happened to be on.[20] In both cases, however, official legal attention was nearly universally unwelcome.

When people were not involved as the objects (or commodities) of smuggling, or in other words, when consumer goods, inanimate commodities, or illicit substances *were* the objects of the smugglers' attentions, official reactions were generally infrequent. Perhaps this was because the cost of detecting smuggling could easily outweigh the benefits that could be produced with the additional revenue that might be collected from an intervention.[21] Nevertheless, when there was any kind of sustained and measurable oversight, it nearly always came from those individual officials who demonstrated a predisposition to be rule-bound.

I mean to suggest here that, within the group of historical actors that I encountered in the archives, two basic categories emerged, much as there are today the same two basic categories. The first consisted of those who, like Dominica's eighteenth-century Governor John Orde, were rule-bound and who believed that any statutes and directives needed to be enforced regularly and consistently, and thus, in theory, fairly. The second consisted of those who knew the rules, but who could not have cared less about what the rules actually were and how to enforce them, so long as they did not have to deal with a problem that might create additional work for them to perform during their tours of duty. The differences ought to be clear: those who were rule-bound generally enforced all of the rules all of the time, even if that meant acting against their own personal interests.[22] Those who were not rule-bound might well be aware of rules, laws, and statutes but did not necessarily behave according to the statutes' prescribed actions. Working through existing archival sources supports the notion that rule-bound officials were frequently harder to observe in many societies, because there were fewer of them, than officers who were not so inclined.

During periods of war, however, governmental oversight of every kind could often be more intense as bureaucrats received more direction and engaged in more frequent communication with their superiors, usually metropolitan officials, or nearby military officers who, then as now, were much more likely to follow the rules than their civilian bureaucratic counterparts. Of course, the very presence of additional oversight made it much more difficult either to sanction smuggling through willful ignorance or even to participate in such actions through corruption. There were simply too many additional sets of eyes to make things comfortable for those who wanted to look the other way or otherwise to profit from their offices in ways that their government employers did not specifically intend.

Similar patterns also emerge when considering the smuggling of people. This contraband traffic generally was tolerated, or at least it was not prevented, unless either (a) slaves were the objects of smuggling activities, or (b) British government officials *believed* that non-British shippers continued to import African slaves after 1808. Soon after ending its slave trade, Britain began to capture any ships of other European states that had been found to be engaging in human trafficking; Britain had effectively become the Atlantic's policeman. Even colonies that had legally legitimate reasons, such as Brazil or Cuba, to rely upon slave labor found their ships being stopped and searched for illicitly obtained slaves.[23] As has been seen in the last chapter, at least one British East India Company official *planned* to send Chinese workers who had smuggled themselves out of China through the East India Company's Malay settlements to work as replacement laborers in newly settled Caribbean islands.[24] Such efforts still relied upon smuggled laborers; the Chinese had broken Chinese laws to get to the East India Company's settlements. But even the most rule-bound officials could still reason that as long as British laws were not broken, such commerce was bearable, if not nominally acceptable.[25]

If patterns of smuggling and anti-smuggling activities, however small, can be identified, it is also possible to identify smuggling relationships that operated on both intraregional and interregional levels. By this I mean that for virtually any given modern world region, it becomes possible to characterize the contraband trade that took place both within it and from it to another geographic region. For example, using the case of the eighteenth-century Caribbean, the area of the world with which I have the greatest historical familiarity, it is possible to identify and generally characterize the intraregional smuggling that took place between the British and French, or between the British and Spanish, islands. So too is it possible to identify smuggling activities between the French Caribbean and North America, or between the British Caribbean and the Spanish Atlantic World. In short, though the products being traded were often quite different in each of these circuits of exchange, whether within one region or across regions, any given region engaged in both kinds of smuggling on a regular basis.

Perhaps one way to look at this is to consider a port in a single region and to examine its smuggling activities over a brief period. This kind of microstudy should help readers understand the ways in which contraband commerce took place and how it is that it became publicly observable from time to time.

Counting in Monte Christi

The most common kind of port in the Atlantic World was neither a large city port, such as Philadelphia or Kingston, not was it an officially licensed "free port" that was designed to get residents of another country to break with their own legal regime in the pursuit of consumption. Instead, the most common kind of ports were neither officially monitored nor legally recognized. Yet they grew up organically, meaning that residents of these towns (and their surrounding hinterlands) naturally engaged with residents of other towns (and regions) in order to get what they needed; they were the free market in operation. They fulfilled, in other words, their Smithian propensities to "truck, barter, and exchange," almost completely outside the gaze of European imperial officials. The principal example of this kind of port to be considered here is Monte Christi, on the island of Hispaniola.

Most world historians have probably never heard of Monte Christi; the same is probably true even for historians of the eighteenth-century Atlantic World. Even so, the town's significance as a place in which the human proclivity to consume fiercely confronted mercantilist regulations designed to check that very behavior ought not be underestimated. Located on Hispaniola's north coast, astride the border that separated the island's French and Spanish colonies, Spanish-controlled Monte Christi illustrated the ways in which colonial residents from all of the American empires rewrote those imperial statutes that served European mercantilist (imperial or state) interests at the expense of local colonial residents. These Caribbean acts of legal noncompliance were, in many respects, more effective in furthering the interests of colonial consumers than those asserted in North America in the decades just before the American Revolution. British North Americans confrontationally and aggressively challenged those policies with which they disagreed in the years after 1763. Yet those who lived in Monte Christi, along with those who came to trade there (including many North Americans), remained superficially supportive of problematic regulations even as they actively and quietly undermined them. Residents of this kind of port city assumed control of their own consumer needs, as Smith believed natural. They did not rely upon European governments to sanction or prohibit their behavior. They simply rewrote law through transgressing it.[26]

Most scholars would consider Monte Christi little more than a minor settlement, given that its usual population consisted of only about one hundred Spanish subjects of no particular means.[27] Nevertheless, during its heyday as a center for contraband commerce in the mid- to late eighteenth century, *several hundred* oceangoing ships annually called into its harbor. That would amount to several ships per inhabitant—an astronomical number for the time period. Many of these vessels came from British North America, where European-imposed laws forbade trade with either the French or the Spanish.[28] Still others came from islands elsewhere in the Caribbean. Because almost all sailings to Monte Christi by ships other than Spanish-licensed vessels violated Spanish law—if not also those of another European state—there is scarce documentation for voyages to the port. Having said that, however, enough ships faced interdiction on their return voyages to leave historians with an ample supply of data on the mechanisms by which the port operated.

Monte Christi's lieutenant governor wrote to William Shirley, governor of the British Bahamas, in March 1760.[29] The Spanish official asserted that an English privateer, based in New Providence (now Nassau), illegally captured five Spanish vessels.[30] The lieutenant governor of Monte Christi claimed that he had licensed the five ships to sail from the port under his control only as far as the neighboring French colony of Saint Domingue. The ships were to return loaded with goods that were required "for the Encouragement of the new Settlement under [Monte Christi's] Government."[31] *British* privateers would thus have had no reason to stop, let alone capture, these ships.[32] Though Britain and France were at war, these were represented to be, at least ostensibly, neutral Spanish ships. Of course, *French* shipping would have been subject to British arrest and seizure—but these particular ships had Spanish licenses. British Governor Shirley therefore endeavored to learn why the ships had been seized before he would answer his Spanish colleague. It is thus possible to see the overlapping national legal regimes yielding to an emerging international legal regime—one that Caribbean residents were negotiating for themselves.

Fortunately for Shirley, the five arrested ships had already been brought into the British Court of Admiralty in Nassau for official condemnation, sale of the cargo, and division of the proceeds. Before any division of the prize could take place, however, the court needed to determine the answer to the question of the ships' nationalities. If they were French ships, they were lawful wartime prizes; the ships and their contents could be divided between the privateers who captured them and the British government. On the other hand, if the ships belonged to Spanish subjects, restitution would obviously be required—as Spain and Britain remained at peace in 1760—since there would have been no legal reason for a British seizure other than the ships' having eluded British customs.[33] Governor Shirley asked the Admiralty Court to share copies of all pertinent documents and depositions.

The court complied with the governor's request. Shirley, who had recently arrived in Nassau after having been governor of Massachusetts, then glimpsed that which was already well known to most regional populations. Shirley learned of Monte Christi's important role in facilitating extralegal exchange by evading territorial, and therefore legal, boundaries. The Bahamian governor remained uncharacteristically diplomatic while standing his ground. Shirley maintained that the English privateers acted appropriately. Moreover, he asserted that Monte Christi had manufactured its own problem. Governor Shirley delicately "reminded" his Spanish counterpart what the captured licenses (or passports), which the Spanish official had in fact signed, actually mandated. The first ship (*Nuestra Señora de Alta Gracia*) had permission to "carry the Effects permitted [by Spanish law], and to bring some eatables and provisions for the use of Monte Christi, and *for no other port*." If the ship's master violated his instructions then any cargo aboard was to be "answerable."[34] The second ship had been instructed to bring "the fruits and eatables of the Earth from the French colonies to Monte Christi for the *Encouragement of the New Settlement There*."[35] A third ship (*Nuestra Señora de Socorro*) was licensed "to carry such Goods as are permitted to the French Colonies, and to bring from thence *some provisions for the City of Monte*

Christi, and no other place."[36] (Emphasis in all quotes above are mine.) The remaining two ships had similar charges.

This meant that altogether a total of five oceangoing vessels received simultaneous permission to bring back produce from the French colony to be consumed in the Spanish port; no mention was ever made of shipping the imported French produce to other Spanish settlements on Hispaniola.[37] But the port's one hundred or so consumers could not possibly have consumed all of the imported "eatables and provisions" on the five ships, given their small number. William Shirley therefore concluded that his Spanish counterpart must have known that the Spanish ships, by bringing to Monte Christi more than could be consumed, were planning to export the French products, quite possibly to British colonies in the region or in North America. This was clearly transgressive behavior.[38] Since British privateers captured the ships in French waters, and France was at war with Britain, the capture seemed legitimate to the British.

But it was worse than all of that; the ships' captains had further evaded the official Spanish legal regime. Rather than confront a colleague, Governor Shirley diplomatically pointed this out. The holds of these captured ships, in contravention of their licenses, contained *no food at all.* The cargo instead consisted of "Sugars, Molasses, Rum, Indigo, and Coffee, the produce and manufacture of the French settlements." They were "without any of the usual and necessary papers for proving them to be the property of Spaniards." Since there was no dispute about the ships having been to French ports on Hispaniola, what was in them must have been French.[39] The cargoes were French, in British eyes, simply because there was no record of duties having been paid either for the export from Monte Christi to Europe or another colony; nor was there a record of duties having been paid for the import into Monte Christi from Saint Domingue. The British admiralty judge therefore could condemn the cargoes as French, making them legal prizes of war.

But what of the ships themselves? Governor Shirley admonished his Spanish counterpart that though enough evidence existed to order the ships condemned and sold, he would see that they were released. What evidence did Shirley have against the ships? He again used the passports that the Spanish governor had approved. The ships did not adhere to instructions; they both had on board products that were not "eatables," such as sugar, and they had far more of it than Monte Christi's small population could ever use, at least before it spoiled. Shirley claimed that "a most unwarrantable and prejudicial Commerce to the Interests of Great Britain is carry'd out with the French of Hispaniola thro' the Channel of Monte Christi, whereby the French are frequently furnished with great Quantities of Money, Contraband, and other

Goods, in exchange for their Sugars and the other produce and manufactures of their Settlements."[40] The Spanish ships had thus given aid and comfort to Britain's French enemies, thereby violating principles of neutrality. But because the ships were Spanish-owned, he allowed them to be returned to Monte Christi with a warning that such behavior was unacceptable. The ships were once again placed in the service of Monte Christi's few consumers and its many traders.

The port certainly had a great deal of experience in dealing with non-Spanish customers; indeed, it made its living from such people. Spanish commercial law appears to have been largely irrelevant in that port. British ships (from Britain, from the North American colonies, or from neighboring Caribbean islands), along with those from other European nations, regularly docked in Monte Christi's harbor, paid the Spanish governor *cash*, and were then given a Spanish license to enter the port. (Non-Spanish ships were not allowed in Spanish colonies; Monte Christi's governor broke Spanish law when he issued these passes.) Next, the visiting ships unloaded their foreign cargoes directly onto Spanish-licensed ships, like those captured by the privateers. The goods being transferred would be counted and then the foreign traders would pay the Spanish governor another fee, usually a piece-of-eight, for every hogshead of molasses or other product that was destined to the French on the frontier's other side. In exchange for this consideration, the governor overlooked the Spanish residents who loaded and unloaded foreign cargoes in the harbor at Monte Christi and who shipped them aboard Spanish boats to foreign ports—and then did the same on the return voyages. They also paid their governor a fee for this service, taken out of the wages they earned for their labors.[41]

In return, the British and other foreign traders received Spanish money and French luxury goods, as well as French sugars, molasses, and other tropical produce, such as coffee. These products then entered the European marketplace as British produce; they usually remained on board the ships and then were clandestinely added to the final tallies at a pre-export inspection in the last American port that they visited before heading to Europe. Tropical products generally fetched higher prices in protected British markets than they did in protected French ones.[42] And because the foreigners paid the French producers in Saint Domingue for their products and goods in advance of them being entered into the market, consumers there benefited doubly. Not only did they get cash before they shipped their produce, they also received a higher price than they would have done by following legal channels. In fact, the port of Monte Christi—and others like it—allowed consumers across the Atlantic World to escape from policies that injured or restricted their consumer propensities. As Lauren Benton claims, albeit in a slightly different context, "local institutional practices sometimes offered opportunities for capital accumulation that colonial agents sought to preserve."[43]

Resorting to diplomatic language, Governor Shirley let his Monte Christian counterpart know that the British had noted Monte Christi's modus operandi. Rather than accuse the lieutenant governor of fraud, Shirley asserted that the Spanish crews found means "to protect their [illicit] French Cargoes with Spanish papers" by using "some misrepresentation or Imposition (as I doubt not it must be) to obtain Certificates from you, Sir, that the same were puchas'd by Subjects of Spain, residing at Monte Christi."[44] Governor Shirley claimed to have seen documentation that a British ship had a cargo of Spanish sugar, purchased at Monte Christi, aboard it. Shirley knew for a fact, he said, that the sugar was French and had been loaded at St. Christopher's. "[T]here is a very large Quantity of the pernicious Trade," Shirley maintained, "carry'd on at Monte Christi."[45] In this way the Bahamian governor revealed some additional ways in which individual consumers—and their agents—found ways to evade European-created rules that obstructed colonial property acquisition and, through it, capital accumulation. Mercantilist policy, without directly saying so, attempted to control consumer demand by using tariffs and prohibitions.

Regional Expansion

If tiny Monte Christi had a sizable amount of organized illicit commercial activity, it should come as no surprise that much bigger and more populous ports, such as Kingston in Jamaica, also regularly participated in illegal commerce. These larger ports, which had more officials visibly stationed in them, faced more consistent and frequent scrutiny. As in the smaller ports, local consumers and their merchant suppliers frequently found ways to challenge the laws that impeded their abilities to "truck, barter, and exchange," while simultaneously impeding any official efforts to enforce the problematic statutes.

Monte Christi was an active port, despite its small size. It regularly employed passive tactics to circumvent the law and operate beyond the notice of enforcement officials. At the same time, larger ports—with more official oversight—utilized much more confrontational and assertive tactics to beat back any governmental challenges to their illegal behavior. Though European merchants had induced their various state and imperial governments to promulgate policies that favored them, the benefits did not apply evenly to all commercial people. In many cases eighteenth-century Caribbean merchants found the restrictions placed upon them to have deleterious consequences for their economic advancement. Many broke ranks with their European counterparts and the policies that they supported. Instead, they forged alliances with their counterparts in other islands and, frequently, on the American continent (or elsewhere in the world). Commerce outside the legally prescribed channels happened with regularity in these places as well.

With Britain and France still fighting a war in July 1761, British Rear Admiral Holmes wrote to the secretary of the Admiralty in London from his Jamaica post. Holmes reported that he had recently offended several Jamaican merchants.[46] He had done so by acting to suppress the illegal trade that he supposed Jamaica's residents carried on with the Spanish and French on Hispaniola. This trade almost certainly took place through Monte Christi, though it could also have been carried on in a few other places on the larger island, as the earlier example in this chapter has illustrated. A number of Jamaica's most prominent residents attempted to get Admiral Holmes to relax his opposition to the trade. They first tried the "soft" approach. But Holmes knew better. In his report to the Admiralty, Holmes claimed that he was "soothed, caressed, and flattered, but all to no purpose."[47] Because Jamaica's traders and other influential consumers could not eliminate his opposition to their lawbreaking with this approach, several prominent Jamaican merchants decided to work behind his back in order to undermine his ability to enforce British commercial policy. Indeed, Holmes believed that the Kingston merchants entered into clandestine deals with French ships to capture or destroy British naval ships. He thought that they had created a sort of private naval harassment force—much like privateers, though without the local governor's approval. Though this might have created a temporary nuisance for the British fleet in the area, the Jamaican merchants' policy failed to have the desired effect. The British Navy had quite literally "gotten in the way" of the island population's propensities to exchange one thing for another when it did not succumb to French harassment.

But the Jamaican merchants were not so easily mollified. Desperate to end their own government's harassment of their contraband commerce, several Kingston merchants clamored for a meeting of their commercial colleagues. In this meeting, they discussed constructing the "proper Measures for the better Protection of the Trade of this colony."[48] There ought to have been nothing wrong with this, since it sounded above board. But when Admiral Holmes learned of the merchants' plans, he became extremely agitated. His pride in and commitment to his profession had been challenged. Holmes believed that the merchant meeting strongly implied that the British Navy could not adequately defend and protect the island's trade from foreign aggression. Why else would the merchants be having such a meeting? He strongly resented the public participation in such a meeting; he also vowed to continue, and strengthen, his efforts to stop illegal trade between places like Jamaica and Monte Christi. Holmes again asserted that the Jamaican merchants were trying to find a way around the British Navy in order to continue their trade. The meeting, he believed, showed them to be nothing but, as he called them, a "Motley Group of Defamators."[49]

After they held their meeting, a number of the most well known and powerful attendees went to Admiral Holmes's house and presented him with "their insolent, false, and abusive letter." Holmes did not reply to their letter. Instead, he became even more convinced that these people had something to hide. They simply *must* be engaged in some clandestine commercial venture. In this instance he practiced guilt by inference and association. He did, however, have current events that supported his view. The ship *Guadeloup* had recently been condemned in Jamaica's Admiralty Court. Like the five Monte Christi ships that ended up in the Bahamian Admiralty Court a year earlier, this ship "had a false Spanish Pass, was navigated by Spaniards, and [was] taken, coming from the [French] Ports in Hispaniola, with French Produce."[50] Holmes believed that the ship and its cargo did not belong either to the Spanish, as claimed, or to the French, as the evidence indicated. He believed instead that the ship's cargo, if not the vessel itself, belonged to several Jamaica merchants—who happened to be participants in the Kingston meeting. These merchants, Holmes maintained, illegally imported French sugar into Jamaica by claiming that the ship used to carry it from Saint Domingue to Jamaica had actually originated in a distant Jamaican port—and therefore was not subject to import duties.[51] In this way the island's merchants increased their rate of return from that which they could have expected had they followed the law and engaged in trade with only Jamaican produce—or paid the heavy duties that were legally required to import foreign goods and produce. Admiral Holmes, who seemed to epitomize the incorruptible official, was outraged that such a scheme could take place at the highest levels of Jamaican civil society.

But outrage about such activities somehow does not seem the appropriate response. The merchants' illegal and extralegal activities and schemes developed because commercial rules and regulations were not properly suited to local economic conditions. Such policies did not allow individual Caribbean residents to assert easily their "propensity to truck, barter, and exchange." As a result, they found the official legal policies under which they lived to be confounding. In order to remedy their situations, many created trading communities that at once allowed them to acquire goods they wanted to consume while simultaneously challenging those restrictions that, when enforced, served to hold their economic growth and development in check. In short, they created new, more pluralistic legal regimes through negotiated authority. Colonial officials charged with enforcement were often frustrated when they got to the Caribbean; it should, however, not be surprising to learn that enforcing unpopular statutes could make life truly miserable for such officials. A fair number of them eventually acquiesced, becoming more like the lieutenant governor of Monte Christi than Rear Admiral Holmes.

The law, especially if we think of it as a European imperial institution, became the largest casualty in the negotiations over the creation of a pluralistic legal regime. The port towns, with their easy access to individuals from different societies and economies, made legal evasions and challenges relatively simple. American ports challenged European ones, at least metaphorically, for control of the ways in which consumption took place across the Atlantic World; similar challenges took place elsewhere around the globe. When all is said and done, the colonial ports facilitated, if they did not specifically encourage, legal transgressions. From the European perspective, this could be seen as a small but consistent colonial rebellion against the state. At the same time, at least from a colonial (Atlantic) perspective, these conflicts point to the creation of new pluralistic legal regimes, where authority is negotiated and where institutions matter much less than considering the law and its relationship to property, just as Benton suggested.[52]

If the broader Atlantic World could be interrogated as a single unit, as these examples illustrate, then it ought to be possible to consider smuggling between the Atlantic and elsewhere, such as India or China. Indeed, Indian opium smugglers exported their product to China, as well as across several more oceans into the nineteenth-century Atlantic World. Such global activities must be viewed as the forerunner of today's drug trade, among other things.[53]

By broadening our geographic focus in this way, it soon becomes possible to identify a fair bit of illicit commerce across a variety of world regions; nevertheless, readers must always remain cognizant that any evidence emerged from the archives as individual cases and stories; this makes it impossible to generate any accurate quantification of identified patterns. By considering opium in the nineteenth century, or illicit drugs of any kind now, it might well be possible to get a qualitative sense of smuggling's scale and geographic reach; but any effort to enumerate clearly the amount of smuggled product is destined to fail, at least absent a statistical model.

So too is it possible, if not exactly desirable, to expand the definitions and understanding of smuggling. For example, it is possible to consider "pirated" or fake products (without regard to the piracy definitional problem itself) being produced in, for example, China and then being imported, sometimes illegally, into many different geographic locations. This would then lead readers to consider copyright laws and violations thereof, as well as the theft of intellectual property. Such subjects are certainly interesting, and related to smuggling in that legally required fees are avoided. They are also related to piracy in that there is a robbery with an identifiable victim that is not the state itself. Even so, these transgressions must generally remain beyond the scope of this book. Because some governments tacitly accept either the fake products or permit the production of such products without the payment of licensing fees, however, readers will be reminded of arguments made earlier in the book. By failing to intervene and prevent such copyright infringement activities, the state may well gain legitimacy with its population; residents are allowed to buy "fake" products at a fraction of the price of legally registered goods. In doing so, government deprives itself of revenue to which it is otherwise entitled; it gains, however, at least theoretically, in its subjects' esteem. If a government does intervene to put a stop to such frauds, one almost certainly might expect that a great deal of international pressure has been brought to bear on it to do so. In this regard, very little has changed from the historical past to the present. Inactivity remains common and it is only heavy external pressure that causes government to be more than slightly responsible to its subjects and citizens.

War, Peace, and Global Expansion

Though contraband trade existed across the modern world at virtually all times, it is possible to make a case that it was much more prevalent in some periods than in others. Categorizing these periods nevertheless remains difficult, though it is at least possible to consider some broader-based patterns, such as smuggling during wartime and smuggling during relatively peaceful periods. As mentioned earlier, smuggling during wartime was in general not tolerated; instead, in some cases, formerly prohibited trade was legalized on the basis that shortages as a result of the war could lead to populations suffering from lack of food and clothing.[54] Many Caribbean residents, for example, were often hard pressed to get much needed supplies from their officially approved channels, especially if there was a blockade in place or bad weather that made shipments arrive late—and spoiled. In many other cases, regular, if frequently illicit, supply routes became irregular. This was often a direct result of the disruptions caused by battles and blockades being instituted more regularly. Governments were busy fighting the enemy, and trying to stop illegally obtained products from entering the protected marketplaces that their colonies had become. Such actions created hardships for the people; yet, more often than not, the people responded by becoming real "free traders" or smugglers and evaded their own governments.[55] In such instances, the population faced shortages whenever the illicit trade was cut off through the increased presence of metropolitan troops; government attempted to make the case that its residents would starve without abrogating commercial policy. In other words, there was a clear recognition that the law, as written, could not provide adequately for colonial residents.

Peacetime, on the other hand, was when all bets came off. Legal enforcement of trading regulation was, at best, erratic—at worst, it was nonexistent. (Of course, from the smuggler's perspective, the best and worst cases would have been reversed.) Most people generally preferred the worst case scenario, as the limited state enforcement actions effectively meant that they could generally flout laws that cost them more than they were willing to pay by smuggling. There were many fewer naval officers, customs officials, military commanders, and law officers in general to interfere with their corrupt intentions and actions. Because of this, local officials could easily be bribed to look the other way if they possessed even a small inclination to enforce the statutes on the book or, for that matter, open and read the statute book to see precisely what was allowed and what was not allowed.

On one hand, the consuming population generally appeared content, insofar as it could gain access to desired products and commodities at reasonable prices, whether legally or illegally. On the other hand, local officials remained happy so long as they (1) were able to govern without too much pushback from their charges and (2) did not have to deal with frequent, oppressive, or micromanaging oversight from their metropolitan and/or imperial masters. Even those who controlled metropolitan or imperial treasuries remained indifferent to smuggling activities half a world away, or even two counties away, as long as they were not getting complaints from rival governments *and* as long as some money continued to enter the treasury. Though the money that entered such coffers was not the maximum amount to which they were legally entitled with strict adherence to the statutes, some money was better than none—especially when the cost of collecting the additional cash was factored into play. Some must have reasoned that it would have cost more to exact better legal compliance than ignoring the lost revenue and pretending that it did not exist.

Because peacetime smuggling was so prevalent, it becomes possible to look at those cases about which we know anything and to determine from them what was being smuggled across legal frontiers, as well as the means by which it was smuggled and, if appropriate, what responses it received. At times when there was no war, more cases of contraband trade were prosecuted than during wartime, where the military effectively dealt with smugglers whom they encountered. A few smuggling cases even ended up in court. Those that actually made it into the legal records generally did so because the perpetrators either took especially bold risks that other smugglers, who sought to avoid the limelight, shunned or they chanced upon an incorruptible rule-bound official at exactly the wrong time, making them especially unlucky. It is from these kinds of records that most of our information about smuggling derives.

All of this leads back to questions raised earlier in this chapter: what was being smuggled and why? The answers to these questions can best be provided with several illustrations. Each of the following stories has been chosen because it is both somewhat representative of the larger patterns of smuggling that are considered here and because, very simply, each of these stories makes for interesting reading. The effect of these tales will, I anticipate, be additive so that readers come away with at least a partial answer to the questions of what was being smuggled, as well as how it was being smuggled.

In 1809, J. M. Cowham wrote to the Earl of Caledon, who was then serving as governor and commander in chief of the British East India Company's Cape Colony.[56] In his missive, Cowham presented a remarkable story—remarkable not so much for its content, but rather for the severity of the smugglers' punishment. A British East India Company ship, the *Camperdown*, was sailing on a return voyage from India to Britain and had just rounded the Cape of Good Hope. Just before Christmas in 1808, the *Camperdown*'s crew got into one of the ship's small boats, from where the ship had been anchored in Table Bay, in order to visit Cape Town. The men began to row ashore. According to the report, the crew was allegedly "coming on shore for the day's provisions" when a clerk to the searcher of the Customs detected on board the small boat "twenty pieces of silk handkerchiefs and fifteen pieces of nankeen." These were prohibited goods.[57] In response, the colony's Court of Justice confiscated their boat, levied a fine, and ordered the sailors' imprisonment for a year.[58]

J. M. Cowham, captain of the ship, wrote to the colony's governor in order to get this judgment against the *Camperdown*'s crew overturned. He saw the verdict as unnecessarily harsh, and he presented his case as a special hardship to himself. Cowham claimed to own the *Camperdown*'s remaining cargo.[59] He asserted that "should the judgment be put in force the impossibility of the men being able to make good . . . the value of the [confiscated] boat" would prove a hardship at a time when things were already tough. He reminded the governor of the "great loss the Camperdown would sustain by reducing her present compliment [of sailors] being already several hands short of her number," in the hopes that he could get what he saw as an excessive sentence against his crew commuted.[60]

Despite making some fairly direct, and even persuasive, arguments, Cowham did not prevail, indicating the hard-line, rule-bound character of the Cape Colony's governor. "It appears the men were not aware of the penalty they subjected themselves to, by such illicit traffic," Cowham wrote, "as they did not in the smallest degree resist the examination by the searcher and the articles being brought on shore in the bags for the provisions (about half past six in the morning) merely to conceal their actions from the commanding officer."[61] In other words, Cowham's crew *was* engaged in smuggling activities. He claimed that the smugglers must have *unintentionally* broken the law, because they were unaware that having imported cloth on board was prohibited. Why else would they have willingly given up their contraband cargoes? The fact that they got caught for, in effect, being stupid enough not to conceal their cargo when the searchers came on board provided proof of their naiveté. Because they lacked even the most basic awareness of what it took to be a real smuggler, Cowham argued that their harsh sentence ought to be immediately commuted.

In fact, however, this did not happen. In the *Camperdown*'s case, the law appeared clear; no foreign cloth could be imported without the payment of duty.[62] Ignorance of the statutory requirements was not enough to get a lawbreaker's charges dismissed, just as ignorance of the law now is not a reason either not to bring charges or to acquit the lawbreakers. Even so, Cowham did not give up his claim. He even got an East India Company official in Cape Town, John Pringle, to write in support of clemency ten days later. Pringle attempted to get the men released by claiming that it was an "impossibility for them to pay the treble value to which they are condemned as I imagine they have nothing in the world but their wages."[63] He appears to have been unsuccessful; the next day, after hearing back from his correspondent, Pringle forwarded the response he received and added that "I cannot interfere any further in a business regularly decided upon by the laws of the Colony."[64] The state had spoken; its interests at this moment in time would take precedence over that of Captain Cowham and the East India Company.

What the *Camperdown*'s crew was smuggling was very small; it amounted to nothing more than a little package of consumer goods that would not fetch much money in what amounted to a small settlement in a remote imperial outpost.[65] As a result, the fines and sentence really did seem completely out of proportion to the criminal act that had been committed. Moreover, the loss of crew to Cape Town's jail would almost certainly have severely harmed Cowham's ability to navigate the *Camperdown* back to Europe according to Britain's legally mandated crew requirements.[66] Perhaps most importantly, however, Cowham would himself have suffered losses as a direct result of having to hire new crewmembers to sail the boat back to Britain, and to pay the contracted crew while it sat in jail. Clearly he was about to bear the cost of his crew's ignorance and in his view this was simply not fair. His tenacity revealed as much about contemporary attitudes toward smuggling as it did about Cowham's personal qualities. It seems clear that such activities were relatively widespread, and that the Earl of Caledon's regime in Cape Town made a determined effort to shut such activities down.[67]

This story, from the early nineteenth century, bears more than a passing resemblance to that of Columba Bush, which was presented in the last chapter. Mrs. Bush's high spending on Parisian couture was certainly on a much grander scale than that of the poor sailors who were arrested in Cape Town in 1808, but there is nevertheless a certain continuity of meaning in the two cases. In both of them, individuals claimed to be ignorant of the laws that they were caught violating. They (or, in the *Camperdown*'s case, their employers) believed that they could negotiate their ways out of the mess that their own actions had created. In the 1808 case, the government was rule-bound. No negotiation seemed possible. In the 1999 case, the government had developed a procedure to avoid becoming rule-bound. Its three-times-the-price of duty penalty amounted to a valiant effort to avoid incarcerating many people for running afoul of the revenue laws. It indicated that the law was negotiable or rather that there were ways for legal violators to be punished in proportion to their crimes. Both cases reveal, however, that many individuals did not take potential legal violations seriously enough, especially when the laws being violated got in the way of individual consumers' ability to accumulate either property in the form of goods or small profits.

Both tales also have something else in common: they are each an example of the smuggling of consumer goods. The nineteenth-century story is one of interregional smuggling: Asian, perhaps Chinese, goods being smuggled into Southern Africa. The Bush tale, though it is also intercontinental in its scope, is more appropriately viewed as intraregional smuggling within the Atlantic World. In both cases the perpetrators claimed ignorance of their crimes. In both instances, the punishment seemed routine, at least in part: Mrs. Bush received a fine of three times the price of the duty she ought to have paid. The ignorant sailors in Table Bay were ordered to make restitution to the owner of the *Camperdown*, which had its small boat seized and confiscated. In addition, they too were fined for their illegal behaviors. As importantly, in both cases, a negative backlash against the outcomes' seeming arbitrariness developed.

Jeb Bush's claim that his wife's smuggling arrest was a "private affair" effectively sought to minimize the crime that she had committed.[68] The news media's failure to question this assertion appears also to imply that this *really was* a private indiscretion that could simply be ignored. That logic, with Jeb Bush's now familiar quote, "I love my wife more than life itself," argues for an interpretation that the actual law being violated had become largely irrelevant.[69] Moreover, it parallels the case of the *Camperdown*. The sailors were represented to have committed a trifling crime—a few pieces of fabric imported at the bottom of a provision bag, which they did not even know needed to be declared to the customs officers—only to be met with a muscular governmental overreaction. The fact that Cowham dared to write to the Cape's governor suggested that he *understood* the punishment not to fit the crime. His belief was relatively common; for individuals to act assertively required significant amounts of energy. As importantly, because the historical and legal records are not filled with more of these kinds of cases, it appears that the *Camperdown* case *really was* an anomaly. Cowham was not necessarily far off base by suggesting that the case be reviewed again, especially once he had pointed out all of the hardships that the punishment would cost him; the punishment did not suit the crime. In other circumstances, a bribe would have neatly done the trick—and no one would have had to go to jail!

Just as it is possible to discuss the smuggling of consumer goods from one legal regime to another, it is also possible to discuss the smuggling of agricultural commodities. Though such crops were generally smuggled across regions, such as tea being smuggled into the Americas or sugar being smuggled into Europe, it is also possible to talk about commodities being smuggled within a single world region. We have already seen French sugar passed off as British through smuggling via Monte Christi, Dominica, other British islands, perhaps even North America. But this was by no means an isolated case. A few examples will better illustrate this point.

Complaints about the illegal importation of French-produced sugar into Dominica, from where it was exported to Britain as British sugar, run through the island's official correspondence, as it had earlier done in the Leeward Islands.[70] One writer claimed:

> The Exportation of French Sugars as the growth and produce manufacture of this Island has formed and doth form one of the most considerable branches of commerce here, and I am certain that a much greater quantity of sugar was exported during the last year than the whole crop of the Island amounted to,

and that an equal quantity will be exported this year. . . . It would not be a difficult matter to point out particular ships both for London and Bristol, carrying from 5 to 600 Hogsheads each, and not one Hogshead on board the produce of this island. . . . [T]his is well known to every person here, except the officers of His Majesty's Customs, who will not know it.[71]

If the accusation was true, and there is evidence that it was, then Governor Orde was right to be so determined to stamp out smuggling. He reckoned in 1787 that about "one half the sugar is made here, the remainder together with most articles the French inhabitants use are smuggled in."[72] The problem, of course, is that his actions further alienated the local population, which increasingly made his job untenable and eventually resulted in his recall to Britain in order to answer the accusations that were made against him.[73] But Orde's experiences were not at all unique. The same sort of thing took place at other times and in other places.

In 1818, British East India Company officials began to express their concern about the ways in which tobacco from Coimbatore province had begun to be smuggled into nearby Malabar.[74] The East India Company's revenue officers in India wrote to company headquarters in London in order to inform their metropolitan officials about "the prevalence of the practice of smuggling tobacco into [Malabar] and . . . the evil consequences with which that practice is attended."[75] The complainants continued to observe that the measures the two regional governments had already taken were insufficient to stem the trade because "the smuggling of tobacco from Mysore is increasing at such a rapid and enormous rate that some rigorous steps must be taken to put a stop to it."[76] At this point, readers should note that the magistrates in India, most of whom were determined to make their particular provinces look good to the London company because their career advancement depended upon it, instigated this particular series of allegations. Though their complaints amounted to little more than petty grievances and allegations, they were sufficient to merit the preparation of a full report.

The chief object of the magistrates' concerns arose from their observations that unequal duties on tobacco in different legal jurisdictions negatively impacted the local population by inciting some of them to circumvent the law's provisions. Those in Malabar, where the price of tobacco was artificially high—a result of the East India Company's monopolistic protections—accepted the decrees of their legal regime, which in turn provided opportunities for tobacco sellers to make high profits. As a result, their neighbors in Coimbatore turned into "public robbers" in order to steal tobacco to resell at a higher price on the other side of the legal frontier.[77] In other words, the price discrepancies caused by the East India Company's duties increased the amount of tobacco smuggling into Malabar, where profits could be had simply by selling illegally imported, perhaps even inferior, tobacco at prices lower than those mandated by applying the East India Company's required import imposts. In response to the smuggling, the East India Company requested that its officers:

> take . . . into consideration whether the present profits of the monopoly might in great measure be secured by a very considerable reduction in the selling price of tobacco, which would at the same time reduce the temptation to smuggling, thus increasing the consumption of government tobacco, and diminishing the expense of enforcing the monopoly and would put a stop to those serious evils resulting from the monopoly which if they cannot otherwise be prevented may make it necessary [that] the monopoly should be altogether discontinued.[78]

It would appear that the East India Company at least understood the effects of its policies on the Indian population of Mysore and Coimbatore; it questioned the sagacity of its taxation policies, as it should have done, because it caused people to find ways to circumvent the law, robbing the state of money that might otherwise have been paid had taxation levels been lower.

A few months later, in June 1817, however, little had changed for the better. Circumstances had forced the magistrate of Malabar to revise the plan for eradicating smuggling. He now proposed combining the police and tobacco departments into one entity—to create a kind of economy of scale, while simultaneously increasing the size of the police force.[79] He envisioned that the new force would be a low-paid police force; he suggested that any additional charges to combine the forces would be small. Indeed, he believed that the men to staff such a force could be easily obtained by simply offering to pay just a small bit more than they were currently earning either as a police officer or as a customs official. Of course, like many at much higher levels, he failed to contemplate that their existing low wages made them susceptible to bribes—therefore facilitating smuggling.

In fact, looking carefully at the magistrate's proposals requires historians to assess whether or not the plan was ever truly intended for implementation, or whether it was simply a way to extract more capital from the East India Company in London for his own purposes. The combined police force could also have been a well-planned distraction, designed more to get the London bosses off his back by focusing them on immediate solutions to a perceived problem of smuggling rather than allowing them to do long-term economic planning. Such planning might well have included reevaluating the role of the tariffs on tobacco or the utility of continuing a monopoly that encouraged contraband trade in order to evade the monopoly's guaranteed prices.[80]

It did, however, become abundantly clear in November 1817 that there really was a smuggling and robbery problem in these regions of the subcontinent and that some sort of official action from the East India Company would be required to put the region's population into a more settled and reliable, and therefore less transgressive, commercial pattern. The acting magistrate of Zilla, a town in Coimbatore, claimed that those living in Malabar had raided territory under his control:

> The moplas[81] from Malabar or Cochin plundered the villages of Marchnail pollam in the Polacky and Condegoon in the Coimbatoor Talook in September last, and on the night of the 1st instant, a party of from thirty to forty plundered the villages of Tondam Moor and Molapollam in the Coimbatore Talook of property worth about 1000 pagodas, slightly wounding and torturing two of the inhabitants.[82]

As East India Company officials, along with local officers in their employ, confronted the violent offenders from Coimbatore, the lawbreakers explained that they had revenge as their chief motive. Just a month before the attack on the village, the Coimbatorese had unsuccessfully attempted to smuggle six hundred bundles of tobacco into Malabar. The revenue officers had seized their contraband commodity, thereby preventing the smugglers either from selling it elsewhere or otherwise earning any kind of capital on it. This became a heavy financial blow to them. The men from Coimbatore admitted that they had planned to dispose of the seized tobacco in Malabar because of the huge price differential between the two territories: the price was near ninety pagodas a bundle in Malabar, while in the region where it was produced, Coimbatore, it would be lucky to fetch only about twenty pagodas in the marketplace. Such an enormous discrepancy in the price could have generated huge profit margins to the Coimbatore producers while depriving the East India Company government of revenues to which it claimed a legal entitlement.[83] All the smugglers needed to do was sell their tobacco for less than the tobacco that had paid the East India Company's taxes.

The Coimbatore residents therefore sought revenge on those who had confiscated their crop. Rather than attacking the revenue officers directly, as the Vietnamese still owners did over a century later,[84] this raiding party declared that it "would come back and murder and plunder the village of the Monigar,[85] who gave the information which led to its [the tobacco's] seizure."[86] The punishment would be swift and direct; law-abiding citizens had effectively reported their law-breaking neighbors and would certainly be paid back for their failure to participate in a smuggling enterprise. En route to their revenge in Malabar, the party came across and attacked "six peons stationed at a pass thro the hill to intercept smugglers." These Malabar residents had "attempted to stop these banditti but they were too strong for the peons to seize, and escaped among the rock and jungles."[87] The local officials, who had to deal with the repercussions of such violence, knew exactly where to place the blame: "This is one of the evil consequences of the monopoly in Malabar."[88] Monopoly, of course, led to trading restrictions, which generated the reason for smuggling in the first place.

The intraregional disequilibrium between identical commodities in neighboring legal jurisdictions contributed to smuggling activities just as frequently, if not more so, than did the interregional smuggling, where such price differentials might reasonably be expected and therefore seemed more normal. After all, environmental conditions diverged and influenced what could and could not be grown. Productive technology was different in each place, and different articles and commodities were frequently manufactured in each place.

Even so, it could just as legitimately be asserted that the similarities between intra- and interregional smuggling were greater than their differences; it was really the tax boundary or frontier, along with the laws that supported them, that mattered most. The differentials in taxes across such boundaries resulted from specific policies, rooted in economic protectionism. They derived from several characteristics of what was once seen as the sign of a strong state all across the mercantile world of the eighteenth century. Governments needed to provide a police force to keep out prohibited or protected goods and enforce tariff restrictions. Moreover, the state needed the ability to check, through price regulation, consumption of articles or commodities that were seen as harmful to the public good. The revenue for such a police force to regulate consumption needed to be generated by those whose trade was being regulated.[89] In short, this was a flawed understanding of political economy; it nevertheless kept these problematic policies in place for longer than they might otherwise have remained.

Protecting the Public Good: The (Pink) Elephant in the Room

It is at this point that a discussion of contraband commerce must necessarily turn away from prohibited goods and commodities and turn toward drugs. These substances, at once consumer goods *and* commodities, additionally have a public health aspect that, because of their negative (or perceived negative) effects and side effects required governments around the world to ban them from being produced or imported.[90] Opium, perhaps the best known of the illicit drugs, was regularly smuggled out of India into China in order to ensure that the East India Company no longer ran an unfavorable balance of trade with the Chinese.[91] There have been several examples of opium smuggling, or rather the violence that opium smuggling has caused, discussed elsewhere in this book. Yet opium was not the only drug to have been smuggled.

Indeed, it might perhaps be a little surprising to learn that, like tobacco, *ganja* was smuggled from one region of India to another. Like tobacco, much of the contraband trade was done in order to break a British monopoly that sought to restrict and control both its recreational and medicinal usage. Beginning in the late nineteenth century, the British government began to find ways to prevent marijuana smuggling from one region of the subcontinent to another.

The Indian government commissioned a report on the subject in 1904, and asked its author to investigate if there was a way to prevent the problem of marijuana smuggling within India that was then taking place. As G. Rainy wrote in the government's report: "The most important question I had to deal with was the opportunities for smuggling afforded by the present system and the extent to which they can be removed or minimised by different administrative arrangements. I have, therefore, taken it as a starting point, and all the details of the existing system have been considered from this point of view."[92]

Rainy's report went over old ground. In 1883–1884, the Bengal Excise Commission had also explored the problem.[93] In that report, the commissioners pointed out their concerns. They observed declining production per unit of cultivation, without specifying its causes. They also saw rising prices, which when combined with declining production made sense. At the same time, the government raised its own licensing fees in order to increase its revenue. The Bengal Excise Commission believed that these factors, in combination with each other, led to an increased number of illegal transactions. Avoiding revenue points when prices were generally high would have meant that consumers paid lower prices than they would have done had the required duties been paid. At the same time, sellers of such products could make tidy profits by keeping profit and not turning it over to the government in the form of taxes.[94] Everyone but the government stood to benefit. As the commissioners explained it:

[I]t must be remembered that the retailer practically fixes his own rate of license fee by competition at public auction, and when he undertakes to pay a high fee for the right to retain an article subject to a high direct duty, he must hope to recoup it in one of the following ways: either by increasing his licit sales to such an extent that the proportion of the license fee to the direct duty may become so small as to make the former practically unfelt, or by compelling the consumer to pay for the article a price high enough to cover both duty and license fee, or by supplementing his licit sales by selling illicitly a large quantity of the article without payment of direct duty.[95]

In short, the British government of India believed that diminishing production and higher prices proved to be an incentive to smuggle *ganja* from one region of India to another. They were concerned enough, in 1884 and again in 1904, to try to understand the reasons behind such illegal behaviors.

According to the report's author, "previous to 1854, the duty on *ganja* was levied in the form of a daily tax paid by the retail sellers of the drug."[96] Moreover, "[t]he usual practice was for the purchasers of *ganja*, armed with passes granted by the Excise Officers of their respective districts, to go to the cultivators of the drug, and purchase from them whatever they wanted, without any interference from the Excise Officers. . . . No weighing and packing in the presence of government officers were deemed necessary in those days."[97]

Beginning in 1854, British officials began regularly increasing the duty to be collected on *ganja*. Yet, oddly enough, "nothing was controlled except its exportation. There was no restriction on cultivation, and there was no check on the outturn."[98] A generation later, however, cultivators were required to take out a license so that the government knew who was involved in growing the product.[99] Of course, no one ever bothered to check the actual amount of land being employed to grow *ganja*, or whether the license matched the realities of growth and production. Becoming aware of the problem, and not wanting to spend the money to hire a staff to survey all of the land under cultivation, the government decided upon a different path. Indeed, the lack of willingness to spend money on enforcing the law probably resulted from government believing that it did not have enough money to enforce the law; the lack of money derived at least in part from smugglers who evaded paying duty.

In this particular instance, government decided to require that *ganja* be sold only to specific people and organizations, which effectively created a government monopoly on *ganja*. Of course, as was true with other government-controlled processes described earlier in this book, smuggling actually increased, as prices would frequently be better on the open market, where different competitors could bid against each other—based on local circumstances and regional demand. This did not escape the attention of those charged with investigating the problem:

> As a class the cultivators of the *ganja* mahal are remarkable in two ways. They are singularly peaceable and law-abiding and they are remarkably wealthy and prosperous. The impression they created on my mind was a most favourable one. I found them uniformly pleasant to deal with, frank without bumptiousness, and courteous without servility. The smuggling that goes on cannot be attributed to any innate criminality on their part—on the contrary, as a body, they are free from all criminal tendencies—it is due simply to the fact that where the temptation is very great and the risk of detection very small, no human virtue is strong enough to resist.[100]

According to the 1904 report:

> [I]t may be assumed that smuggling is, as it certainly ought to be, impossible after the *ganja* is stored in the public warehouses. All smuggling must now take place between the time the crop is ripe and the time when it is stored in the public warehouses, i.e. roughly speaking between the 1st of February and the 31st of March. This means a great abbreviation of the smuggler's chances. He can no longer smuggle comfortably at his leisure. He must take time by the forelock and seize the advantage of the fleeting moment.[101]

But the report's author indicated that while the policy had shifted, behavior did not necessarily shift along with it; smuggling continued unabated. Moreover, the government monopoly did not guarantee that *ganja* would not otherwise enter the market. It secured the marijuana supply but it did not commit to getting it into the hands of consumers. It then did not satisfy the market, which took things into its own hands.

Theft from the public warehouses soon became a problem or, even more frequently, "green *ganja* is sometimes stolen from the field and smuggled into the tracts in Bogra, Dinajpur, and Rajshahi immediately adjoining the *ganja* mahal."[102] In other words, individuals without licenses harvested unripe *ganja* from the fields in order to keep it out of government warehouses and make a profit on it—by smuggling it into nearby territories without paying the appropriate taxes. Consumer demand could therefore be satisfied. The author of the report claims that engaging in contraband commerce was not something that those who held official government licenses did, but his case seemed less than compelling. It would have been very easy for such people to deliver a portion of their harvest, keeping some of it back to ensure against bad payments from the legally mandated channel—at once satisfying consumers *and* maximizing their own profits.[103] It would also have been easy for them to look the other way as others made off with part of their harvest, in exchange for later payment—after the crop had been smuggled and duty effectively evaded. In any case, both of these possibilities were really about supplies being made available to satisfy consumer demand at acceptable prices.

The Indian official who authored this *ganja* report claimed that virtually all government officials were very keen to make sure that all smuggling activities were consistently prevented. He suggested two ways to guarantee this. First, the penalties for smuggling needed to be increased. "[S]muggling can only be dealt with by lessening the temptation or by increasing the risk of detection. Now, obviously, if the penalty of detection is very heavy, if the mere suspicion of smuggling entails the most serious consequences . . . the cultivator will think twice before he runs the risk of incurring such a penalty."[104]

Though this position is clearly true, it would also have been highly impractical. In other words, eliminating smuggling altogether, even if it was possible, would certainly have cost more than the increased revenue full legal compliance would have generated.

Second, he wanted to prevent the possibility of bribery. His argument made a plea for paying enforcement officials more, in order to exact better compliance and ensure that they would be compensated fairly for their work—and, therefore, not be forced to accept bribes in order to make ends meet.[105] By singling out *ganja* smuggling here, he explicitly suggested that all prevention officers be compensated for making a "bust." If officials were paid enough to be able to refuse bribes, and therefore be in a position to forgo what a smuggler could offer, the practice, he believed, would disappear:

> In *ganja* smuggling cases large rewards [for arrests and seizures] are invariably given. In the present year a case was detected in which opium had been smuggled from Nepal to Rajashi and *ganja* taken back in exchange. The Deputy Inspector who was successful in arresting the smugglers was given a reward of 400 [rupees]. All the Deputy inspectors were anxious to detect smuggling cases in hopes of promotion. . . . It can hardly be said that the smugglers corrupted all the officers. No doubt the smuggler could afford to bribe on a handsome scale, but considering the high rewards that are given, he would probably find it cheaper to pay the duty, than to pay the Excise Officer a sum large enough to close his mouth.[106]

This tension between smugglers and law enforcement staff existed throughout the modern world, in virtually all of the places that I have examined.

Nevertheless, tensions were even greater when people were involved as the objects of smuggling. In some cases, those who smuggled themselves fled from abject poverty or otherwise simply sought increased economic opportunities elsewhere. They stole themselves away in vessels, hoping to emerge from them in another locale. They bribed their way across borders, if they could not simply cross them. In many of these cases, representatives of the state, or those who worked in its highest orders, provided assistance.[107]

For example, three members of the Texas National Guard were charged with human smuggling in 2007. The three were paid about $1,500 to $2,000 each for running illegal immigrants into the United States from the Mexican border; they were officially supposed to prevent such illegal crossings. "According to the federal complaint, [one member of the National Guard] Private Torres was driving 24 illegal immigrants in a white Ford van leased to the National Guard," when he was stopped at a border checkpoint north of Laredo.[108]

Private Torres escaped detection by working with another guardsman, who was also in on the scheme, by appearing to do National Guard business, and then leaving the checkpoint in the service lane, thus avoiding an immigration inspection. The next night, as he attempted to bring these migrants further north, Border Patrol officers stopped him. These agents thought that they saw people hiding in his van; the officials did not appear to offer any additional reason for impeding Private Torres's journey. At that point, Torres admitted his corrupt activities, and identified a superior officer, Sergeant Pacheco, who he claimed had paid him between $1,000 and $3,500 a trip, for each of the seven times that he had taken Mexicans from the border to Dallas.[109] Those illegal immigrants who were arrested were generally believed to have paid around $1,500 to get across the border and to Dallas. It was clear that this was a way for the National Guard officers to earn additional income; that they did so several times before this arrest once again shows just how easy it was for antismuggling laws to be broken. There is an implicit level of trust, even when it is obvious from observed actions that such trust is not fully warranted.

Even so, the penalties that these men faced for smuggling were significant—if the state decided to seek maximum penalties. According to the press, no decision was immediately made about how to proceed: "the men were ordered held in the Webb County jail in Laredo on $75,000 bail, pending a preliminary hearing . . . or a possible federal indictment on smuggling conspiracy charges, which carry penalties of up to 10 years in prison and fines of up to $250,000."[110]

Of course, the cases were nothing new. According to the *Times*, "since the 2004 fiscal year . . . 282 employees of Customs and Border Protection working on the border from California to Texas have been investigated for corruption, 52 of them [from January to June 2007], compared with 66 for all of last year." Homeland Security did not know how many of these cases were related to human smuggling, or even how many convictions it had obtained.[111] Perhaps as importantly, the Guardsmen's lawyer's response ran parallel to that of Jeb Bush defending his wife: "Obviously, it's a crime," his lawyer said. "But it's not a serious crime like supplying cocaine or marijuana."[112] All of those involved pleaded guilty in August 2007 and in February 2008; the first of the men was sentenced to three years imprisonment and three years of supervised release for running a "sophisticated" operation. Perhaps what was most telling is not that the government scored a conviction—the violations were, after all, clearly demonstrable. Rather it is that the Immigration and Customs Service issued a press release when it had secured its convictions, recounting the story and explaining the rationale for the punishment.[113] It was as if it was telling the press, in order to tell the people, that illegally smuggling people across the border would result in punishment that was severe, as opposed to some sort of lesser sentence because the crime was not serious. What makes this case significant is the crime of corruption—of the police actually being involved in illegal activity.

D'oh!

Detecting smuggling, of course, was notoriously difficult since there were never enough police or customs officials to check all activities and every transaction at all times. Most illegal exchanges, therefore, went unchecked and unobserved, which is precisely the way smugglers liked it. Nevertheless, *consumers* of smuggled products often inadvertently tipped off law enforcement officers by failing to purchase a product that, because access to it was regulated, they ought to have purchased. The article or commodity then remained unsold, alerting anyone who cared to pay attention that something not quite right had taken place; the problem was especially apparent to those who happened to be rule-bound and therefore predisposed to pay attention. Enforcement officials who chose to do so would then be able to act against legal transgressors, providing more evidence of just what was being smuggled and allowing them to assert ways to prevent it. Two examples will help to illustrate this point more clearly.

In the fall of 1784, Martinique's French colonists had their houses and shops searched for English and American flour. The French troops who searched door-to-door seized somewhere around three thousand barrels of flour. As might be expected by a seizure this large, word quickly spread to neighboring islands. Such searches, after all, were extremely rare and therefore extremely newsworthy. According to the newspaper report that appeared in the Bahamas, "it is apprehended the same thing will take place at Guadeloupe, where the seizures would prove much more considerable."[114] The colonial merchants who sold flour could not be supplied quickly enough with French flour, so they turned instead to dealing in contraband as an expedient way to satisfy their customers. Indeed, what they did was fairly common in the Caribbean; European flour took too long to arrive from Europe, and when it did, which was infrequently, it was often spoiled.[115]

As earlier indicated, government seizures on this scale were very rare in any of the American colonies or, indeed, in any society. But, as might be expected in this case, a clear precipitating event with the regular supply of French flour prompted the enforcement action. Ships that arrived in Martinique from France, after their long Atlantic crossings, found "the market overstocked and their own Flour without demand." The merchants who had sent the flour, and who presumably had to endure the losses for spoilage and unsold flour, complained to the government "for a prevention of the contraband trade."[116] It was this complaint, the press speculated, that resulted in the seizures. In circumstances like these, the merchants who agitated for protectionist laws were the ones who had to agitate for their enforcement; government doubly lost. It had to spend money to recover money that it was owed as a result of laws, which had been designed to ensure an adequate revenue stream, being ignored. It goes without saying that other merchants, such as those in Martinique who bought and sold flour, were also the ones responsible for breaking the laws in the first place.[117] Here there was clearly a rupture between merchants, based on their geographic location and its accompanying realities.

Such problems were not unique to the Caribbean. Indeed, half a world away, the same sort of problem was revealed in the first part of the nineteenth century. Colonists at Cape Town acted in a legally evasive, if eminently sensible, way. Soon after newly appointed East India company representative John Pringle arrived in the Cape Colony in 1808, he wrote to the East India Company with a conundrum. He could not determine from looking at customs documentation how tea had been imported into Cape Town. He just did not see much imported tea listed in the customs records:

I cannot ascertain from [the Custom House Returns] in what manner the Colony has been supplied with Tea . . . either there must have been a considerable quantity remaining on hand previous to that period [before Pringle arrived], or it must have been smuggled, the quantity being maintained being totally inadequate to the consumption for even a very short time.[118]

Suspecting smuggling, but having no real proof, Pringle observed that tea importation did not closely match the probable consumption for a population of Cape Town's size. He was almost certainly right; after all, the colony's governor would soon seize a small boat engaged in smuggling cloth, which provoked a response that the punishment was disproportionate to the crime. It seems, then, clear that everyone but a few zealous government officers knew that smuggling into the Cape Colony was tolerated. Nevertheless, by making his observations, and by not keeping them to himself, and by reporting them to his East India company masters, Pringle may have worked against his own interests as an official who actually had to interact and do business with colonial residents. By tipping off his bosses in London that residents of the Cape Colony may have been eluding tariffs and smuggling tea, he risked an order from the East India Company to act against any smuggling that he found. In turn, this could easily have put him into the unenviable position of having to take legal action against those whom he had to lead and upon whose support successful government rested (absent a major police or military state). Acting too harshly against them, as has been argued earlier, could lead to open rebellion and still more clandestine activities. Acting against them would, as well, cost money—which, as earlier indicated, was not certain to be made up by increased compliance with impost collection.

But not all traders and residents were involved in economic subterfuge. Some actually were proponents of increased compliance and enforcement. Examining the activities of another merchant who got caught up with the law, this time in twentieth-century India, revealed a clandestine trade in the sugar substitute, saccharine. In 1924, this trader wrote that "Saccharine is dutiable at Rs. 20 per lb." At the same time, he commented that it was on sale in Bombay for Rs 12 to 13—meaning that it was being sold on the open market for less than the cost of import duty. Since saccharine was not produced in India, the "Honest Trader" knew that it must have been smuggled into the colony. As he wrote, "I am one of the dealers of such commodities and have had the goods in stock for a long time remaining unsold and there will be many who have honestly ordered direct from manufacturers, suffering heavy loss on account of smuggling."[119]

Here there was a plea for the government to act: " I shall thank the Government if it takes immediate steps to stop this."[120] He clearly understood that he was being undercut in the marketplace, even though he adhered strictly, or so he claimed, to the laws that governed the marketplace. His plea was for government to intervene and enforce the laws already on the statute books by collecting the duty. If consumers in Martinique and Cape Town bought smuggled products with the connivance of merchants, here was a merchant who was ready to call out his competitors for participating in a fraud against the government. Of course, this too could have been a ploy to achieve his own monopoly by removing his contraband-dealing competitors from the market place.

Doing as the fair trader wished, however, would have potentially meant an even greater problem for government officials, who risked rebellion for intervening in areas that had customarily tolerated smuggling. Moreover, it would have risked alienating the much larger numbers of saccharine consumers who were paying prices significantly below what the full price of saccharine ought to have been with duty factored into it. As one might have expected, government did not respond to the fair trader's pleas. It simply could not afford to risk alienating the majority of the consuming population in order to placate one of its law-abiding citizens, or rather one who claimed to be law-abiding. (For all we know, he could have been a smuggler of some other product.) As importantly, it is also possible that government's failure to act could have transformed the fair trader into a somewhat less honest trader. In such a way, smuggling became a tolerable act.

And in such a way, smugglers were made.

"Smugglers Alarmed," c. 1830. This illustration is part of a two-picture series, with the other illustration entitled, "Smugglers Attacked." National Maritime Museum, Greenwich, London

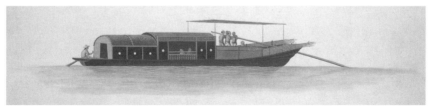

"Tsap-shee-Sheun. A Custom House Boat Employed to Prevent Smuggling." Inscribed, "Patrol boat against smuggling." Opaque watercolor, China/Canton style. Originally published/produced in 1800–1805. © The British Library Board (Add.Or.1984).

SIR JOHN ORDE BARᵀ

Vice Admiral of the *White Squadron.*

MITIS ET FORTIS

Pub by I. Gold, 103, Shoe Lane, 1 April 1804.

"Sir John Orde Bart," in an 1804 portrait by George Romney. Orde was a rule-bound Governor of Britain's Dominica colony in the late eighteenth century. National Maritime Museum, Greenwich, London

"Douanier du Port/French Port Customs Officer," nineteenth-century lithograph. National
Maritime Museum, Greenwich, London

"Smugglers," painting, late eighteenth century, by George Morland (1763–1804), who specialized in images of rough, mostly rural characters. This coastal scene, which has been attributed to him but is most likely a contemporary copy, depicts the popular topic of smuggling. In the late eighteenth and early nineteenth centuries, a scene like this fulfilled the audience's appetite for romantic and adventurous narratives, which was also reflected in contemporary literature. National Maritime Museum, Greenwich, London

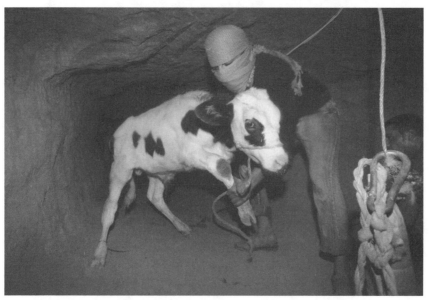

A masked Palestinian man lowers a cow into an underground chamber as Palestinians continue to smuggle supplies and animals though tunnels between Rafah, in the southern Gaza Strip, and Egypt, November 2008. Photo by Abid Katib/Getty Images

"Rigging Out a Smuggler," cartoon by Thomas Rowlandson. *Women played significant roles as smugglers, though this is not documented extensively in the existing record. Even so, women consumed smuggled goods regularly and, as this cartoon illustrated, were prepared to smuggle products themselves using feminine clothing as a means of hiding illicitly obtained articles. This woman was smuggling tea and alcoholic beverages, among other products. National Maritime Museum, Greenwich, London*

"The Opium Ships at Lintin in China," 1824, from a painting in the possession of John Gover, Esq. The large number of ships at Lintin shows how important a port it was for those who were illegally importing opium into China. There were not a large number of Chinese boats to interdict the trade. Indeed, the Chinese ships here were most likely complicit in the trade, as the story in chapter 1 indicates. National Maritime Museum, Greenwich, London

Three boats seized from suspected Somali pirates are cleaned in the sea off the French warship Le Nivose on May 3, 2009. Somali pirates claimed on May 3, 2009, that they hijacked a Pakistani-owned ship, even as France and the Seychelles nabbed fourteen more suspects in the intensifying international hunt for high-seas bandits. Photo by Pierre Verdy/AFP/Getty Images

"Why Polly, You An't on the Smuggling Tack, I Hope!" lithograph by William Heath, 1830. This lithograph can be seen, along with the Rowlandson cartoon earlier depicted, as an indication of the degree to which women were involved in smuggling ventures. National Maritime Museum, Greenwich, London

"Board of Trade and Customs House at Chennai (Madras)," watercolor drawing by John Gantz, 1822. © The British Library Board (WD1363)

Peruvians smuggling bottles of natural gas from Ecuador cross the International Canal (Aguas Verdes, Peru), which defines the boundary between the two countries, January 31, 1995. Photo by Jaime Razuri/AFP/Getty Images

A line of beer smugglers wind their way into Vietnam from the People's Republic of China, March 25, 1994. Photo by David Hume Kennerly/Getty Images

CHAPTER FIVE

—␣␣—

Smuggling, "Custom," and Legal Violations

Smuggling Meets Corruption

Though smuggling activities have been widespread, and typically remain so in most societies that charge import duties, many governments are also generally lax in enforcing their own statutes prohibiting tax and tariff evasion. They see such an evasion of rigor as necessary—not only as a cost savings, where the expenses of vigorous and consistent law enforcement exceed the revenues produced from exacting full legal compliance, but also as a way of maintaining good relationships with those who live under their governments' authority. Indeed, one of the principal reasons that contraband commerce and its ancillary activities are tolerated, if not covertly encouraged, has much to do with ensuring the government's legitimacy in the eyes of its population.[1]

Government could explain away its lack of action, if not its lack of attention, with any number of excuses, such as a lack of money to pay for consistent enforcement actions or the prosecutors' inability to develop strong legal cases, whether caused by a lack of incriminating evidence or a failure to compel witnesses to testify. Contraband traders and their customers, in other words, were rarely convicted, and even more rarely prosecuted.[2] If prosecution took place and convictions were secured, it seems purely to have been done in order to make an example out of the contrabandists, as the last chapter revealed with the case of the National Guard smugglers. Whether or not there was a deterrent effect is impossible to measure; most likely there was not. Moreover, in some cases, governments even denied the existence of any smuggling activity whatsoever; this was a favorite tactic of many eighteenth-century colonial governors in the Americas.[3]

At the core of this chapter rests a small but significant question. In which ways, or how, did government officials deviate from the legal policies and practices that they represented in order to tolerate smuggling? In the modern world, at least, many governments have adopted the idea that government somehow gains its legitimacy from the consent of the governed.[4] Taking this idea of *consent* and applying it to contraband commerce raises another series of questions. Chief among them is whether a population that has agreed to be governed by laws must accept *all* of the laws that are created by its officials, especially those that impede and curtail the population's own consumer behavior.[5] Such a rhetorical question suggests its own negative answer. Sometimes it is simply easier to ignore the law than it is to challenge it and the government that created it, knowing that it could lead to the government's toppling.

In more cases than not, governments passed laws that regulated consuming populations who lived within their territories; nevertheless, both governments and consumers generally and widely understood that statutory law in practice could do little to modify or otherwise transform consumer behavior. Each side had its own reasons for going along with the charade that legislation could be generally effective as a tool that regulated consumption. Government knew that by passing laws that did not provoke open rebellion it could claim to represent the will of its population, therefore achieving a kind of legitimacy. At the same time, the population understood that by simply failing to obey the laws, without entering into open rebellion (especially after 1776), it could achieve a degree of autonomy that might not otherwise be possible.[6] Thus, commercially restrictive laws and policies effectively broadened consumer markets by generating smugglers, who really were engaged in free trade, because they were willing to provide the goods that the consumer market sought at prices that the consumer market was willing to pay. As Adam Smith said, "an injudicious tax offers a great temptation to smuggling."[7]

What makes this so interesting is that most governments knew that this proscribed behavior was taking place. Nevertheless, governments continued to promulgate commercial restrictions across the globe, with full cognizance that such laws would never be adequately, if even at all, enforced. That they still bothered to inscribe the laws into the statute books was more a sign of government asserting its prerogatives than a genuine effort to serve the needs of the local populations whom they governed.[8] In this sense, a state's legal systems acted to demonstrate their authority to other states' legal systems, as well as to show their populations that the legal regimes were not irrelevant.[9] This effectively ensured that there was a certain kind of harmonization between various legal regimes, if not of specific laws then of a more generalized recognition of the utility of legislation that regulated goods crossing from one side of a national border to another. For example, Britain *needed* to regulate commercial activity because Spain did so, and vice versa; France needed to regulate commercial activity in Vietnam because Britain regulated commercial activities in India, and so on. Of course, some states gradually removed their trading restrictions over time, effectively liberalizing commercial laws and practices in order to show other states that somehow "free trade" amounted to a good thing. Such liberalization nevertheless came as *a response to* smuggling, along with the recognition that subject populations ignored bothersome restrictions.[10]

The situation throughout many places in most of the modern world could be summarized as follows: smugglers broke the law. They were, therefore, criminals who ought not to have been rewarded for any legal transgressions they might have committed; yet most of them eluded detection, effectively rewarding them for breaking the laws. At the very same time, government always had an interest in generating compliance with its laws, or at least convincing its subjects that the majority of their neighbors were law-abiding subjects. Such legal compliance, as measured by the lack of prosecutions, could then be portrayed as evidence of popular support for the government more broadly. On the other hand, consumers were going to consume, because they had to do so in order to survive; it was in a certain sense a matter of calories. From a consumer's perspective, there need be no limit on consumption beyond what Adam Smith asserted was natural and appropriate in his *Wealth of Nations*.[11] Smuggling was therefore a perfect compromise in that both sides appeared to be following the law; the population's extralegal and illegal trade was off the books. Government could claim that smuggling was nonexistent even as people continued to engage in illegal trade.

Rather than risk violence, government representatives found ways to tacitly *permit* contraband trading activities by cutting back on enforcement actions, by turning the other way when smuggling took place, and not insignificantly, even by allowing officials charged with legal enforcement to get away with accepting bribes. (This might be one of the earliest examples of the modern adage "government for sale.")

Up to this point, this book has generally been concerned with the ways in which smugglers were able to negotiate tacitly with their governments, as well as neighboring governments. It has not really yet considered those who helped to facilitate bribes and, in many cases, keep those smugglers who were caught outside the law's grasp. The rest of this chapter will thus consider what those who accepted payment to avoid performing their legally required duties communicated to others through their actions. Colonial and other state officials engaged directly with members of the public through bribery and corruption. They engaged in the way that government was supposed to engage with those whom it governed, just not legally. In other words, there was a direct discussion between those who made and enforced laws and those who had to obey them. Government officials in the European capitals, since this is where many governments were based in the ages of colonialism and imperialism, remained blissfully unaware of what activities their minions were engaged in half a world away. Indeed, it was their reliance upon others to enforce the laws for them that allowed the laws to be undermined which, coincidentally, actually bolstered the state and provided it a level of greater legitimacy than it might otherwise have had.

Some local officials were attached to the military, but many others were not. In reality, civilian officials and military officials sometimes found themselves on opposite sides of the enforcement question, as has earlier been described.[12] The military officials, most of whom reported up a chain of command that crossed an ocean or two and went back to a European command center, were not really directly engaged with local and colonial populations. Instead, their contact with colonial populations usually came through other governing officials, and in this they were very precise and exacting. By contrast, civilian officials, though also faced with a long chain of command that went back to government offices in Europe, interacted much more directly with local populations. They therefore bore the brunt of any hostility arising from discontent about legal enforcement from those whom they governed.[13] One way that local officials coped with such popular discontent, and the way that they made their own lives easier, was by accepting bribes to act against the interests of their official employer.

But how do we know this to be true? It is not as if large numbers of local officials, or even small numbers of them, left detailed account books indicating the amounts that each of them received, from which individuals they received it, and what statutes they agreed to ignore as a result.[14] Rather unsurprisingly, corrupt officials only infrequently wrote down that they had accepted a bribe or charged a fee to look away from illegal activities (and who could blame them, really?). While it is certainly true that some of these few instances ended up in court cases, many other local officials who accepted bribes and/or who were otherwise corrupt ended up having their stories told second- and third-hand, so that they show up in obscure places within the archives.[15] Most regularly, the "fees" that corrupt officials charged their subjects received only ancillary mention in a third-party court case, deposition, or report. These third parties were themselves already in legal jeopardy, so they may well have stood to benefit from exposing those local officials who helped to facilitate their corrupt actions. Even so, such stories amount to a kind of buried treasure. They also provide a roadmap to official corruption as it related to commerce, both intra- and interregional.

The available evidence for this official corruption also ranges across this book's entire time span; there are dozens of accusations of corruption, which, as previously discussed, must be considered only a very small proportion of the corruption that actually occurred. Though anecdotal, such illustrations reveal the ways in which official corruption operated in tandem with smuggling. Most accusations come in the form of a criticism or denunciation from someone whose bribe did not procure the desired results or whose actions to apply the law fairly or equally were unfairly met with perceived corruption. All of these examples help to demonstrate the law's pliability, especially when distance from government and local conditions encouraged or required it. They also demonstrate the ways in which corruption helped to relieve tension between those who governed and those who consumed in many societies, in a sense restoring their governability.[16]

Bogus Seizures

For example, in 1764, two Rhode Island merchants, Daniel and John Jenks, accused Spanish colonial officials in Trinidad of refusing to return their captured ship and its cargo after the war between Spain and Britain had ended the previous year, in 1763.[17] Their story, which itself unfolded over a period of several years, points to a number of important issues about the ways in which smuggling populations interacted with governmental officials. It also serves as yet another illustration of the pitfalls of smuggling during wartime, as opposed to peacetime, which has been discussed earlier in this book.

The Jenks brothers owned the sloop *Kinnicut*, which was sailing from Dutch Suriname back to New England in March 1763. It contained a cargo of molasses, as well as linen and chinaware that had been imported from Europe.[18] (The vast majority of the cargo, not unexpectedly given commercial patterns of the day, consisted of molasses.) The Jenkses valued their cargo at £2,566. Within a week after leaving Suriname, a Spanish schooner captured the ship and called it a prize of war. The governor of Trinidad, Don José Antonio de Gil, owned the Spanish schooner; Juan Baz commanded its crew of forty-two sailors.[19] The *Kinnicut* had been captured by a privateer vessel, which just happened to be owned by the Spanish colonial governor who stood to profit greatly from its arrest, not just in his official capacity as governor but also as an owner of the seizing vessel itself.[20] The Spanish ship took the captured *Kinnicut* into port at Trinidad. When the American ship's crewmembers appeared before the governor, they protested that the war between Spain and Britain had already ended, and that they ought not to have been arrested and their ship and its cargo seized. Moreover, they argued that the ship and the crew must be quickly released from captivity or, if not yet possible, that the crew and the ship be brought in front of the Spanish equivalent of the British Vice-Admiralty Court for an impartial determination of how to dispose of the *Kinnicut* and its cargo. Trinidad's governor, however, had other ideas.

The Spanish colonial government in Trinidad continued to hold the ship in port, so that neither its crew nor its New England owners had any access to the goods on board. Moreover, the *Kinnicut*'s crew was imprisoned, despite a very clear peace treaty provision that required their return to British territory.[21] After another week or so in captivity, Spanish authorities gathered the *Kinnicut*'s crew together and took them to two different Spanish territories in the Caribbean, where they were "released." Six crewmembers were landed "on a desolate part of the Main, where none but Savages inhabited." A few days later, the captain and three other *Kinnicut* crewmembers were landed on Tobago.[22] None of them received any kind of food or water when they were put ashore. The record provides no answer to the question of what happened to those abandoned on mainland South America, though it implies that they were forever lost. Those on Tobago, however, were able to escape in a canoe (from where this canoe came is not clear) to nearby Grenada, only a few days after they had been marooned.

It should be apparent by now that Gil, the governor of Trinidad, and Baz, his captain, stood to benefit from the *Kinnicut*'s capture. Rather than adhering to Spanish law and the treaty that ended the war between Spain and Britain, which required them to return the boat to its legal owners, Governor Gil essentially tried to eliminate those who were potential witnesses to the illegal actions of the boat he owned and licensed. More properly, that is what the British owners *claimed*: "[T]his Dispersion of the British Ship's Crew, on distant and uninhabited Places, appears to have been done with a barbarous and wicked Design, that the Said Crew might perish and no more be heard of them, to prevent any Remonstrance being made."[23]

The New England owners of the *Kinnicut*, upon learning of what had happened to their ship, its crew, and cargo, presented a "Memorial to the King," in December 1763. They urged George III to intervene with the king of Spain (Charles III) in order to get the Spanish government to make restitution for their illegitimately obtained and confiscated cargo. Perhaps as significantly, it was also illegal for the Spanish to have imported molasses from Dutch Suriname into Spanish Trinidad. The *only* way that such importation could legally have been justified was if the importation came as a legal prize of war. The British ambassador to Spain made precisely that point when he protested against the Spanish action. The Spanish governor and his employee, the privateer, responded by writing memorials back to Spain, sending along copies of their examination of the British crew.[24] Apparently, Governor Gil's remonstrations and documents completely failed to persuade King Charles III, who agreed with the British claim against him and ordered the governor to make restitution to the British North American owners of the *Kinnicut*. Moreover, the king ordered Baz to be punished for setting the British crew ashore without any provisions or boat, or other means of escape. In short, Trinidadian corruption was reversed in Spain. But this still did not guarantee a happy outcome.

All that the owners Jenks needed to do to reclaim their property was to prepare a power of attorney to be sent along with those whom they hired to go to Trinidad in order to collect the royally decreed reparations. So, the Jenks brothers hired Captain Gideon Manchester to travel to Trinidad. Upon his arrival there, he was to meet with Governor Gil to demand and receive payment for the Jenks brothers' debt. Manchester brought with him a power of attorney that allowed him to act on behalf of the New England merchants.[25]

When Manchester arrived, however, the governor kept him waiting for several days before he would agree to see him. There can be no doubt that he used this time to scrounge some money to pay off Manchester. After a few days, Gil offered to pay Manchester 332 pieces of eight and three ryals, which was only a small fraction of the total amount owed, given the cargo's value; this pittance was completely unacceptable to Manchester.[26] Gil claimed, however, that his offer effectively accounted for the entirety of the proceeds that he received from the sale of the ship and all of its contents. Manchester refused to believe this, so he left Trinidad empty handed. The Spanish governor had basically ignored a legally binding document from his own sovereign. In fact, Governor Gil sought to keep the personal gains he had made from his corrupt actions, so he felt justified in not being attentive to the king's orders. The truth of the matter soon revealed itself.

The governor of Trinidad had waited for some short period after both the *Kinnicut*'s capture and his marooning of its crew. He then ordered that the ship and its cargo be sent to St. Eustatius, a small Dutch island known for its support of "free trade." Once in St. Eustatius, the *Kinnicut* was sold to the

Dutch residents for a hefty profit.[27] Upon learning this, the Jenks brothers again turned to the British government for help in collecting their cash. If a colonial governor could get away with ignoring a royal order by lying to those who sought to enforce it, then such cases, now including corruption, would need to be pursued through other channels, being of course cognizant of the delays that were involved in eighteenth-century transatlantic communications. It is sadly at this point that this tale leaves the historical record. The British government continued to press the case, but its outcome was never revealed. For his part, Governor Gil remained as Trinidad's governor for several more years.

This particular story is significant to understanding contraband trade not because of the amount of the claimed damages, which were sizable but not especially extraordinary, but rather because it deftly illustrates the problems of legal enforcement within the Atlantic World's (and by extension other) colonies. In this case, the Spanish governor—assuming the surviving British legal documents are accurate—actively subverted his own king's direction in order to accumulate personal profit. While he did not allow Dutch goods to be directly smuggled into Trinidad, likely because no one there could afford to buy them, he nevertheless managed to transfer stolen property into his own personal wealth accumulation. Governor Gil was yet another poorly paid public official. He had, at the same time, responsibility for enforcing local and imperial laws and policies and ensuring that his personal financial interests were not ignored. This classic problem of political economy was extremely widespread and, in the eighteenth century, there was no clear way to avoid it, beyond the maintenance of virtuous behavior.[28]

From a legal perspective, Governor Gil had multiple opportunities to set the matter right, at least according to law. Instead, he chose to side with his private employees, the crew of the ship that captured the *Kinnicut*. These put him on the wrong side of both international law, as represented by the Paris Peace Treaty, and direct Spanish royal orders. Because he personally owned the ship that captured the British *Kinnicut*, he stood to benefit from both the *Kinnicut*'s condemnation and its sale. This was, then, a chance for handsome profits indeed. Moreover, Gil's ruler was across an ocean, and would not likely be challenging him. (That the sovereign did so was more a result of international pressure than typical law enforcement in this area.) Gil controlled a small territory, fairly distant from the metropole, and certainly peripheral to the economic mission of the Spanish Empire. He therefore had few eyes watching him, at least officially. The more central to the imperial economic mission, the more likely people would be paying attention. His

choice of siding with his crew indicated that he was aware of which constituents were most important for his success as a colonial administrator.

Gil simply had to satisfy his most important constituents—those people
who lived in Trinidad. This was a sparsely settled colony under Spanish rule.[29]
Its population, like that of Monte Christi mentioned in the last chapter, was
relatively small and not especially affluent. As a result, island residents would
have had little use for the captured molasses; they could not have afforded
to buy it at a high price. What they would have had use for, food supplies or
European goods, was much more easily obtained in neighboring French and
British islands—as well as in the Dutch free port of St. Eustatius, where the
ship was eventually sold. Selling the ship at that entrepôt allowed those with
money to purchase the molasses as well as other goods that could be at once
sold and consumed in Trinidad. The problem is that any goods obtained in
St. Eustatius would almost certainly have entered Trinidad illegally, as they
would not have been from Spain. It would have been highly improbable for
a Dutch colony that regularly supplied Spanish colonists with non-Spanish
goods to sell those same colonists Spanish goods, which were otherwise in
short supply—and the reason that Spanish colonists went to St. Eustatius in
the first place. In this way, Gil enabled smuggling to take place.

Governor Gil was right, in a sense, to send the molasses to St. Eustatius
for sale, as there would not only have been more buyers, but more buyers who
were willing to pay more cash. Purchasers would have gotten a good bargain
and Gil would have had enough money, at least for a while, to keep himself
happy while looking the other way as his subjects smuggled goods that they
needed into Trinidad from St. Eustatius and other neighboring non-Spanish
islands. He had created a win-win situation for himself and for those who
lived under his rule, perhaps explaining his long tenure on the island. The
problem, of course, is that the merchants Jenks successfully, and unusually,
rallied their government to support their claims; this was certainly made
much more feasible by the clear violations of the Treaty of Paris that the
seizure represented. Though the corrupt officials in the colonies had many
opportunities to thrive, doing so when there were high levels of scrutiny significantly diminished their success rates for flaunting the law. Gil got away
with as much as he did because he was peripheral—and because he could
claim to his employers in Europe that he tried to comply but was prevented
from so doing by local circumstance. That sort of explanation might have
worked for those with no real knowledge of the colonies. The greater the
connection, however, the harder it would have been to avoid more pro-
nounced scrutiny.

Corruption in Legal Regimes

Judges in many states and societies also had ample opportunities to become corrupt whenever smuggling was involved. The archival record is heaving with accusations of such behavior.[30] In most places, and especially in European colonies, it remained terribly difficult to eradicate corruption, given the terrible salaries that local officials were paid. In Britain's colony of St. Vincent, acquired with the 1763 Peace of Paris, where colonial officials were paid less than in Britain's more established Caribbean islands such as Jamaica or Barbados, bribery appeared rampant and, in many case, smuggling was at the core of the corruption.[31]

In 1794, the colony's Vice-Admiralty judge, Nathaniel Weeks, was indicted for "unlawfully, illegally . . . and by colour of his said office as Sole Judge" receiving £750 in a corrupt transaction. According to his accuser William Barton, Judge Weeks stated to him that this was the amount that Barton and his co-captors would be required to pay in order to get a condemnation for a legally captured prize-ship during a period of war.[32] In other words, the captors would have to pay the judge a fee in order to gain access to the proceeds of a ship that they believed they had legitimately captured. This is, in many respects, the flip side of the previous example from Trinidad. In that case, officials refused to release an illegally captured boat. In this case, they refused to condemn a legally captured boat, at least not without payment of a large fee. Of course, if true, the accusation demonstrates an earlier point: the nature of colonial officials' salaries made bribery something that was intrinsic to their job performance.

For example, if an Admiralty judge such as Nathaniel Weeks received more pay to condemn a ship and its cargo than he did to acquit a ship, then he had an incentive to issue a condemnation unless someone could pay him more again to change his decision.[33] In this particular case, again assuming that Barton's accusation was accurate, it is likely that the Vice-Admiralty judge demanded more than what he would have gotten from either a condemnation or an acquittal. It was as if he had set a minimum price, and he was determined to get it—even if it meant stepping outside of the law and his commitment to enforce it. If he had decided to acquit the ship and return it to its owners, then he would have received nothing and might even have caused the ship's contents to be sold elsewhere, which would not have especially helped the local population, his neighbors, upon whom he depended in order to live in St. Vincent. By convicting the vessel, he helped his local friends and other members of the population by assuming that they could purchase its condemned cargo; he did not necessarily enrich himself much, if even at all. This simple fact almost certainly explains why he would have resorted to bribery and extortion.

Judge Weeks and his accuser, William Barton, would therefore both have benefited from the ship's condemnation. But Barton was averse to handing over any more money to the Vice-Admiralty judge than he was otherwise obliged to do by the law itself. There could have been several reasons why this was the case. At root, though, paying more to the judge would have meant less available cash. By demanding a bigger after-sale share of captured ships' proceeds, judges had the ability to corrupt the system even further. And smuggling was virtually always involved in some way or another.

Because this ship was a legal prize capture, taken during the war, otherwise prohibited goods on board the ship could legally be imported into St. Vincent. A condemnation then would have made widely available in St. Vincent objects and products that normally had to be smuggled into the island; the condemnation would also have benefited the treasury, because duty would then have been collected on the imports. An auction of a captured ship, therefore, would have brought normally smuggled goods into a place legally—increasing the state's coffers and still supplying products to residents at a lower price than normal duty rates would have dictated. During peacetime, such goods would have been prohibited—and been subject to smuggling. Judge Weeks argued that if everyone in his society was to benefit from an action that he took, he too should benefit from this action—as he was also a part of this society. Even so, additional opportunities for corruption were present with these kinds of import-export activities. Many of these regularly involved the customs collectors themselves.

Customs collectors were regularly accused of charging more for their services than they were legally allowed to do; it is likely that such allegations represent the tip of an iceberg rather than more isolated illustrations.[34] With their low salaries, customs collectors faced frequent opportunities for corruption. That the collector of the customs could be guilty of such an infraction might have been surprising to European officials, who relied upon them to document imports, though not to residents of the colonies—who relied upon them to do just the opposite. Governments placed the burden of enforcement upon people who would have to act against their own self-interest as consumers to prevent illegal traffic. Moreover, if they prevented such traffic, they could wind up hurting those who were much closer in proximity to them than were their employers. States were almost certainly aware of this, though there was little that they could do to change the practice:

> I have received his Majesty's Commands to signify to you His Royal Pleasure that you do take the most effectual Care that no Officer of the Customs, his Deputy, or any Clerk employed by either of them within your government, do, on any pretense whatever, demand, exact or take more than the Fees established, or cause any unnecessary delay to shipping.[35]

Customs Collector William Brown, in New Orleans, was much more direct in his corruption than was Nathaniel Weeks, again assuming that the accusations made against each man were accurate. In 1809, a kind of "all points bulletin" was sent out around the Caribbean; such communiqués appear to have been extremely infrequent. Governor Hugh Elliott of St. Christopher wrote to the Earl of Liverpool to inform him that "Lt. Bainbridge waited upon me, and stated that the object of his voyage to these islands was to apprehend the Collector of the Port of New Orleans who had absconded."[36] The official notice that Bainbridge presented to Governor Elliott stated that "William Brown, collector of the Port of New Orleans absconded . . . on the 13th [November 1809] taking with him in gold one hundred and fifty thousand dollars of the public money, and you are called on for your aid in apprehending him."[37] Indeed, low salaries and constant exposure to tax collection provided such large opportunities for corruption. Because bookkeeping was so far behind, it is possible to imagine how such a large sum would have been able to accrue in the first place. How a poorly paid customs collector could have managed such a feat then becomes much easier to understand.[38]

Nothing is known about whether or not Brown was ever captured, but it is more likely than not that he made his escape, no doubt with the complicity of one or another local official who was willing to accept a bribe. What these small illustrations reveal is not only that customs collectors could be unaware of the crimes over which they ought to have had control such as smuggling, but that they were frequently participants in them or, at the very least, they benefited from them through either deliberately looking the other way as goods remained undeclared and were imported or from turning corrupt in one of several ways.

The Public-Private Partnership in Crime

If local officials could be accused of being susceptible to demanding and accepting bribes, some of them, perhaps a great many of them, also connived with their neighbors to import otherwise prohibited goods. In order to do so, they sometimes had to fend off the metropolitan governments' attempts to stop their own corrupt employees from, well, being corrupt employees.

In many of these instances, the military, which did not owe any sort of allegiance to the local populations, took it upon themselves to eradicate smuggling activities.

On 24 December 1763, Dominica's British commander, Joseph Partridge, complained to Rear Admiral Tyrrell, who was stationed off the coast of Dominica. Tyrrell was commander in chief of the Leeward Islands. Partridge reported that Tyrrell's men "came here and searched the Vessels in the Harbour, without any information," and that this "distressed the trade of this new colony, upon which the merchants laid a petition before me."[39] It was clear that Partridge was trying to satisfy the formerly French, or newly British, merchants by complaining about his own government's behavior; after all, his job required that he live on the island with them and govern them according to directives coming from across the Atlantic.[40] He therefore objected to an announced search of ships in the harbor: he even attempted to appeal to Admiral Tyrrell's sense of British nationalism. Partridge maintained that *legally* allowing French sugar to be imported into British territory would actually "greatly increase his Majesty's revenue," by increasing the duties that the Crown would collect.[41] In other words, Partridge tried to suggest that there was an advantage to government itself if it overlooked its own laws, which forbade the importation of French sugar into Dominica in French ships. But he went too far with his argument.

In fact, Admiral Tyrrell knew that Partridge had earlier issued a false clearance to some French boats that had brought the sugar from neighboring French islands into British territory, simply in order to pass it off as British produce from Dominica, from where it could be re-exported to Britain. Partridge himself was clearly complicit in smuggling sugar into Dominica for this purpose; it is not certain whether he accepted any payment for providing a false clearance or whether he was inclined to violate his own country's laws simply because he wanted to make the task of governing this newly acquired British island, with its French subjects, somewhat easier. After all, he *was* willing to work with local residents.

Admiral Tyrrell did not hesitate to discard Partridge's red herring of an argument. Tyrrell knew about the harbor search, and had himself given his blessing to it, long before it had taken place. He had, of course, refused to inform Partridge in advance that it would happen, figuring that such notice would allow Partridge to hide his activities. Admiral Tyrrell did not believe that he owed any duty of further explanation to anyone in Dominica, especially not to conniving Partridge. "I don't think I am in the least obliged to inform you from whence I derive that Power [to search for contraband]."[42]

But it is the rest of Tyrrell's response to Partridge's complaint that is so important to understanding the ways in which local colonial officials, as they tried to negotiate a difficult legal terrain, could easily fall victim to corruption. The strict constructionist Tyrrell chided the more accommodating Partridge to be more attentive to the laws:

> You say that you hope I shall take this new colony into consideration, which in its infancy ought rather to be assisted than distressed. I am to inform you that the Protection of the Trade and the Prosperity of the Colonies, in general, has and always shall be the chief objects of my care and attention. And I take the liberty further to acquaint you that instead of dictating to me what I am to do, had you taken the pains of reading over the laws of your country and acts of trade, you would have avoided the censure you now labour under, of giving a false clearance to a sloop.[43]

Tyrrell informed Partridge that he had ordered that falsely cleared sloop seized in the harbor of St. John's, Grenada, a neighboring island, and that he would be referring the entire case to the Board of Trade in London. He claimed that the island's population practiced widespread corruption: "I am not only credibly informed but find . . . that the Custom House Officers give fictitious clearances on purpose to defraud his Majesty of his Revenue which Infamous practice I hope will be represented . . . to the Surveyor of the Customs." They "knowingly connive at the fraudulent importation and exportation of French sugars, French Rum, etc."[44]

Nothing further appears in the British records about this case, nor could I find anything about it in French colonial archives. In many ways, however, that fact is beside the point. What *is* relevant here is that this case illustrates the differences in action between legal authorities within a single state. Though the laws were generally clear in describing what was permissible and what was not, the implementation and interpretation of those laws were clearly at odds with each other. The disconnect between Tyrrell's legally exacting interpretation and Partridge's accommodation, or corruption, in this case of sugar smuggling, illustrates the ways in which the colonists gained the upper hand over state policy specifically because they were able to maneuver around the law with the help of those who should have stopped them from doing so. The diffusion of power brought about by multiple authorities with multiple responsibilities in multiple jurisdictions allowed a great deal of illegal activity to take place without very much of it ever being observed. Those who were caught *really* were the unlucky ones, who happened to be in the wrong (right) place at the wrong (right) time. They knew that Admiral Tyrrell, and others like him, could not be everywhere at once.

Corruption deeply permeated most, if not all, levels of any given society as well; as has been seen, even the courts, with judges who got paid different amounts based upon what action they took, could be complicit in facilitating illegal trade. In May 1792, Captain John Drew wrote to Admiral John Laforey to complain that though Drew had ordered his men to suppress the smuggling trade around Carriacou, a Grenadine island, he had been undermined from accomplishing his mission. It is not that these British naval officers were unsuccessful at picking up smugglers and their ships; indeed, they were quite good at it. Rather, in this case, "on the day following [the arrest, the captured ship was] delivered . . . to the collector of the Customs at Grenada and libeled . . . for trial."[45] Of course, Captain Drew was very clear to indicate in his letter to the admiral that he had previously checked with Grenada's attorney general about the legality of his seizure of smuggling ships. He claimed that the attorney general informed him that he had made a perfectly legal seizure.

Once the seized ship made it to the Court of Vice-Admiralty in Grenada, however, the judge "ordered the Vessel and Cargo to be restored" to its owners because seizing officer John Drew was not authorized, in his view, to make seizures.[46] Captain Drew disputed this, naturally. He believed that he was "fully empowered by the 27th section of the Act for regulating the production of manifests to delegate my power to any of the officers of the ship I command for such purpose."[47] And he had a concurring opinion from Grenada's attorney general. In fact, Drew believed that most reasonable people would agree with him, because those with whom he consulted agreed with him. The problem for Drew, therefore, became one of refuting the Vice-Admiralty Court judge's reasoning. The judge was, of course, a local resident of Grenada—not a British naval officer.[48] In his professional capacity, and with his local knowledge, the judge knew that condemning the cargo could hurt his neighbors by denying them access to goods that they needed or wanted, especially if they had to pay more for them. On the other hand, he also knew that if he ordered the cargo released, he could actually benefit his fellow residents of Grenada by making its products, otherwise forbidden from entry without payment of steep duties, available for local consumption—even if they had to be exported, as was likely, and then smuggled back into the country.

Such a choice must therefore have seemed clear to the judge: when it came to a choice between hurting the state for whom he worked and which paid him, however minimally, by denying it access to its legally mandated revenue stream, or hurting one's neighbors by taking either necessary goods or affordable luxuries out of circulation, local officials nearly always chose to hurt the state. Like their Spanish counterparts in the region, British officials who lived in the colonies constantly had to balance local needs against imperial interests. Though there were officials who believed in strict construction, as discussed in the last chapter, they certainly appeared to have been a much smaller cohort than those who were willing to be more flexible. Nevertheless, their enforcement actions made it challenging for the majority of those who believed that they needed to negotiate with their populations and tolerate illegal trade in order to survive. In a perverse kind of way, the state actually gained respect and legitimacy from the local populations when it *did not* enforce the letter of the law and, instead, overlooked an amount of illegal activity that could not be waived off as entirely insignificant.

Corruption and the toleration of smuggling, however, was not just the prerogative of colonial and imperial officials. As one might expect, such activities also went back into Europe as well as into other societies. It is, of course, difficult to detect, because to do so required reading past all of the European complaints about residents of far-flung empires and territories. Reports of fraud, nevertheless, could be gleaned from examining archival materials from most societies; what appears is almost certainly a very small proportion of what actually took place.

In 1762, an anonymous New England resident, most likely in Marblehead, Massachusetts, wrote to Mr. Clarke, then serving as the collector of the customs in Barbados. The letter claimed that "a certain house in Old France is engaged in procuring French passports and letters for any Vessel that shall carry provisions to any of their [colonial] settlements."[49] The fact that a New England author was informing a Barbadian government official, even one as lowly as Customs Collector, about the way in which his neighbors and countrymen planned to skirt French law is really quite remarkable. The author goes on to state that the letters "are signed by the two principal secretaries of France and sealed with the King's seal," and that they direct any French subject to assist those who possess the letters so that "they are not molested or interrupted on any Account in the prosecution of their Voyages."[50]

According to this letter's author, these false French passports—made in France—were for sale in Boston as well as in the British Caribbean, at a cost of about $200 each. British North American purchasers were informed that if they encountered British naval ships while they were en route to French territory, the fraudulent passports were to be destroyed in order to avoid the punishment that would come for claiming enemy nationality.[51] At the same time, the letter alleged that the forgers offered, for the sum of $100, an opportunity to purchase a letter that would serve in place of the official passport.

It is clear that, if the author's information is accurate, the French government in some way was behind this attempt to defraud the British government of revenue. As a result of holding these passports, British traders could claim to be French traders, and therefore could call into French Caribbean ports in order to obtain otherwise prohibited cargo or cash. They could then return to British territory and pass off their cargoes as British, thereby avoiding customs duties. It was also possible using this system for British ships to trade directly with French European ports, in violation of both countries' legal policies. The French residents benefited from this too—as they would have gotten access to British products that were otherwise prohibited at prices that did not take customs duties into account. What is perhaps most striking about this is that the French government was willing to look the other way, even as its own laws and policies were violated. The French did so because the benefits to its citizens generally came at the expense of the British treasury, which collected neither import nor export duties. During a war, this could have been especially significant. Depleting your enemy's treasure was one way to gain the upper hand in such a conflict.[52]

Having said that, however, the author of this particular letter also attempted to explain *how* he had come to learn about this scam in the first place. The information he possessed was so detailed that knowledge of it would have had to come from someone who had seen and perhaps used such a document for the prosecution of some illegal trade. "I had engaged one of them," the author wrote, "with no other view than to secure a vessel with a large cargo I was unloading in case she should have fallen into the enemy's hands."[53] If true, the author was simply trying to protect his cargo from seizure by a French privateer when sailing between two British territories. At the same time, the false passport could also have aided smuggling ventures to elude detection if they happened to be stopped and questioned by a local official.

The quality of the document, however, revealed that the author also feared being detected in a French port, where he should not have been and, not coincidentally, where many British ships went during the Seven Years' War. What becomes clear from this letter, and the narrative that it presents, is an observation that all levels of government officials were involved at one time or another in violating their own country's laws. Though there is no direct evidence in this case that the French monarchy was selling false passports, it is very clear that the false passport documents had attached to them a French royal seal. And, because there was such a seal on the document, someone with more than a passing familiarity with the royal seal would have had to have been involved in its production, if it was to have any chance of fooling enforcement officials.

False passports facilitated smuggling by allowing ships to claim to be something that they were not, thereby evading duties and other fees. Such documents continued to be an issue that was raised repeatedly, at least through the first part of the nineteenth century. And, yet, European governments (and indeed others) could never find an effective way to stop them from being trafficked. This was almost certainly because various people who were part of the government, and who knew how passports were made, benefited from their sale in some way: either as purveyors of the fake documents or as consumers of the products that were illegally imported by using them as cover.[54] When the British Admiralty received a copy of a bogus U.S. passport in 1800, it was clear that American officials were involved in producing them.[55]

The British government's response to the detection of these documents was quite clear:

> We apprehend no prosecution can be carried on with effect against the Persons concerned in the transaction stated. Persons making use of such fictitious papers for fraudulent purposes may, by the manner in which they try to use them, make themselves liable to prosecution, but this must necessarily depend on the particular circumstances. If it should be deemed important to prevent the making and altering of such fictitious papers in the country by punishing the act as a crime, it seems to us that some legislative provision must be obtained for that purpose.[56]

In an opinion that seems to be a harbinger for many more recent decisions, the legal interpretation that the government provided for this case suggests some moral culpability of the perpetrators for using such false documents to facilitate a particular transaction. But it also stops short of referring to such actions as somehow fully illegal. In other words, there was no explicit statute banning this particular action of making counterfeit passports. If such bogus passports could be used as part of committing another legal transgression, such as a boat claiming to be from a country from which it was not in order to import otherwise prohibited goods, action could then be taken—for violating the commercial laws rather than for being in possession of a forged document, however knowingly this document was held. Such an interpretation again shows that in order for a state or government to achieve legitimacy with its population, it somehow needed to tolerate questionable or illegal actions, which could clearly be seen as benefiting the population at little cost to the government itself other than a bit of lost revenue.[57]

Eighteenth-century Atlantic colonial officials and European government representatives, of course, did not have a monopoly on finding ways around inconvenient laws; such patterns of lawbreaking continued across time and space. In the years after the Opium Wars, British merchants in Canton considered local Chinese officials to have been corrupt.[58] They even accused Charles Elliott, the British superintendent of trade in China, of handing out bribes to high-ranking Chinese officers: "Such rumours . . . plainly prove that it is believed possible some of the High [Chinese] Imperial Officers can take bribes . . . it is the surest evidence of the decay of Government."[59]

Though Charles Elliott dismissed the accusations against him as baseless, his argument in response seems more about practicing diplomacy than it does about confronting the issues behind the accusations. As he said, referring to himself in the third person:

[I]t is certain that Elliott could never think of offering a bribe to Keshen, because the high English Officers dare not do such things, and would not be so foolish if they did dare. . . . How in any case could [Keshen's] receipt of large sums of money be concealed from his followers: and even if he should forget his own duty to his Prince [the Emperor], how should he forget that his family was in the Emperor's power?[60]

Elliott, and through him the British government, sought to avoid offering any support for overtly illegal and immoral activities, lest British sailors and traders get ideas about perpetrating illegal and immoral activities closer to home (which, of course, they already had). The fact that Elliott wrote about bribery to his superiors in England actually suggests that the British already had such ideas: "[U]pon the side of the English Officers, must it not be clearly perceived that if great concessions are purchased by Bribes from high Officers, by rapid degrees every thing must be purchased by bribes from inferior officers, down even to lowest conveniences and necessaries of life, permission to buy and sell, permission to come and to go, permission to have servants, permission to write."[61]

Such a downwardly deteriorating spiral would lead right to the widespread corruption of fair trading practices, smuggling, which Elliott at least claimed he wanted to avoid in China or anywhere else. What becomes clear from this logic is a kind of complete unwillingness to admit that corruption was already widespread among both the Chinese and the East India Company employees who were engaged in trade. (Lest we forget, at the end of the day, these were opium traders, after all.) Clearly the Chinese laws and British East India Company policies that discouraged opium smuggling had been widely ignored. But now the drug smugglers accused each other of being corrupt, by accepting bribes![62]

Elliott's remonstrance against corruption's interaction with trade came much too late. Indeed, in 1820, evidence already existed to show not only that Chinese officials were willing to accept bribes, but also that British East India Company employees were willing to pay them. And while punitive action was sometimes taken against this corruption on both sides, it had the quality of being much more about showing punishment, perhaps as a future deterrence, than about dealing with the underlying issues concerning corruption, trade, and more generally, what that said about government legitimacy as it strove to regulate trade.

Indeed, the East India Company wrote to its secret committee of factors in Canton during the spring of 1820:

[I]t appears that a small quantity (about 10 or 12 pounds) of opium was discovered on board the *Essex*, while proceeding to Canton . . . it was seized by the Chinese officers and . . . to prevent the imposition of a heavy fine on the security merchant, as well as any further restrictions on the Trade, Marhop the Security merchant of the *Essex* compromised the affair by the payment to the inferior Chinese officers of the sum of 6000 dollars.[63]

The *Essex*'s Captain Nesbitt denied any knowledge of opium being taken on board his boat at Bombay. He claimed that the gunner, an inferior officer, must likely have placed it there without his or any other person's knowledge or permission; whether such clandestine action was even plausible remains a mystery. The East India Company governors were not really that concerned about the issue of bribery, since they seemingly factored it into the possible and necessary costs of doing business in China. Rather the company's directors were concerned, as was Elliott, that Chinese officials could come to *expect* bribery, thereby raising the costs of doing business in China. Moreover, this could lead to further dishonest activities that again drove up costs, such as Chinese officials making a habit of finding contraband opium on their inspections of company ships, even if the British had not loaded such products, simply as a way to augment their own incomes by demanding a bribe in order *not* to confiscate the entire ship. Though smugglers did not want to be *required* to pay bribes to carry out their own illegal activities, they were not completely averse to paying bribes if necessary to evade punishment for their crimes, so long as the whole matter could be kept under wraps. Such reasoning again suggests that they were most interested in carrying out fully free trade, with no restrictions.

As for the *Essex*, the East India Company determined to get to the bottom of the question about the origins of the opium, though it is not clear that they ever did. The ship and its crew was recalled to London so that they could be properly examined by British officials and, if necessary, company policy be properly adjusted:

> The consequences which are likely to follow from the discovery of opium on board of any of our ships in the Canton River are so serious that every effort must be used to prevent so destructive a practice. For this purpose immediately after the arrival of the *Essex* in the River Thames, a most particular inquiry will be entered upon, the results of which will be made known to you, with such further directions as the nature of the case may appear to require.[64]

Subsequent history of the East India Company shows that it repeatedly paid bribes, but that it tried to avoid doing so except when absolutely necessary to prevent a much bigger loss of cargo.[65]

Nor were the East India Company, the British, and the Chinese governments the only organizations to wrestle with the corruption of their own officials and others who had duties in either regulating or checking contraband commerce. As the next example illustrates, both the French and their Vietnamese trading partners were prone to corruption and "legal flexibility" in precisely the same areas. In this case, too, smuggling had become, in a sense, a way to legitimize other illegal activities.

The French government wrote to its "Chief of the Expeditionary Force to [Gulf of] Tonkin" on 4 September 1885:

> The Report of the President of Quin'hon, which you have transmitted to me, by your letter of 2 July last, signals the existence of a local customs office, which is directed by the friendly Mandarins who collect taxes on merchandise transported from one point to another on the Annam coast. These exactions of the Mandarins . . . constitute a flagrant violation of article 12 of the treaty of 6 June 1885. Under its terms, the Customs, in all the Kingdom of Annam, must be entirely entrusted to the French administration. Please . . . assure the strict observation of this article of the Treaty.[66]

In this document, the French complained that local Vietnamese officials, as they had done in the past, continued to collect customs duties, even though they had signed a treaty that guaranteed that the French were to be the sole agents for the collection of customs duties. The Vietnamese "mandarins" continued to collect customs on the coastal trade. The French, however, wanted this activity stopped because officials believed that it violated international law in the form of the 1885 treaty, which they also believed entitled them to the revenue stream that the coastal trade generated.

In order to achieve its aims here, the French government offered to increase its contributions to legal enforcement in order to prevent the previous Vietnamese rulers, the mandarins, from continuing their practice of charging and collecting imposts on imported goods from China, as well as on the coastal trade within Indochina. It was much more important to the Paris government that its colonial state officials gained power and authority through controlling the monopoly on import duties (and ensuring the validity of their treaty) than it was to preserve the idea of local control; the French wanted to demonstrate their own authority to local Vietnamese residents, even if it meant risking the alienation of the local officials upon whom they otherwise depended. It was not at all clear that the French understood that the "mandarins" could have turned the population against them with ease; all they would have needed to do was assert that the French were preventing their neighbors from engaging in their customary trading patterns. This would have meant diminished access to familiar goods and products. It would also have resulted in increased unhappiness and, perhaps, increased smuggling to avoid French duties.[67]

In this particular case, the French government simply wanted to ensure that those whom it considered corrupt treaty violators, in other words those who were more concerned with lining their own pockets than helping the French institute their version of colonial rule and its accompanying legal system, were actually prevented from engaging in legally prohibited practices. But from the Vietnamese mandarins' perspective, collecting taxes on imports became a way for them to demonstrate their outward positions of authority to their neighbors. The tax income that resulted also provided them revenue that would otherwise have gone to the French, further allowing them to accumulate wealth at a faster rate than most of their neighbors. This in turn helped to ensure a better livelihood for themselves and their families. Of course, as this document also illustrates, French colonial officials appeared more interested in demonstrating their own authority by suppressing the Vietnamese import duty collections than in actually putting that revenue to any sort of productive use. As a result, with this single example, it is possible to see the contest over legitimacy focused around illegal importations and tax collections. Those who controlled the law's creation did not necessarily control its enforcement; smuggling took place precisely because this gap created the space for it to occur.

French colonial officials, unsurprisingly, won this particular contest because the Paris government, in the heyday of imperialism, proved perfectly willing to increase the number of officials and boats in service that could be used to suppress the local Vietnamese mandarins' ability to collect taxes.

In other words, unlike in some of the earlier cases of smuggling, the French state prepared itself to enforce vigorously its right to tax the Vietnamese, in order to pay for bringing French government to Vietnam. This represented a change from, for example, some of the ways that European governments in the eighteenth-century Caribbean, including the French, demonstrated both a reluctance and an inability to spend money in order to exact this more careful statutory compliance with antismuggling revenue policies.[68]

Yet local imperial officials, those who were on the ground in l'Indochine—in this case "*Monsieur Le General Commandant en Chef du corps expédition-naire du Tonkin*"—might have had exactly the opposite in mind; they might have been much less inclined to support a greater revenue force for fear of a backlash from the resident Vietnamese. Governing a large population of Vietnamese speakers in a long-established society would surely have been easier with the consent, or at least a lack of organized resistance, from Vietnamese officials.[69] Moreover, by allowing the "mandarins" to continue to collect some taxes while the French ramped up their imperial enterprise and its activities, the net gains to the French might well have been equal to or even exceeded the total lost revenue that the Vietnamese claimed through their tax collection. Yet only those French on the ground in Annam would have known this. Like those in the Caribbean over a century earlier, colonial officials would have had to ignore orders from home even as they claimed to be scrupulously obeying them in order to get along with a much larger population of subjects on the ground. In this respect, they could have gained legitimacy with the colonized populations. In other words, they would have had to allow contraband commerce to exist in all but the most egregious of cases. There is no positive evidence that this happened in Vietnam, though there is some that it did elsewhere in Southeast Asia.[70]

Conclusion

Most contraband trade in empires around the world was not stopped—either because, as was argued earlier, it went undetected or because, as has been argued here, official corruption allowed it to continue. Because of these simple facts, it was colonial residents or local indigenous populations all across the world that prevailed over the strict rule of law, at least in this regard. Smuggling was simply their vehicle for gaining leverage against a state that sought to regulate their consumption activities and patterns. Contraband trade both led to, and was facilitated by, the bad behavior of corrupt or indifferent officials, who used bribes as a way to avoid forcing a strict compliance with the letter of the law or the legal regime in which they lived. Whether forging a passport, or using a fraudulent one, whether making a false conviction in order to extract a bribe, or failing to comply with an imperial directive while claiming strict adherence, or developing a systematic way to extract additional income from one's neighbors, local residents of all shapes and sizes found ways to subvert state and imperial authority through smuggling. They had thus effectively, perhaps even spectacularly, negotiated with the state.

Conclusion

Smuggling is free trade, yet some of free trade's biggest proponents could also be counted as among smuggling's fiercest critics. They have couched their complaints by distinguishing *free* trade from *fair* trade. For them, "free trade" represents exchange without any restrictions whatsoever. But, as we know all too well, most "free traders," whether historical or contemporary, have been expected to follow all manner of legal and commercial regulations imposed by legal regimes around the world. Such proscriptions were not historically part of any *moral* code, nor are they now. Nevertheless, having a moral compass certainly helps all kinds of commercial participants.

Trading policies, which almost always have some sort of restrictions lodged within them, have historically come from the state itself, or even more recently through supranational institutions such as the World Trade Organization (WTO). In contrast to "free trade," *fair* trade consists of commercial activity that, while it is carried out according to governmental policies and prohibitions, simultaneously utilizes the principle of "fellow feeling," about which Adam Smith wrote over two centuries ago.[1] Fair trade practitioners are honest, or *so they claim*. They portray themselves as virtuous, in line with idealized visions of how trade ought to be run. Moreover, by claiming the mantle of "fair trade," such dealers allow their customers to share in those feelings of virtue as well. Individual consumers, who can now freely purchase fair trade products such as coffee and chocolate, clearly expect that those who have produced what they have paid extra to consume have been paid a fair, if perhaps not quite a living, wage. If such consumers were to think about this for more than a few seconds, perhaps some even do, they would likely presume that the government in which the fair trade labor had taken place had not been defrauded of any revenue.[2] Fair trade is, then, a way for both consumers and their governments (or other regulatory agencies) to ensure that cheap products are not coming at the expense of the manufacturer, agricultural or otherwise, of such products. Nor does fair trade deprive the state in which that producer resides and works of its share of any revenue to which it is entitled. Fair traders can thus make living within the law, and being socially conscious while doing so, a virtue. In this regard, fair traders clearly have challenged the practices of smugglers.[3]

Fair trade could thus be said to represent both a *consciousness* and a *conscience*, which of course clearly begins to distinguish fair trading practices from all of the illicit activities that have gathered themselves around the act of smuggling. Such transgressions are rich, as we have seen. So too are they widespread, and not only geographically. From obtaining products to exporting them without paying all legally mandated taxes and duties, from shipping goods and people through unauthorized channels to evading duties and permissions upon their entering a new market, from purchasing goods whose origin is unknown to knowingly failing to stop smugglers or accepting bribes to permit their crimes to proceed, a very wide group of individuals have historically and contemporarily been complicit in the act of smuggling. The list of such activities could go on, of course, but I hope that readers can by now identify most of the activities that surround smuggling as it existed—*and as it still exists*. Fair trade, of course, is not theft; it is after all predicated on the ideas of virtue and fellow feeling. Smuggling, by contrast, is clearly theft, though, as I have argued earlier, its victims are much less visible than most other criminally injured parties. Fair trade sounds very attractive to many people precisely because it allows individual consumers to imagine themselves as part of a body politic when they perpetrate that most individual of acts—consumption. That idealized body politic is honest and just; moreover, it treats everyone equally before the law. In short, it is *fair*.

It is also, unfortunately, imaginary. As this work has suggested, smugglers and their customers very probably outnumber fair traders in many societies around the world; this is nothing new, they always have. The number of willing consumers of smuggled goods seems virtually without limit. Without ascribing guilt to readers of this book, it is probably safe to say that most people think nothing of carrying more goods across a national border than the duty-free allowance ordinarily permits. Nor would many people hesitate to travel across an international boundary in order to buy life-saving medication at a lower price than might be possible if they simply stayed home.

There have, as well, been countless instances of individuals hiring domestic workers, nannies for example, whose working papers are never inspected, if even they exist—and on whose behalf taxes are not paid.[4] There are larger stories, too; factories of illegal meatpackers, individuals who have smuggled themselves across a border in order to work to support families at home.[5] Apparently, distribution for products produced with smuggled labor is easy to arrange if, as is often the case, the price is right. Many consumers like to imagine themselves to be fair traders, yet many of them are anything but. Their actions eat away at the body politic of which they clearly consider themselves to be a part.[6]

While the producers of fair trade goods may well earn more than they otherwise might, though perhaps still less than a real living wage, there is no guarantee that consumers of their products are paying enough to ensure that all of the appropriate taxes will be submitted to both the importing and exporting governments. So, even those who are willing to pay more for fair trade goods may not be doing as much as they hope or think they are toward strengthening their national body politic or aiding the global economic system. Sometimes, even, their neighbors look at them with disbelief: "Why would someone willingly pay more for 'the same' goods that are cheaper without the fair trade label?" It is as if consumption has become *either* about paying the lowest possible price or, using Veblen's concept of "invidious comparison," engaging in conspicuous consumption.[7] Gone are the market principles about which Adam Smith wrote in *The Wealth of Nations*. Virtuous consumption and production, self-regulation, even self-awareness, seem now to be relatively scarce, as this book has shown that they have also been many times in the historical past. Nevertheless, a clear rhetoric continues to exist; it encourages people to support the very same ideas of virtue and fellow feeling that are so easily transgressed, often without even consciously doing so. Marketing has in this regard trumped substance. As a result, the body politic, civil society, has increasingly found itself at odds with its own government. This may be a pitfall of living in a classically liberal, or even a neoliberal state, where individual interest is put first and the legal regime is expected to bend to popular will. As this book has shown, however, this is nearly an impossible task.

But even that proposition is not universally true. Consider this story, related to me by a close friend. This friend purchased some jewelry in a country other than the one in which she lives. She did so in order to make a gift for her daughter; the price she paid abroad was much less than she would have paid in her own country. She then took the jewelry on the plane with her and returned home. When she landed at her country's international airport and retrieved her baggage, she saw the green lane, where those with nothing to declare would pass, and she also saw a red lane, where those with something to declare were supposed to go and make their declarations, in order that they could pay duty on the goods that had been acquired abroad. She could easily have walked through the green lane, along with most of the people on her flight, and taken her daughter's jewelry illegally into the country. No one would have been any the wiser.

Her conscience, however, did not allow her to do that (unlike, say, Columba Bush, who in any case spent far more money than my friend and actively lied on a printed declaration; there was no printed declaration in my friend's country). She entered the red lane. There were no customs officials there. In fact, there was no one in this lane but her. So she went to the customs office. It was closed. She knocked on the door, and waited for someone to arrive. Finally, after at least ten minutes, a customs officer appeared. My friend explained the situation to her and told her she has bought a pair of diamond earrings; the customs officer looked at her with befuddlement—as if to communicate that she was crazy for stopping when she could simply have walked through unchecked. Why would someone volunteer to pay? Why would someone seek out the state's representative to hand over money that could easily not have been handed over? My friend wanted to pay what she owed, so the customs officer obliged. She gave her a bill, and she paid it before leaving the airport. What became clear to my friend was that government expected her to cheat; its officials even made it easy for her. But my friend refused, and for her trouble was viewed suspiciously. I think that makes her an honest "fair trader."

Not many people would have gone to such lengths to assuage their consciences. I've even asked this question of my students over the years—hypothetically, of course. I polled my large lecture classes—most of whose members, perhaps as many as 90 percent, have traveled abroad—about whether or not they are always scrupulously honest about declaring everything they bring back to the United States on their customs form and paying duty if necessary. The general response has been one of laughter and derision, as if to say that they have viewed such governmental forms as highly irrelevant. When I then referred to them as smugglers, and shared with them some of the stories that appeared in these pages, they began to contemplate whether their actions, unwitting or deliberate, might some negative repercussions for the civil society in which they live and the government that rules over them. Just as my friend did not want to be a smuggler but the state appeared to be indifferent, my students could not conceive themselves to be smugglers in any way, but they were. That made them very uncomfortable, at least until I changed the subject several minutes later.

Such an experiment has always served as a useful teaching tool for me, as I regularly teach both a lower-division survey of world history and an upper-division survey on classical political economy. At the core of both of these classes is a central question about the role that government should play in the lives of the individuals who live under its rule. Both historically and theoretically, my students leave with more complicated ideas about not just what the theoretical relationship ought to be in practice, but also about what is *right*. Though it is not so easy to measure improvements to critical thinking, it has nonetheless been observable to me that the questions that students asked as they considered both theory and practice over the course of a semester grow increasingly sophisticated. What is more, many of them came to understand that smuggling (along with other kinds of illegal actions) ought to be considered a test of the boundaries that exist between citizens (or subjects) and the state over what the role of government in people's lives should be.

Whether one believes in "big government" or not, it is absolutely essential that some form of government and legal regime exist in every society. One does not need to accept a Hobbesian version of the world, or even a Machiavellian one, to understand that government provides certain functions to its population. Whether it is protecting individual life or property, or waging war against others, the state in virtually every society has one or more important functions. Once such a simple premise becomes accepted, and my students always accept it, it then follows that the state, or government, requires revenue in order to exist.

Therein lies the problem for smugglers, and virtually every other tax evader. *Someone* has to pay taxes and fees in order for the government to be able to carry out its functions. While it is certainly true that many governments do not provide adequate protection for either their citizens or their markets, and while it is no less true that many individuals do not see themselves in any way connected to their governments, the problem with smuggling is that it *further* undermines the ability of government to perform its job fairly or adequately at precisely the same time that it erodes many individuals' belief in the state's relevance to them. The eighteenth- and nineteenth-century moralists, in this regard if not in others, were not far off the mark when they complained about smuggling denying the state and society their due.[8] In fact, smuggling and its participants create a vicious circle, which is extremely tough to escape.

Left unchecked, smuggling leads not only to the corruption of officials—and these pages have shown that there has been no shortage of them historically—but also to a profound challenge to the legitimacy of government itself. It is one thing to be able to identify those in the employ of government who flagrantly (or not so flagrantly) violated the law that they were paid to uphold and enforce. It is quite another thing to participate in an enterprise that allows every individual to consume what he or she wants, at a price that he or she wants to pay, without a single thought about the origins of the consumed product. It is even scarier to contemplate that such unfettered consumption might well have the deleterious effect of undermining the government, which is the very organization that protects the same individual consumer's life, property, and even the right to consume.

There is, then, a very clear trade-off. Yet most people do not see it, or rather they choose not to see it. If government is to survive, it must support itself through taxes. It can get taxes from any number of sources, but ultimately it must get taxes from those who live under its authority. No matter from which source it draws its revenue, those who pay taxes and fees must understand that they *are* getting something in return. That return is, at the very least, protection and civility. Government, in other words, provides the very services that make civil society function, well, *civilly*. Government is therefore as dependent upon civil society for its nourishment as civil society is dependent upon government for its protection. The relationship between the two is not, as some have so recently argued, parasitic. Quite the contrary, government and civil society exist, and must continue to exist, in mutually beneficial symbiosis.

This last sentence might well disturb some readers, but it needed to be said. It certainly will not make me popular with the low-tax crowd. These are the people who believe that they pay too much in taxes but that they don't have enough money to buy their dream Porsche, their twenty-room estate, perhaps even a coveted Hermès Birkin bag. In order for government to exist, and provide even the most minimal of services, it requires that people pay their taxes. This is a simple fact.

Even so, this topic became a significant issue during the 2008 American presidential election campaign and has lingered into the global financial crisis discussions in 2009. Vice President Joe Biden (D-DE) claimed during the campaign that anyone who made over $200,000 in an Obama presidency "is going to pay more. . . . *It's time to be patriotic . . .* time to jump in, time to be part of the deal, time to help get America out of the rut." In response to another interviewer, a Republican pundit responded, "I don't think people think that paying taxes is something that is patriotic."[9] The complex idea that paying taxes is the price for participating in a legal regime that stabilizes civil society and permits individual freedom (including consumption) had been reduced to a discussion of patriotism.

The issue again appeared later in the campaign. Republican candidate for vice president, Governor Sarah Palin (R-AK), attacked Biden's stance:

> Now you said recently that higher taxes or asking for higher taxes or paying higher taxes is patriotic. In the middle class of America . . . that's not patriotic. Patriotic is saying, government, you know, you're not always the solution. In fact, too often you're the problem so, government, lessen the tax burden on our families and get out of the way and let the private sector and our families grow and thrive and prosper.[10]

Palin's statement attacked the idea that government has a role to play in the lives of its citizens; it is, then, not based in any coherent understanding of political economy. Her antigovernment rhetoric implied that the patriotic thing to do would be to eviscerate the state. This is not logical, given what patriotism actually is. In other words, to be a patriot, there needs to be a government, which in turn requires revenue to exist. And that revenue is, of course, provided by taxes. It therefore stands to reason that if *necessary* government services—determined in any variety of ways, according to the government's prescribed role—cannot be provided with existing revenue, the government needs to get more. It can do so by raising taxes, or it can do so by more vigorously enforcing existing revenue laws. That could require new laws, such as those passed on the eve of the American Revolution, or it could simply mean that customs collectors perform more vigorous border checks and that consumers returning from abroad pay the duty that they might owe. Paying taxes, in this way, does indeed become a patriotic act.

New York Times columnist Thomas Friedman made a similar point in his regular commentary on 8 October 2008. He wrote:

> I grew up in a very middle-class family in a very middle-class suburb of Minneapolis, and my parents taught me that paying taxes, while certainly no fun, was how we paid for the police and the army, our public universities and local schools, scientific research and Medicare for the elderly. No one said it better than Justice Oliver Wendell Holmes: "I like paying taxes. With them I buy civilization."[11]

Friedman had it right; the rest of his column eviscerates Palin's position on the subject by tying the need for taxes to essential services that government provides. One can disagree with what those services are, but one cannot disagree that they must be paid for with taxes; there is no alternative. Indeed, it is *patriotic* to pay taxes, but even that is insufficient. Paying money to the government is, as Oliver Wendell Holmes claimed, a mark of living in civil society. Indeed, it is part of what makes society civil. Paying taxes, and not engaging in smuggling or consuming smuggled goods, being a "fair trader," really does appear to be the only way that individuals can ensure that civil society can continue to exist for their neighbors.

It is, however, possible to engage in a debate about the nature of the taxes, and whether the taxes are laid on appropriate goods and services. So, too, is it possible to consider the role of government in supporting regulations that, seemingly, benefit one group of people over another. Every legal regime has a mechanism to do so, or at least it should. Moreover, there are supranational institutions, such as the WTO, that can help with this kind of issue. But it is crucially important that while those debates are taking place, individuals and corporations (who are often treated in some legal regimes as individuals) continue to pay their taxes, imposts, and duties. Failure to do so would not only make the debates impossible to continue but, eventually, they would result in a bankrupt system and a failed state. There are more than enough of those in the historical past and the contemporary present to go around; we don't need to see any more of them. In this, Adam Smith's logic was impeccable. Paying taxes, even bad ones, protects both individual and public morality; if the taxes are bad, the public can negotiate better ones through available mechanisms to change bad policies and governments. Moreover, paying taxes will guarantee that the concept of "truck, barter, and exchange" can happen with equality of opportunity and equanimity for all who live under a particular legal regime.

—∿—

Notes

Preface

1. Very few smugglers kept diaries or, at least, diaries that have survived; among the very few that remain is John Rattenbury, *Memoirs of a Smuggler, Compiled from His Diary and Journal: Containing the Principal Events in the Life of John Rattenbury, of Beer, Devonshire, Commonly Called the Rob Roy of the West* (London, 1839). There is also a North American diary allegedly written by John Howe, entitled *The Journal Kept by John Howe While He Was Employed as a British Spy; Also While He Was Engaged in the Smuggling Business* (Concord, NH, 1827). The author of this book claimed to be a smuggler, but doubts about the existence of this author have since been raised. See William Daniels, "Specious spy: The narrative lives and lies of Mr. John Howe," *Eighteenth Century: Theory and Interpretation* 34, no. 3 (1993): 264–86. Daniels argues that Howe was a creation of the work's publisher, Luther Roby, and that the character was an amalgamation of Henry DeBerniere's experience in the American Revolution along with the experiences of others who were familiar to the publisher. It is important to note at this juncture that because primary sources written by smugglers are so scarce, historians have become dependent upon other kinds of sources, prepared by those who rarely participated in smuggling activities, in order to characterize contraband commerce. A similar argument has been made about Southeast Asian smuggling during the nineteenth century in Eric Tagliacozzo, *Secret Trades, Porous Borders: Smuggling and States Along a Southeast Asian Frontier, 1865–1915* (New Haven, 2005), esp. pp. 6–7.

2. For the idea of legal regimes, see Lauren A. Benton, *Law and Colonial Cultures: Legal Regimes in World History, 1400–1900* (Cambridge, 2002), esp. pp. 1–30. Because contraband trade and smuggling by definition involve subjects, citizens, and laws from multiple countries, the records of any single country will be inadequate to the task of full

legal analysis. Indeed, this is exactly the sort of problem that makes the study of smuggling a comparative subject at its most basic or, at its broadest conceptualization, a global problem in need of the world historian's wide-angle lens.

Furthermore, identifying and investigating every judicial case is itself a terrifying prospect, yet efforts to do so would in no way guarantee that every issue of contraband trade and other smuggling activity would be represented in these cases because so many of these activities went undetected.

It is also important to note here that identifying a single case in *one* country's judicial records would in no way assure that a complete understanding of exactly what happened could be obtained, precisely because at least two countries' laws are involved in smuggling activities. To complicate matters even further, many legal records have been destroyed, either through disasters, such as seventeenth- and nineteenth-century fires in London's Customs House, or through more willful destruction by corrupt officials.

3. See, for example, Alan L. Karras, "Caribbean contraband, slave property, and the state, 1767–1792," *Pennsylvania History* 64, no. 5 (1997): 250–269; "'Custom has the force of law': Local officials and contraband in the Bahamas and the Floridas, 1748–1779," in *Florida Historical Quarterly* 80, no. 3 (2002): 281–311; "Smuggling and Its Discontents," in *Interactions: Transregional Perspectives on World History*, ed. Jerry Bentley, Renate Bridenthal, and Anand Yang (Honolulu, 2005), pp. 206–227; and "Transgressive Exchange: Circumventing Eighteenth-Century Atlantic Commercial Restrictions, or the Discount of Monte Christi," in *Seascapes: Maritime Histories, Littoral Cultures, and Transoceanic Exchanges*, ed. Jerry Bentley, Renate Bridenthal, and Kären Wigen (Honolulu, 2007), pp. 121–34.

4. In many respects, the decision to mine European archives, especially British and French archives, came about for two reasons. First, these archives are generally well organized and I had already developed a way to extract information from them about smuggling in the eighteenth-century Caribbean. I therefore hypothesized that it would be relatively easy to do the same for other world regions. Second, and more importantly, much of modern world history after 1800 could be described as being, to some degree or another, caught up in an exchange between indigenous populations and Europeans, especially the British and, to a lesser extent, the French. In short, this proved to be an efficient way of expanding the scope of the book's research while not making it completely unmanageable.

5. Aline Helg, in *Liberty and Equality in Caribbean Colombia, 1770–1835* (Chapel Hill, 2004) presents a fine discussion of smuggling in South America, esp. pp. 72–74. Also see the forthcoming article in *Slavery and Abolition* by Linda Rupert, "Marronage, Manumission, and Maritime Trade in the Early Modern Caribbean," which considers slave smuggling between the Caribbean and South America.

Chapter 1

1. See, for example, William Mathew to the Board of Trade, 8 March 1751, The National Archives: Public Record Office (henceforth TNA: PRO), CO 152/41, Kew. This document concerns smuggling between the Danes and the British in the West Indies.

There are also many discussions of smuggling into and out of Martinique in 1822, for example, in FM/SG/*MAR/CORR/55, Centre des Archives d'Outre Mer (henceforth CAOM), Aix-en-Provence. For information on the illegal East Indian Trade, see "Illicit Trade in Spices at the Molucca Islands. Exertions of Mr. R. T. Farquhar to Prevent the Same," 1801, in India Office Records (henceforth IOR) F/4/92/1858, British Library (henceforth BL), London.

2. For one example that attempts to explain and estimate the economic role that smuggling plays in both national and global economies, see the collection of articles in part I of Jagdish Bhagwati, ed., *Illegal Transactions in International Trade: Theory and Measurement* (Amsterdam, 1974), pp. 9–46. Also see C. G. F. Simkin, "Indonesia's Unrecorded Trade," in ibid., pp. 157–71.

3. G. Rainy, ICS, "Report on the Manufacturing and Smuggling of Ganja," Joint Magistrate on Special Duty, Calcutta, 1904, p. 12, IOR, V/27/625/5, BL.

4. This is similar to a point that Lauren Benton makes in the introduction to her forthcoming book, *A Search for Sovereignty: Law and Geography in European Empires, 1400–1900* (Cambridge, 2009). The laws of empires and states need to be connected to their geographies, especially as they relate to enforcement.

5. It is quite possible to relate discussions of smuggling to emerging and evolving definitions of the state throughout the modern world. An extended discussion on this subject appears in chapter 3. It is also the subject of the excellent book on smuggling in late-nineteenth-century Southeast Asia by Eric Tagliacozzo, *Secret Trades, Porous Borders: Smuggling and States along a Southeast Asian Frontier, 1865–1915* (New Haven, 2005).

6. For example, exports of sugar to Britain from one Caribbean island, Dominica, outstripped its registered production, tipping off governing officials that the island was illegally importing sugar from neighboring French islands in order to re-export the French sugars as British produce. See, for example, "Extract of a Letter to General Melville from his Correspondent in Dominica," dated 8 May 1785, TNA: PRO, CO 71/9, f. 357.

It is possible to estimate the size of the smuggled product by matching the production data against the export data. Sadly, however, the archives do not contain full sets of either data point.

7. See, for example, Jack P. Greene, *Negotiated Authorities: Essays in Colonial Political and Constitutional History* (Charlottesville, 1994), esp. pp. 15–24. The question really concerns the ways that states governed individuals who resided at some distance from the metropolitan center. Also see Lauren A. Benton, *Law and Colonial Cultures* (Cambridge, 2002), pp. 210–65.

8. For one treatment of the relationship between economic policy and state legitimacy see Jürgen Habermas, *Legitimation Crisis*, trans. Thomas McCarthy (London, 1976), esp. pp. 70–75, 96–97. For a more lucid treatment, see Rodney Barker, *Political Legitimacy and the State* (Oxford, 1990). It is not my intention to get drawn into the extensive theoretical debates on legitimacy but rather to raise the debate as a way for readers who are interested in the sociological theory to find additional reading.

9. See, for example, the pamphlet, "An Examination of the British Doctrine Which Subjects to Capture a Neutral Trade Not Open in Time of Peace" (London, 1806).

10. There is much that could be said about the emerging role of the government during the early modern era. For political economists, the role of the state (or prince) is clearly articulated in chapter XIV of Machiavelli's *The Prince*. This book, which was first published in 1515, suggests how European rulers envisioned the state's purpose as chiefly that of waging war. By the time that John Locke wrote, a century and a half later, political thinking had evolved so that the state's chief aim was the protection of private property. See John Locke, *Two Treatises of Government*, Book II, Chapter IX. The evolution of this concept is discussed in more detail in chapter 3 of this book.

11. For a discussion about the expanding role of consumption in political economy, see chapter 3.

12. See Lauren Benton, *Law and Colonial Cultures*, esp. pp. 212–14. It could also be argued that land-based empires, such as Russia and the Ottoman Empire, incorporated new territories into their empires solely to benefit their own coffers. More people and more land meant more opportunities for regulation (or extending regulation), which increased the revenue base. In so doing, limitations on outside contact were almost always applied, further increasing the legal regime's power over new people.

13. See Lauren Benton, *Law and Colonial Cultures*, esp. pp. 31–79. Also see John Francis Davis, *The Chinese: A General Description of the Empire of China and Its Inhabitants* (London, 1836), esp. v. 1, pp. 3–128, and v. 2, pp. 430ff.

14. For one example of this, see Roy Moxham, *The Great Hedge of India* (New York, 2001). Moxham's concern is with the British-built customs hedge in India, which was designed to keep salt from freely flowing across borders from territory that was not controlled by the East India Company to territory that was. His quest to locate the customs hedge proved elusive for most of the book, but he reveals much history and political economy in the process.

15. For a discussion of merchants and their relationship to government, at least in Britain, see John Brewer, *The Sinews of Power: War, Money, and the English State, 1688–1783* (New York, 1989), esp. pp. 206–17. Also see John Reeve, *A History of Shipping and Navigation* (London, 1792), for a thorough discussion of trade laws and their application to America, along with some specific legal cases that clarified the legal issues involved.

16. There is a plethora of material on people of all classes participating in smuggling. This particular passage is taken from G. P. R. James, *The Smuggler: A Tale* (Paris, 1845), p. 3.

17. For an example of this in China, see Davis, *The Chinese*, v. 2, pp. 446ff. I have also discussed this in "Caribbean contraband, slave property, and the state, 1767–1792," in *Pennsylvania History* (Special Supplemental Issue, volume 64, Summer 1997): 250–69.

18. For Smith's discussion, see Smith, *An Inquiry into the Nature and Causes of the Wealth of Nations* (London, 1776), Book I, Chapter II, paragraph 1. Also see John Locke, *Two Treatises*, Book II, Chapter XI, "Of the Extent of the Legislative Power," for the relationship of government to preserving property.

19. See Jack P. Greene, *Negotiated Authorities: Essays in Colonial Political and Constitutional History* (Charlottesville, 1994), pp. 43–77, for one discussion on this subject; for another discussion, see Benton, *Law and Colonial Cultures*, pp. 12–18.

20. The Spanish phrase "Obedezco pero no cumplo," which literally means "I obey but I do not comply," was regularly used by Spanish officials to respond to Spanish government regulations. It effectively gave them the leeway that they wanted to interpret laws in their own way at their own place of residence.

21. "Prepared remarks of Attorney General Michael B. Mukasey before the American Bar Association," 12 August 2008, as quoted in Eric Lichtblau, "Mukasey won't pursue charges in hiring inquiry," *New York Times*, 12 August 2008.

22. Much of the earlier historical work on smuggling and contraband trade has been anecdotal and antiquarian, without being analytical in any way. This has meant, for example, that there have been many stories told, generally concerning one state or region, but no explanation or context for the kind of described behavior that has been presented. For several examples of this kind of work, see Joseph Jefferson Farjeon, *The Compleat Smuggler: A Book about Smuggling in England, America and Elsewhere, Past and Present* (London, 1938), and A. Hyatt Verril, *Smugglers and Smuggling* (New York, 1924).

23. There are basically three kinds of commercial statutes, but smuggling treated them all roughly the same. The three kinds are those that were designed to raise revenue, those designed to regulate some social aspect of consumption such as preventing the import of addictive substances, and those that derive from international treaty obligations.

24. The distinction was not lost on practitioners of these activities; see, for example, a song entitled "The Citizen's Procession, or the Smuggler's Success and the Patriot's Disappointment: Being an Excellent New Ballad on the Excise Bill" (London, 1733). Smugglers are here associated with the mob, and are juxtaposed against the fair trader and honest trader. Also see Robert Hardy, *Serious Cautions and Advice to All Concerned in Smuggling: Setting Forth the Mischiefs Attendant Upon That Traffic; Together with Some Exhortations to Patience and Contentment under the Difficulties and Trials of Life* (London, 1818). This sermon distinguishes the different acts involved in smuggling: funding it, actually doing it, or dealing in smuggled objects as either a buyer or a seller.

25. G. P. R. James, *The Smuggler: A Tale*, p. 4.

26. The historical record is full of smugglers who got caught in the wrong place at the wrong time; indeed, that is usually the only reason that smugglers got caught in some locations. See the *Memoirs of a Smuggler, Compiled from his Diary and Journal: Containing the Principal Events in the Life of John Rattenbury, of Beer, Devonshire, Commonly Called the Rob Roy of the West* (London, 1839). Rattenbury's life story, at least according to him, was replete with examples of him finding himself in the wrong place at the wrong time.

27. See Governor Orde in Privy Council, 4 July 1789, TNA: PRO, CO 71/16.

28. The French *exclusif* had more restrictions on commerce between France and its colonies than did the British Navigation Acts, which were, in any case, being whittled away by Britain's 1766 Free Port Act. That act had opened up some local Caribbean ports, including Dominica's capital, Roseau, to non-British commerce. See Frances Armytage, *The Free Port System in the British West Indies. A Study in Commercial Policy, 1766–1822* (London, 1953), and Jean Tarrade, *Le commerce colonial de la France à la fin de l'Ancien Régime. L'évolution du régime de «l'Exclusif» de 1763 à 1789, etc.* (Paris, 1972).

29. British trading policy did not have a merchant monopoly in the same way that the French system did; French Caribbean planters believed that selling their sugar in Britain's more open sugar market would fetch them a higher price. See Robert Louis Stein, *The French Sugar Business in the Eighteenth Century* (Baton Rouge, 1988), pp. 76–79.

30. The pattern also worked in reverse. British merchants regularly complained about the way that French residents of Martinique illegally imported non-French products, when the British controlled the island. They paid for them by illegally exporting French sugar as British produce. See, for example, Mr. Grove to Mr. Leslie, 19 May 1784, TNA: PRO, CO 71/8, as well as J. Orde to the Privy Council of the Board of Trade, 1 September 1787, TNA: PRO, BT 6/41, ff. 205–11.

British industry was in its earliest stages, but the quality of most objects, at least those in the Caribbean, appeared to favor the British as supplying better value for money than anything being shipped over by the French. There are similar occurrences in Southeast Asia in the nineteenth century; British textiles were passed off as French ones because they were perceived to be of better quality and a better price. See Dossier L-22(4), with material dated 1886, in Fonds Ministériels, Série Géographique, */Indo/AF/227, CAOM.

31. Indeed, the issue of colonial versus imperial interest is not an insignificant one. Island residents, like those in colonies around the world, frequently complained of chafing under the weight of laws that seemed antithetical to their interests because they had been designed to benefit those in the metropole. See Greene, *Negotiated Authorities*, esp. pp. 20–23, and Benton, *Law and Colonial Cultures*, esp. pp. 80–126. Benton's assertion of this problem as a jurisdictional conflict strikes me as inherently useful.

32. In fact, in my reading of significant amounts of local Caribbean correspondence from a wide variety of the islands in the eighteenth and early nineteenth centuries, John Orde stands out as one of the most rule-bound and dogmatic believers in London's legal authority. There can be no doubt that he was the most likely British official to take legal action against those over whom he ruled whenever he believed that they transgressed the statute books. There is more correspondence about smuggling in Dominica's Colonial Office Papers than there is in virtually any other set of island papers that I examined (including the earlier-mentioned Jamaica and Barbados) in Britain's National Archives. See, for example, TNA: PRO, CO 71/16, 71/17, and 71/18, NA for many examples of Orde's preoccupation with smuggling, as well as his ongoing conflict with the island's judges and council, who were far more inclined to tolerate it. Perhaps this is because he was a former naval officer.

33. A very clear statement of the way in which the Navy handled the division of the proceeds when naval officers were involved in the seizure of ships at sea can be found in the Order in Council, 1 June 1763, TNA: PRO, ADM 1/3866. For a more general discussion of the procedures used in the Vice-Admiralty courts in the Americas, see Carl Ubbelohde, *The Vice Admiralty Courts and the American Revolution* (Chapel Hill, 1960), pp. 15–16.

34. Governor Orde in Privy Council, 4 July 1789, TNA: PRO, CO 71/16.

35. Ibid.

36. Stewart to Orde, 2 July 1789, TNA: PRO, CO 71/16. The island's Legislative Council generally sided with Orde, at least initially. See the Resolution of the Council, 9 September 1789, TNA: PRO, CO 71/16. But the following year, things had deteriorated. Stewart had himself deposed to make a complaint about Orde; see "Deposition before Anthony Bertrand, Esq.," 1 July 1790, TNA: PRO, CO 71/17. Orde claimed that he was going to replace Stewart, which caused Stewart to take action.

37. There are many illustrations of these cases in the Colonial Office Papers found in TNA: PRO, CO 71/17 and CO 71/18.

38. See Proclamation, 15 April 1790, TNA: PRO, CO 71/16.

39. See James Bruce to Grenville, 10 November 1790, TNA: PRO, CO 71/18. Also see Orde to Grenville, 8 January 1791, and R. Wells, Acting Comptroller of the Customs, to Orde, 13 December 1790, TNA: PRO, CO 71/18.

40. Orde to Dundas, 13 June 1792, TNA: PRO, CO 71/23. Orde was concerned that Dominica's large number of French residents encouraged collusion with Martinique and Guadeloupe in efforts to smuggle goods and sugar between the islands. He also became increasingly concerned with the colony's refusal to appropriate funds to strengthen the island's defenses as war between Britain and France approached. But Dominica's residents did not withhold anything from him that other governors had actually extracted.

41. Lintin is a small island at the mouth of the Pearl River, near Canton (which is now called Guangzhou) harbor; it is ten miles south of Whampoa, not far from Macao and Hong Kong. See Davis, *The Chinese*, v. 1, pp. 120–121.

42. See "Extract from a Secret Letter to China," 2 April 1828, IOR, F/4/958/27188(2), BL, p. 87.

43. See ibid.

44. The reasons for the prohibition would have been to promote the social well-being of the Chinese population by denying them access to a product that could become addictive and debilitating. The state had created such a law for an ostensibly different reason than most protectionist European laws of trade. Nevertheless, a parallel between the two kinds of legal prohibitions can easily be made. The ideology behind many European trading restrictions was designed to promote virtuous consumption (i.e., limit luxury consumption), and otherwise serve as a check on improper consumer behavior.

45. "Extract from a Secret Letter to China," 2 April 1828, IOR, F/4/958/27188(2), para. 88ff., BL. Also see J. A. Mackay, *From London to Lucknow* (London, 1860), v. 2, p. 526, for an excellent and clear statement of the opium smuggling problem. Though the Chinese government did not respond to this particular attack, it nevertheless found itself generally aggrieved about the British positions toward opium and its importation.

46. "Extract from a Secret Letter to China," 2 April 1828, IOR, F/4/958/27188(2), para. 93, BL (emphasis mine).

47. Indeed, the 1844 treaty between China and Great Britain mandated that "The Chinese Superintendent of Customs at each port will adopt the means that he may judge proper to prevent the revenue suffering by fraud or smuggling." See Treaty between England and China, 1844, TNA: PRO, CO 129/1, f. 228, p. 10.

48. For a general discussion of laws related to smuggling into China, as well as the punishments that the state provided to Chinese subjects, see *Ta Tsing Leu Lee: Being the Fundamental Laws, and a Selection from the Supplementary Statutes of the Penal Code of China*, trans. Sir George Thomas Staunton (London, 1810). In particular, Book V, "Duties and Customs," of the Third Division (Fiscal Laws), discusses punishments of salt and tea smugglers as well as other smugglers more broadly defined; see pp. 148–57. Also see section xxxiv of the First Division; it states that foreigners are subject to the laws of China (p. 36). In addition, edicts dealing with the interpretation and application of these policies to European merchants in Canton are found in appendix XI, pp. 515–24.

49. On the opium trade and the Chinese state, see Davis, *The Chinese*, v. 2, pp. 452–57. Also see Carl Trocki, *Opium, Empire, and the Global Political Economy: A Study of the Asian Opium Trade 1750–1950* (London, 1999), esp. pp. 88–93. A brief discussion of the opium ban into China can be found in "An Explanation of the Peiho Massacre," in Mackay, *From London to Lucknow*, v. 2, p. 525.

50. Van Tuê is located between Hanoi and coastal Haiphong; though it was remote, it was near roads that passed from the coast to the capital, and would have been a prime location for the transshipment of smuggled products.

51. John Gillespie, in *Transplanting Commercial Law Reform: Developing a Rule of Law in Vietnam* (Aldershot, 2006), esp. pp. 49–55, argues that French law was largely irrelevant to most Vietnamese villagers, except those who had to deal directly with the French. That attitude is surely represented here. From the French perspective, efforts were being made in the early 1940s to standardize the administration of justice (p. 51). Such a practice represented a change from the earliest French experience in Vietnam, as described in Milton E. Osborne, *The French Presence in Cochinchina and Cambodia: Rule and Response (1859–1905)* (Ithaca, 1969), pp. 84–88.

52. Telegram, 6 January 1940, INDO/RSTNF//5451, CAOM.

53. Five piastres amounted to around fifty francs, which had been the fixed exchange rate after 1930. The bribe was not very large, something like US$2. For a discussion of this currency relative to others, see https://www.globalfinancialdata.com/index_tabs.php3?action=showghoc&country_name=VIET_NAM (accessed 31 July 2008).

54. Telegram, 6 January 1940, INDO/RSTNF//5451, CAOM.

55. Ibid. It is important to note for the record that the officials who had been beaten were clearly wearing their uniforms. The official French inquiry was very much concerned with this point; the French questioned how much the villagers might have known as they tried to consider whether this was an attack on two individuals who could not be corrupted or an attack on the French state. That the officials were wearing uniforms suggests that the villagers were attacking the French state itself, just as the other two stories in this chapter depict violence against clearly identifiable officials. The violence, in other words, was targeted against those who tried to stop the smuggling and contraband activities.

56. There is a good and extended discussion on illegally distilled alcohol in India, noting in particular that the problem was greater in outlying and more remote areas. See "Report of the Commission Appointed by the Government of Bengal Excise Commission to Enquire into the Excise of the Country Spirit of Bengal, 1883–84," IOR, V/26/323/4,

BL, pp. 50–58, for a view on illegally distilled alcohol in India. The Vietnamese case is, in some ways, much more mundane as the issue really was about taxes and fees rather than about any moral shortcomings of those who consumed alcohol.

57. Telegram, 6 January 1940, INDO/RSTNF//5451, CAOM.

58. Ibid. The events portrayed here are not dissimilar from a story related in Bradly W. Reed, *Talons and Teeth: County Clerks and Runners in the Qing Dynasty* (Stanford, 2000), pp. 172–75. The personnel in China were, of course, different but the story that Reed relates reveals the local population's utter disgust with those who were charged with enforcing the tax laws.

59. Indeed, even the French government was aware of the problems of enforcing the law in the interior of the colony. Arthur Girault, in *Principes de colonization et de legislation coloniale* (Vol. 2: Notions administratives, juridiques, et financiers, 5th edition, 1929), asserted that collecting taxes and otherwise enforcing the law in places interior to the colony ran the risk of alienating the population while producing only a very limited return. Girault instead argues for collection of duty on coastal imports and exports as being a simpler and fairer way to achieve revenue; see pp. 731–32. The same general position is visible to Lauren Benton, in *Law and Colonial Cultures*, pp. 127–66. The cases amount to jurisdictional conflicts, whether within a particular empire, between two states, or between a previously existing state being colonized and its new colonial ruler.

60. Robert Hardy, *Serious Cautions and Advice to All Concerned in Smuggling: Setting forth the mischiefs attendant upon that traffic; together with some exhortations to patience and contentment under the difficulties and trials of life* (London, 1818).

Chapter 2

1. See, for example, some of the news stories on Somali pirates in April 2008: "Piracy's new wave; Big ransoms, technology give plunder on high seas new allure," *Chronicle Herald* (Halifax), 24 April 2008; Johan Lillkung and Xan Rice, "Focus: Ocean terror: They opened fire with machine guns and rockets," *Observer* (London), 27 April 2008; and John J. Metzler, "Ahoy! Pirates in Somalia's troubled waters," *China Post* (Taiwan), 3 May 2008. As a study in contrast, see the *New York Times* story on smugglers that appeared on 27 May 2008. This story, which did appear on the front page (on a slow news day, right after a holiday) focused not on smuggling so much as on the ways that officials at the U.S.–Mexico border become corrupt. The story's focus was thus not about smugglers, per se, but rather about officials who tolerate smuggling and what they receive for this toleration in return. As always, the smugglers and their customers remain in the shadows.

2. An unscientific search of book and article databases returned, for example, 1,214 Library of Congress entries with the word "pirate" in the title, compared with 271 that had "smuggling" in the title. A search of the article database FirstSearch revealed 503 entries for "smuggling" as a keyword and 1,129 for "piracy" as the keyword. Though these are purely anecdotal illustrations, they provide quantifiable demonstrations of the relative attention that scholars have paid to these important subjects.

3. There is a large literature on piracy; it is not my intention to discuss the vast majority of it here. For a few illustrations of pirates creating victims and those victims identifying their attackers see Alexander Exquemelin, *Buccaneers of America*, trans. Alexis Brown (Mineola, NY, 2000), pp. 92–97; Virginia West Lunsford, *Piracy and Privateering in the Golden Age Netherlands* (New York, 2005), p. 155ff; and Carl Trocki, *Prince of Pirates: The Temmengongs and the Development of Johor and Singapore, 1784–1885* (Singapore, 1979), p. 67ff.

4. In defining smuggling, John Wesley argued that there are many types of smugglers, especially including "all those who sell anything that has not paid the duty." Even so, he also numbers among the smugglers "those who buy tea, liquors, linen, handkerchiefs, or anything else which has not paid the duty." John Wesley, *A Word to a Smuggler* (London, 1793), p. 1.

5. Marcus Rediker, *Between the Devil and the Deep Blue Sea: Merchant Seamen, Pirates, and the Anglo-American Maritime World* (Cambridge, 1987), p. 261; also see Lunsford, *Piracy and Privateering*, p. 105. See also J. S. Bromley, "Outlaws at Sea, 1660–1720: Liberty, Equality and Fraternity among the Caribbean Freebooters," in *Bandits at Sea*, ed. C. R. Pennell (New York, 2001), esp. pp. 170–71, and Kenneth J. Kinkor, "Black Men under the Black Flag," in ibid., esp. pp. 195–202. For an alternate discussion of who served as a pirate, see Robert J. Antony, *Like Froth Floating on the Sea: The World of Pirates and Seafarers in Late Imperial South China* (Berkeley, 2003), esp. pp. 16–17 and 82–104.

6. Wesley, *A Word to a Smuggler*, p. 1.

7. See Marcus Rediker, *Villains of All Nations*. Also see Carl Trocki, *Prince of Pirates*.

8. A notable exception can be found in Trocki, *Prince of Pirates*, esp. pp. 62–67. Modern pirates have sometimes discussed their goals of escaping the socioeconomic order in which they find themselves as a reason for their actions. A number of them also focus on the increased consumption that their crimes allow them. Hence there is a bit of a paradox—pirates want to escape their socioeconomic position but end up participating in it even more, as a result of increased consumption. Piracy thus becomes not a utopian escape but a means for upward mobility and advancement. For an example, see "Piracy's new wave," *Chronicle Herald* (Halifax), 24 April 2008.

9. George Lipscomb, *A Journey into Cornwall* (Warwick, 1799), p. 227.

10. For example, see Anne Pérotin-Dumon, "The Pirate and the Emperor: Power and the Law on the Seas, 1450–1850," in *Bandits at Sea: A Pirate Reader*, ed. C. R. Pennell (New York, 2000), pp. 25–54. This story is also told in Douglas R. Egerton et al., *The Atlantic World: A History, 1400–1888* (Wheeling, IL, 2007), esp. pp. 133–35.

11. Pirates were unlicensed robbers on the high seas, while privateers had received licenses from government to attack enemy ships. The lines between the two groups were clear legally, but in times of peace, complaints were regularly made against privateers who acted against non-enemy shipping, which of course made them into pirates. A good, if simple, discussion of the distinction between pirates and privateers can be found in David Cordingly, *Under the Black Flag: The Romance and the Reality of Life among the Pirates* (New York, 1995), pp. xvii–xviii. Also see Lunsford, *Piracy and Privateering*, esp. pp. 9–34, for a good discussion of the role of privateers in the early Dutch economy.

12. See Alexander Exquemelin, *Buccaneers of America*, pp. 56–57, for a discussion of a very early incidence of picking off ships from the Spanish treasure fleet. There are many other illustrations of raids against Spanish settlements and their residents in the Americas in this work (e.g., pp. 135–42). A more general history of such behavior can be found in Nigel Cawthorne, *A History of Pirates: Blood and Thunder on the High Seas* (London, 2003). Also see Anne Pérotin-Dumon, "The Pirate and the Emperor," in *Bandits at Sea*. There is, as well, a passing mention of this in J. H. Elliott, *Empires of the Atlantic World* (New Haven, 2006), p. 224.

13. See Derek Johnson, Erika Pladdet, and Mark Valencia, "Introduction: Research on Southeast Asian Piracy" in *Piracy in Southeast Asia: Status, Issues, and Responses*, ed. Derek Johnson and Mark Valencia (Singapore, 2005), esp. p. xi, for a good discussion of definitions of piracy. Also see Anne Pérotin-Dumon, "The Pirate and the Emperor," in *Bandits at Sea*, pp. 29–55.

14. This process is discussed in some detail in Antony, *Like Froth Floating on the Sea*, pp. 122–23. Though he considers the case of the South China Sea, the same processes occurred elsewhere around the globe. For a discussion of the establishment of colonies in the Anglo-Caribbean as they related to pirates, see Marcus Rediker, *Between the Devil and the Deep Blue Sea*, esp. pp. 56–61.

15. A brief discussion of the *flota* can be found in John Robert McNeill, *Atlantic Empires of France and Spain: Louisbourg and Havana, 1700–1763* (Chapel Hill, 1985), p. 6. Also see Archibald Campbell to William Pitt, 18 October 1790, TNA: PRO, FO 95/7/4, ff. 481–85 for a good contemporary discussion of the *flota* in global perspective.

16. See Nigel Cawthorne, *A History of Pirates: Blood and Thunder on the High Seas* (London, 2003), esp. pp. 51–76, for a general discussion of this history as it relates to pirates.

17. See Egerton et al., *Atlantic World*, p. 135; Cawthorne, *A History of Pirates*, pp. 77–106; and David J. Starkey, "Pirates and Markets," in *Bandits at Sea*, p. 115.

18. In a very real sense, the Europeans recognized criminals simply because they contributed cash to the European treasuries, which really amounted to a bribe. That the money came through direct attacks on a fellow state was generally inconsequential to the European states. See Anne Pérotin-Dumon, "The Pirate and the Emperor," in *Bandits at Sea*, pp. 29–55. Also see John L. Anderson, "Piracy and World History: An Economic Perspective on Maritime Predation," in *Bandits at Sea*, pp. 82–106, and Egerton et al., *The Atlantic World*, p. 134.

19. See Richard S. Dunn, *Sugar and Slaves: The Rise of the Planter Class in the English West Indies, 1624–1713* (Chapel Hill, 1972), esp. pp. 3–22. Also see Rediker, *Between the Devil and the Deep Blue Sea*, p. 58.

20. The argument was a bit disingenuous, since most other European states were not happy with the Treaty of Tordesillas and its division of new territories between the Spanish and the Portuguese; they wanted to be able to establish their own colonies there. See Dunn, *Sugar and Slaves*, pp. 3–18, as well as Arthur Percival Newton, *The European Nations in the West Indies, 1492–1688* (London, 1933), for an extended discussion of the inter-European rivalry in the Caribbean.

21. See Anne Pérotin-Dumon, "The Pirate and the Emperor," pp. 34–35, 37, 41–44.

22. Of course, it is also important to remember that Spanish policy was not exactly benevolent to those Amerindians who produced the bullion by extracting the ore from which it was made. Indeed, some might even argue that Spanish policy toward the native American populations actually made it easier for pirates to acquire territory in the Americas, since the Amerindians were so completely dis-enamored of the Spanish, their settlement and extraction activities. See, for example, Elliott, *Empires of the Atlantic World*, p. 224.

23. Indeed, scholars have noted this and have worked on laying these themes in front of their readers. For an excellent overview of this aspect of the literature on piracy, see Rediker, "The Seaman as Pirate," in *Bandits at Sea*, pp. 140–48, and Bromley, "Outlaws at Sea," in *Bandits at Sea*, esp. pp. 175–82.

24. See Peter Earle, *The Pirate Wars* (London, 2003), esp. pp. 89–108 and 159–80.

25. This is perhaps an oversimplification of a very nuanced and complex argument about the law as it interacted with pirates that Lauren Benton makes in "Legal spaces of empire: Piracy and the origins of ocean regionalism," *Comparative Studies in Society and History* 47 (2005): 700–24.

26. See, for example, Hans Turley, *Rum, Sodomy, and the Lash: Piracy, Sexuality, and Masculine Identity* (New York, 1999), pp. 1–27, for a brief discussion of life on eighteenth-century pirate ships. See also Rediker, "The Seaman as Pirate," and B. R. Burg, "The Buccaneer Community," in *Bandits at Sea*, pp. 211–43.

27. On independent living: Alan L. Karras, *Sojourners in the Sun* (Ithaca, 2002), pp. 211–15. Also see Bromley, "Bandits at Sea," esp. pp. 176–84. It was clear that many pirates and buccaneers did not succeed in their quests for independence, though they may have improved their economic lots considerably over what they might otherwise have been. Marcus Rediker, in "The Seaman as Pirate," refers to the distribution of booty as "one of the most egalitarian plans for the disposition of resources to be found anywhere in the eighteenth century" (p. 144). Of course, such equal distribution did not ensure a comfortable retirement with income generated from a landed estate. There is a good discussion of these issues in the South China Sea in Antony, *Froth Floating on the Sea*, pp. 122–38. Finally, a very general discussion of modern-day piracy (along with other crime at sea) can be found in William Langewiesche, *The Outlaw Sea: Chaos and Crime on the World's Oceans* (New York, 2004).

28. Among those rights and privileges was the pirate's legal standing. See Benton, "Legal Spaces of Empire," esp. pp. 704–10.

29. Again, see Benton in "Legal spaces of empire."

30. See Anne Pérotin-Dumon, "The Pirate and the Emperor," pp. 45–48.

31. "Examination of William Blackstock, before the Honorable Gilbert Fleming, Esq., Lieut. General and Commander in Chief of all His Majesty's Leeward Charibbee Islands in America," TNA: PRO, CO 152/45, ff. 136–38.

32. The ship was later valued at £150,000, and was said to have come from Mexico and to have been en route to Spain. See "Proclamation by Gilbert Fleming, 8 December 1750," TNA: PRO, CO 152/45, f. 165.

33. Ibid.

34. Blackstock certainly meant New Bern, North Carolina, which was about forty leagues via boat from Ocracoke.

35. A brief mention of Rhode Island's connection to piracy against the Spanish can be found in Elliott, *Empires of the Atlantic World*, p. 224. Even so, the Colonial Office papers for Rhode Island contain many illustrations of smuggling in Rhode Island; it was perceived to be one of the hotbeds of contraband trade, though there are no statistics to prove this claim. Rhode Island historians have connected the *Liberty* incident, in which customs collectors were attacked and the ship destroyed in 1769, to the American War for Independence. See John Russell Bartlett, ed., *Records of the Colony of Rhode Island* (Providence, 1861), v. 6, p. 593, as well as Sidney James, *Colonial Rhode Island: A History* (New York, 1975), p. 319. For additional reports of Rhode Island's involvement in the smuggling trade, see Joseph Wanton's response to the Customs Officials at Boston, July [n.d.] 1769, TNA: PRO, CO 5/1282, pp. 209–10, and the "Copy of a Letter from the Collector and Comptroller to the Commissioners of the Customs at Boston, 27 July 1769," TNA: PRO, CO 5/1282, p. 173. There is also additional discussion of this incident in the documents of TNA: PRO, CO 5/1282.

36. "Examination of William Blackstock, before the Honorable Gilbert Fleming, Esq., Lieut. General and Commander in Chief of all His Majesty's Leeward Charibbee Islands in America," TNA: PRO, CO 152/45, ff. 136.

37. Ibid. This is from where the £150,000 estimate of the ship's worth derives. The crew discovered 150 bags of coins on board. The Spanish galleon that unloaded these coins, then, almost certainly was part of the treasure fleet. In fact, it is likely that Owen Lloyd knew the contents of the ship and wanted to prevent this sum of gold being turned in to the governor of North Carolina. It certainly provides a plausible explanation for why he hatched a scheme to steal the ships in the first place.

38. "Examination of William Blackstock, before the Honorable Gilbert Fleming, Esq., Lieut. General and Commander in Chief of all His Majesty's Leeward Charibbee Islands in America," TNA: PRO, CO 152/45, ff. 136. Cochineal was a red dye produced from insects; it was one of the main exports from Spanish Mesoamerica.

39. Ibid.

40. Admiral Rodney to Philip Stephens, 6 March 1781, TNA: PRO, ADM 1/314, p. 46.

41. In general, those who gave information that led to condemnation and sale would receive a third of the money that was left after auction. The idea here was for Blackstock and his friend to split a third of the goods that they themselves had helped to steal, by identifying its location to local officials without revealing how they came to have knowledge of this. They surely reasoned that once their shares as informants were paid, they would be in the clear for their earlier crimes, and in any case they could leave the territory.

42. "Examination of William Blackstock, before the Honorable Gilbert Fleming, Esq., Lieut. General and Commander in Chief of all His Majesty's Leeward Charibbee Islands in America," TNA: PRO, CO 152/45, ff. 136.

43. Ibid. The violent character of pirates was well known and one of the main reasons that pirates received capital sentences. See Rediker, "The Seaman as Pirate," p. 154, and *Between the Devil and the Deep Blue Sea*, pp. 24–27.

44. "Proclamation," by Gilbert Fleming, 24 November 1750, TNA: PRO, CO 152/45, f. 165.

45. "Proclamation," by Gilbert Fleming, 8 December 1750, TNA: PRO, CO 152/45, f. 167. The Admiralty Board in London was also made aware of the case—and the diplomatic remonstrances that were then going on. See Gilbert Fleming to the Earl of Sandwich, 13 December 1750, TNA: PRO, ADM 1/3818, p. 78.

46. See Gilbert Fleming to the Lords of Trade, 22 December 1750, TNA: PRO, CO 152/41. Fleming was concerned that the population, which was admittedly complicit in robbing the pirates, was an accessory to piracy and therefore liable to capital punishment.

47. See "Memorial of Hay and Kingsley, Merchants in St. John's, Antigua," [n.d.] 1771, TNA: PRO, CO 5/119/2, f. 230.

48. For a brief discussion of Danish commercial and free port policies, see Neville A. T. Hall, *Slave Society in the Danish West Indies: St. Thomas, St. John, St. Croix*, ed. B. W. Higman (Baltimore, 1992), pp. 21–22. Frances Armytage, in *The Free Port System in the British West Indies. A Study in Commercial Policy, 1766–1822* (London, 1953), also makes several passing references to St. Thomas and the Danish position relative to free trade.

49. Crab Island was the British name for Vieques, which is only eight miles off the eastern coast of Puerto Rico. Hay and Kingsley claimed that it was "generally deemed to belong to Great Britain though uninhabited." It certainly was not yet settled; the Spanish did not begin their efforts to settle it until the nineteenth century.

50. See "Memorial of Hay and Kingsley, Merchants in St. John's, Antigua," [n.d.] 1771, TNA: PRO, CO 5/119/2, f. 230.

51. Ibid.

52. Ibid. The reference to what was not on board referred to European produced goods. There was no mention of "poles," which could themselves have been the object of a contraband commerce.

53. This point is discussed in much greater detail in the next chapter.

54. "Report from Foreman of Grand Jury, 7 April 1809, in Correspondence of Recorder of Prince of Wales with President of India Board," 1807–12, IOR, G/34/197, ff. 137–38, BL.

55. Ibid.

56. Ibid. The problems with piracy, and accusations of piracy, continued unabated. While the British and other European governments were trying to enlarge their regional presence and strengthen the state, they also recognized that they had to deal with local rulers, many of whom profited from piratical raids in the region. See, for example, *An Exposition of the Political and Commercial Relations of the Government of Prince of Wales Island with the States on the East Coast of Sumatra from Diamond Point to Siack* (Prince of Wales Island, 1824), esp. pp. 4–5.

57. Ibid. Carl Trocki, in *Prince of Pirates*, suggests that this concern came about after the formation of Singapore in the 1820s. As he said, "Following the Foundations of Singapore, Europeans in the Malay world came to be deeply concerned about Malay piracy" (p. 76). But it is clear from these records that this concern predated the

foundation of Singapore; the European presence in the region always sought to be free from pirates. For a relatively modern discussion of pirate raids in the region, see Owen Rutter, *The Pirate Wind: Tales of the Sea Robbers of Malaya* (London, 1930), republished by Oxford University Press in 1986. Also see Eric Tagliacozzo, *Secret Trades, Porous Borders: Smuggling and States along a Southeast Asian Frontier, 1865–1915* (New Haven, 2005).

58. For one example of smuggling activity through Prince of Wales Island, see chapter 3.

59. Commodore of the H. C. Yacht Nereide to G. W. Salmond, Esq. [Acting Secretary of Government], 18 April 1829, IOR G/34/145, BL.

60. Ibid.

61. Ibid. It is possible to make this claim because the British East India Company gave a vague reference to some of the goods that were on board the plundered ship. The phrase "and other goods" after a clear enumeration of other cargo seems highly suspicious. It was as if the authors only wanted to list cargo whose legality could not be disputed.

62. Ibid. There has not been much historical work on Malay pirates done in English. For one example, see Samuel Dickinson, *The Pirates Own Book, Or Authentic Narratives of the Lives, Exploits, and Executions of the most Celebrated Sea Robbers* (Portland, 1837), esp. pp. 204–20, which discusses Malay pirate attacks around the same time as that discussed above.

63. Discussions of illegal video and software copying, for example, can be found in "Seoul waging war against illegal copying," *Korea Times*, 6 April 1999, and Natalie Alcoba, "Counterfeit DVD lab busted: Four arrested: 20,000 pirated movies seized from two stores," *National Post* (Canada), 29 August 2006. These are but two small examples. The manufacture and selling of counterfeit luxury goods is discussed in Carolyn Batt, "Bargain hunters sustain shady counterfeit world," *West Australian* (Perth), 16 June 2007, and "South China police seize 2.6m-dollar worth of counterfeit products," Xinhua news agency (Beijing), in English, 25 August 2007. Also see the OECD report, *The Economic Impact of Counterfeiting and Piracy* (2008), available from www.oecd.org/sti/counterfeiting (accessed 27 November 2008).

64. Johan Lillkung and Xan Rice, "Focus: Ocean terror: They opened fire with machine guns and rockets," *Observer* (London), 27 April 2008.

65. See Xan Rice, "Focus: Ocean Terror," *Observer* (London), 27 April 2008.

66. "Somali pirates seize French yacht," BBC News online, 4 April 2008, available from http://news.bbc.co.uk/1/hi/world/africa/7331290.stm (accessed 8 June 2009).

67. Associated Press, Somalia, "Hostages on French ship freed, and six pirates and loot are seized," *New York Times*, 12 April 2008.

68. See John Tagliabue, "Suspected pirates arrive in Paris," *New York Times*, April 17 2008.

69. Ibid.

70. Ibid.

71. Ibid.

72. John S. Burnett, "Captain Kidd, human rights victim," *New York Times*, 20 April 2008.

73. See, "Report: Arrested 'Pirates of *Ponant*' related to Somali president," Deutsche Press-Agentur (German Press Agency), 5 May 2008. The most famous of these was Henry Morgan, who became lieutenant governor of Jamaica in 1675, as well as, unsurprisingly, a judge of the Vice-Admiralty Court. He was replaced as governor in 1682; see *Oxford Dictionary of National Biography* (Oxford, 2004), v. 39, pp. 121–28.

74. "Pirates take crew of Spanish fishing boat to shore: Report," Agence France-Presse, 22 April 2008.

75. Elizabeth A. Kennedy, Associated Press, "Two wives, a home, $90,000; They're the perks of being a pirate off Somalia," *Hamilton Spectator*, 24 April 2008.

76. This might not be true of all smugglers, since many drug smugglers, especially those associated with the big cartels, sometimes resort to violence when other avenues appear to be closed off to them. Perhaps the cleanest claim to make here is that violence occurs only when smugglers can think of no other way out, and the alternatives that they see are just not palatable to them.

77. Kennedy, "Two wives, a home, $90,000," 24 April 2008.

78. "Piracy's new wave: Big ransoms, technology give plunder on high seas new allure," *Chronicle Herald* (Halifax, Canada), 24 April 2008.

79. One place to see the wild pirate spending sprees was in Port Royal, Jamaica. See Dunn, *Sugar and Slaves*, esp. pp. 155–58, 177–86. For a firsthand description of piratical life, see Alexander Exquemelin, *Buccaneers of America* (Mineola, NY, 2000). Also see C. H. Haring, *The Buccaneers in the West Indies in the XVII Century* (London, 1910).

80. See Rediker, *Villains of All Nations*, pp. 70–76, 99. Also see Antony, *Like Froth Floating on the Sea*, p. 132ff.

81. "Piracy's new wave," *Chronicle Herald*, 24 April 2008.

82. Ransoms generally get split between those who bankroll the attacks—they generally reside in places relatively close to Somalia, such as Kenya and the United Arab Emirates—and those who carry them out. Ringleaders are believed to net several million dollars from each raid, making modern piracy much less egalitarian than it might seem and much more akin to big business. Lillkung and Rice, "Focus: Ocean terror," *Observer*, 27 April 2008.

83. John J. Metzler, "Ahoy! Pirates in Somalia's troubled waters," *China Post*, 3 May 2008.

Chapter 3

1. For a good historiographical discussion of slave fertility and the Caribbean slaves' general inability to reproduce, see Kenneth Kiple, *The Caribbean Slave: A Biological History* (Cambridge, 1984), esp. pp. 104–19. Also see Richard Sheridan's excellent *Doctors and Slaves: A Medical and Demographic History of Slavery in the British West Indies, 1680–1843* (Cambridge, 1985), esp. pp. 222–48.

2. A brief biography of R. T. Farquhar can be found in IOR, O/6/8, pp. 597–601, BL. Farquhar began his East India Company career as a writer in 1794, and became an

assistant to the accountant for the Board of Revenue in Fort St. George in September 1795. His career advanced until 1801, when his efforts to take control of Ternate Island caused him to lose control of the island and exclusively take up commercial affairs. He briefly held the Government of Prince of Wales Island from February to September 1805. He then traveled back to India, and eventually England, before once again returning to India in 1810.

3. R. T. Farquhar, "Observations on the Proposed Plan of Introducing Chinese Settlers at Trinidad and the Other West India Islands and Establishing a New Branch of Commerce, by Opening a Direct Intercourse between the East and West Indies," [n.d., 1805] Add. Mss. 13870, pp. 89–104, BL.

4. Ibid., f. 91.

5. See *Ta Tsing Leu Lee*, Fifth Division, Book III, "Protection of the Frontier," pp. 232–39. The Chinese state considered those who left China without a license to be deserters. Punishments were severe: those who merely evaded the frontier were punished with beatings; on the other hand, those who "had communication with the foreign nations beyond the boundaries" were to be strangled to death after incarceration. Officers who connived at this were equally punishable, though in capital cases they were merely banished. Moreover, anyone who might be providing information to foreigners outside of China would, upon conviction, be beheaded; it is clear that the Chinese state took a very dim view of its subjects interacting with foreigners. Hence, those who risked smuggling themselves out of China were clearly contravening the law, and those who accepted bribes to aid them, or simply looked the other way, also put themselves in legal jeopardy.

6. The history of Prince of Wales Island is a bit like some of the Caribbean Islands that changed hands repeatedly; it shifted several times between the Dutch and the British. Sir Home Popham, in *A Description of Prince of Wales Island* (London, 1805) mentions the Chinese and Malay migrations to the island and sees the Chinese especially as potential military recruits. See esp. pp. 28–29. For a discussion of establishing its judiciary, which itself was complicated given that it was not in India but governed by the East India Company and the British Crown, see TNA: PRO, TS 11/369, folder 1159.

7. Farquhar, "Observations," f. 90.

8. Modern economists generally consider "full employment" to be around 95 percent of the population. Such a statistic was obviously not kept in a remote trading outpost in 1805, but it seems a dubious proposition that it would have been achievable in any case.

9. Farquhar, "Observations," f. 91.

10. Farquhar, "Observations," p. 91ff.

11. For two examples of works that depict smuggling as a series of unconnected anecdotes, see Joseph Jefferson Farjeon, *The Compleat Smuggler: A Book about Smuggling in England, America and Elsewhere, Past and Present* (London, 1938), and A. Hyatt Verril, *Smugglers and Smuggling* (New York, 1924).

12. Economists have attempted to estimate the scope and scale of illegal trade; from the historical perspective, this is not as important as explaining and interpreting such

behavior. For one such series of approaches, see J. N. Bhagwati, ed., *Illegal Transactions in International Trade* (Amsterdam, 1974).

13. This subject is discussed in various places and at various times in Lauren A. Benton, *Law and Colonial Cultures: Legal Regimes in World History, 1400–1900* (Cambridge, 2002). See, for example, the discussion on pp. 18–26.

14. See *Ta Tsing Leu Lee*, esp. p. 238, for a discussion of the illegal exportation of merchandise and the penalties for those involved in that, and pp. 148–57 for general treatments of smuggling. Moreover, it is worth considering the various other ways that the Chinese regulated trade and the accumulation of profits. See pp. 164–67.

15. I have relied on the *St. Petersburg Times'* version of this event; many other newspapers, mostly in Florida, carried the story. See Jo Becker, "Bush: Wife meant to hide shopping spree from me," *St. Petersburg Times*, 22 June 1999. Also see Rick Bragg, "Governor explains wife's lie to Customs," *New York Times*, 22 June 1999, p. 14; Judy Hill, "Well, at least she has the clothes," *Tampa Tribune*, 25 June 1999; Andrew Marshall, "Bush's wife is caught smuggling clothes," *Independent* (London), 25 June 1999; and Charles Rabin, "Customs: First Lady declined a chance to amend declaration," *Miami Herald*, 20 June 1999, p. 1B.

16. Becker, "Shopping spree."

17. Ibid.

18. Title 19 of the U.S. Code as it currently stands only uses incarceration in very rare circumstances for violating the customs laws.

19. Becker, "Shopping spree" (emphasis mine).

20. Ibid.

21. Only Jane Wolfe, in "The hazards of trying to sneak it in," *New York Times*, 11 June 1999, sec. 3, p. 8, managed to have a full discussion of the problem, the degree to which it was widespread and the ways in which the Customs Service has responded to the increase in smuggling. Carl Hiaasen, in "First-class faux pas," *Miami Herald*, 27 June 1999, p. 1B, also understood the basic problem. He argued, "Columba Bush's brush with customs was no invasion of privacy. A law was violated, albeit clumsily, by the wife of a well-known, up-and-coming, political figure."

22. See A. Balu, "Nothing to declare," *India Tribune*, 22 September 1999.

23. See Benton, *Law and Colonial Cultures*, esp. ch. 1. Also see her discussion of Indian legal boundaries interacting with those of the European colonizers in "Legal Spaces of Empire," esp. p. 714ff.

24. The popular notion that wealth was measured in terms of money or bullion is discussed in Adam Smith, *The Wealth of Nations*, Oxford ed., Book IV, chapter 1 (Oxford, 1993), pp. 276–78. Smith obviously disputed this conceptualization and thought that adoption of governmental policies designed to maximize bullion acquisition was detrimental in the long run.

25. See, for example, J. M. Cohen, ed. and trans., *The Four Voyages of Christopher Columbus* (London, 1969), esp. pp. 56–57, 61–62, and 143, and Bernal Diaz, *The Conquest of New Spain*, ed. and trans. J. M. Cohen (London, 1963), esp. pp. 87–88, for illustrative examples of the Spanish lust for gold as core to the colonizing enterprise.

26. See, for example, Henry Kamen, *Empire: How Spain Became a World Power* (New York, 2003), p. 287ff. Kamen points to an overreliance on credit to fund Spanish expansion into the Americas. Like others, he did not believe that the treasure that Spain extracted was sufficient to fund imperial growth.

27. A discussion of Spain's relationship to silver, and its role in the Spanish and European economies, can be found in several places. See, for example, Dennis O. Flynn, *World Silver and Monetary History in the Sixteeenth and Seventeenth Centuries* (Aldershot, 1996), esp. ch. 8. Also see John R. Fisher, "Mining and Imperial Trade in Eighteenth-Century Spanish America," in *Global Connections and Monetary History, 1470–1800*, ed. Dennis O. Flynn, Arturo Giráldez, and Richard Von Glahn (Aldershot, 2003), pp. 123–32.

28. See, for example, Flynn, *World Silver and Monetary History*, esp. ch. 8. Also see A. García-Barquero González, "American Gold and Silver in the Eighteenth Century: From Fascination to Accounting," in Flynn et al., *Global Connections*, pp. 107–21.

29. See Kamen, *Empire*, esp. pp. 285–329. Also see Fisher, "Mining and Imperial Trade," and González, "American Gold and Silver."

30. See John Robert McNeill, *Atlantic Empires of France and Spain: Louisbourg and Havana, 1700–1763* (Chapel Hill, 1985), p. 50. For a brief discussion of evolving Spanish trading policy, see Carla Rahn Phillips, "Trade in the Iberian Empires," in *The Rise of Merchant Empires: Long Distance Trade in the Modern World: 1350–1750*, ed. James Tracy (Cambridge, 1990), p. 76ff. The dismantling of Spain's restrictive trade policies is discussed in James Lockhart and Stuart Schwartz, *Early Latin America* (Cambridge, 1984), pp. 362–63. Also see Kamen, *Empire*, for a description of early acts of avoiding restrictive trading laws, p. 437. A brief general overview of the Spanish trans-Atlantic economy in the eighteenth century can be found in David Ringrose, *Spain, Europe, and the Spanish Miracle, 1700–1900* (Cambridge, 1996), pp. 83–105.

31. Very general accounts can be found in Ralph Davis, *The Rise of the Atlantic Economies* (Ithaca, 1973), pp. 176–93, and Niels Steensgaard, "The Growth and Composition of the Long-Distance Trade of England and the Dutch Republic before 1750," in Tracy, *Rise of Merchant Empires*, pp. 102–52. See also Jonathan Israel, *Dutch Primacy in World Trade, 1585–1740* (Oxford, 1989), esp. pp. 237–44 and 313–26, for a discussion of the rise of the Dutch in the carrying trade around the Caribbean. A more specific account of poor Spanish sailors engaging in contraband trade can be found in Pablo E. Pérez-Mallaína, *Spain's Men of the Sea: Daily Life on the Indies Fleets in the Sixteenth Century*, trans. Carla Rahn Phillips (Baltimore, 1998), pp. 105–7.

32. Smith, *The Wealth of Nations*, Book IV, ch. 8 (Oxford edition, p. 358).

33. Henry Kamen, in *Empire*, laments the Spanish inability to supply their own slaves, instead requiring them to be procured by foreigners, either through the officially licensed *asiento* or through a contraband commerce in slaves; see pp. 430–31.

34. See John Orde to Dundas, 13 June 1792, TNA: PRO, CO 71/23.

35. Max Weber detailed the problems of bureaucratic office holders who had to rely upon collecting fees and taxes from those whom they served. Indeed, he argued that such people be paid salaries and effectively professionalized as a way to avoid

such problems. Though he wrote in the twentieth century, he described problems in a system without an effective and functioning bureaucracy that were certainly applicable in the eighteenth and nineteenth centuries. See Max Weber, "Bureaucracy," in *Max Weber: Essays in Sociology*, ed. Hans Gerth and C. Wright Mills (Oxford, 1946), esp. pp. 204–9.

36. For a brief discussion of the significance of contraband trade and the role of corruption in facilitating it, see J. R. McNeill, *Atlantic Empires of France and Spain*, pp. 196–200. Also see William S. McClellan, *Smuggling in the American Colonies at the Outbreak of the Revolution* (New York, 1912).

37. Smith, *The Wealth of Nations*, Book I, ch. 11 (Oxford edition, pp. 157–58).

38. Smith, *The Wealth of Nations*, Book IV, ch. 8 (Oxford edition, pp. 376–77). By "production," Smith refers to those who manufactured and otherwise produced goods having their goods and products moved into a protected market, which translated to a higher price for consumers.

39. See Adam Smith, *The Wealth of Nations*, Book IV, ch. 2. In this section, Smith provides a wide-ranging critique of the problems that arose under the European mercantile system.

40. Adam Smith, *The Wealth of Nations*, Book IV, ch. 8 (Oxford edition, p. 378).

41. See Smith, *The Wealth of Nations*, Book I, ch. 11 (Oxford edition, p. 157). Smith never had much sympathy for merchants, calling them an "unproductive class" who depended for their subsistence upon "proprietors and cultivators" (Book IV, ch. 9, p. 385). The alliance between merchants and the state is also addressed in Linda Colley, *Britons: Forging the Nation, 1707–1837* (New Haven, 1992), pp. 61–71.

42. These are all discussed in Book V of *The Wealth of Nations* (Oxford edition, pp. 393–444).

43. The idea of luxury in Adam Smith's work is briefly discussed in M. J. D. Roberts, "The concept of luxury in British political economy: Adam Smith to Alfred Marshall," in *History of the Human Science* 11:1 (1998): 23–47. Another brief discussion can be found in Istvan Hont and Michael Ignatieff, "Needs and Justice in the *Wealth of Nations*: An Introductory Essay," in *Wealth and Virtue: The Shaping of Political Economy in the Scottish Enlightenment*, ed. Istvan Hont and Michael Ignatieff (Cambridge, 1983), pp. 8–9. See also Smith, *Theory of Moral Sentiments*, ed. D. D. Raphael and A. L. Macfie (Oxford, 1976), Book IV, ch. 1.6–1.10, pp. 180–184.

44. A good general overview of the increasing usage of sugar consumption in Europe can be found in Sidney Mintz, *Sweetness and Power* (New York, 1985), pp. 121–50 and p. 180ff. Mintz refers to this as "intensification" and "extensification." This refers to sugar's increasing role in the diets of Europeans from all social and economic orders.

45. See Smith, *Theory of Moral Sentiments*, Book I, ch. 1.1.4–5, p. 10, for a discussion of fellow feeling. Also see Book VI for an extended discussion of Smith's views on virtue.

46. See Book VII of *Theory of Moral Sentiments* for Smith's discussions of various connections between the law, virtue, and fellow feeling.

47. Slaves were not seen as cost effective, when compared to free labor. See Adam Smith, *The Wealth of Nations* (Oxford edition, pp. 81, 238, and 349).

48. Smith, *The Wealth of Nations* (Oxford edition, p. 348ff.). Note that Smith never stated this, but this section of the work, when combined with the repeated attacks on mercantilism, leads to this conclusion.

49. John Locke, *Two Treatises on Government* (London, 1824), Book II, sections 221–222.

50. Thomas Hobbes, who wrote earlier in the seventeenth century than Locke did, addressed the issue of taxation as well; he argued for a tax on consumption, rather than income, which leads to a certain kind of progressive taxation if those who were poor consumed less than those who had more money. Even so, it was not the kind of progressive taxation that we consider today; it was much more like a Value Added Tax. For an excellent discussion of Hobbes's ideas of taxation, see Dudley Jackson, "Thomas Hobbes' theory of taxation," *Political Studies* 21:2 (June 1973): 175–82. For a discussion of Locke's views of taxation, see Martin Hughes, "Locke on taxation and suffrage," *History of Political Thought* 11 (1990): 423–42, and "Locke, taxation, and reform: A reply to Wood," *History of Political Thought* 12 (1992): 691–702. The second article is a response to the critique of the first piece by Ellen Meiksins Wood, "Locke against democracy," in *History of Political Thought* 12 (1992): 657–89.

51. Smith, *The Wealth of Nations*, Book V, ch. 11 (Oxford edition, p. 451).

52. See Karl Marx, "The German Ideology," as it appears in *The Marx-Engels Reader*, 2nd ed., ed. Robert Tucker (New York, 1978), p. 184ff.

53. See Marx, "The Communist Manifesto," as it appears in *The Marx-Engels Reader*, 2nd ed., p. 475.

54. Friedrich Engels, 1791 postscript to Marx, "The Civil War in France," which appears in *The Marx-Engels Reader*, 2nd ed., p. 628.

55. For one example of Marx pointing out the pitfalls of corruption and its exposing a failing system, see "Corruption at Elections," *New York Daily Tribune*, 4 September 1852. It also appeared in the *People's Paper* of 16 October 1852.

56. See John Stuart Mill, *Utilitarianism* (New edition, 1887), ch. 2, pp. 14–15.

57. See Mill, *Utilitarianism*, pp. 134–39.

58. Jeremy Bentham, "An Introduction to the Principles of Morals and Legislation," in *The Works of Jeremy Bentham* (New York, 1962), ch. 3, p. 14 (emphasis mine).

59. The panopticon concept can be found in Jeremy Bentham, *The Panopticon Writings*, ed. Miran Bozovic (London, 1995), pp. 29–95. A description of the felicific calculus can be found in *Principles of Morals and Legislation*, ch. 4.

60. An excellent discussion of Jeremy Bentham's views of empire—including administration and taxation, which were generally not positive, but contradictory over the course of his career—can be found in Jennifer Pitts, *A Turn to Empire: The Rise of Imperial Liberalism in Britain and France* (Princeton, 2005), esp. pp. 107–21. She also notes the difference between Bentham and the Mills in this regard. The main point here is that Bentham was critical of British imperial rule—and taxation was a significant part of that rule.

61. ·An excellent discussion of issues around legitimacy of government can be found in David O. Friedrichs, "The legitimacy crisis in the United States: A conceptual analysis," *Social Problems*, vol. 27, no. 5 (Jun., 1980): 540–55. Also see Habermas, *Legitimation Crisis*, trans. Thomas McCarthy (Boston, 1975), pp. 98–100.

62. See ibid. The American War for Independence is a good example of what governments ought not to do. Indebted, the British government after 1763 began to pass laws designed to raise revenue—but they also enforced a series of laws already on the books, which caused the rampant smuggling to become more difficult. Protests against such legal enforcement were not framed as government preventing smuggling from taking place; rather, they were phrased in such a way as to criticize the state for being unrepresentative of the people's will and unresponsive to their needs. The hard line that the British government took created a crisis of legitimacy. Failing to negotiate with its population made its own situation worse. See McClellan, *Smuggling in the American Colonies*, and John W. Tyler, *Smugglers and Patriots* (Boston, 1986).

63. This would prove increasingly significant, as European traders became more involved in commerce with the Chinese. Knowing that they tolerated a certain amount of illegal activity proved useful, and gave the European traders an excuse for their bad behavior. See *Ta Tsing Leu Lee*, pp. 543–44. This is a translation of clauses referred to earlier, in the section on dealing with foreigners. The clauses promise punishment to all who are found out, from those who engage with foreigners in commerce in other places to public officials who do not stop such activities or who have been "combined with or connived at" such interaction. Intent matters here, as those who were simply neglectful of their duty would be demoted, while those who were actively participating would be executed. Those who were neglectful could redeem themselves by "securing the offenders, and in bringing them to condign punishment" (p. 544).

64. Indeed, this is a very important point; China considered those who left its territories to be traitors to the body politic. See *Ta Tsing Leu Lee*, p. 232ff. If state officials, who apparently looked the other way at illegal migration, became aware of the situation, and the proposed uses for the migrants, the Chinese government might have become even more restrictive toward permitting its subjects to cross the border by demanding that the borders be closed as the law itself proscribed. Of course, as Bradly W. Reed reminds us in *Talons and Teeth: County Clerks and Runners in the Qing Dynasty* (Stanford, 2000), local Chinese officials were generally prone to corruption or, at least, engaged in tacit negotiations with the local populations (esp. pp. 200–266).

65. See note 2 in this chapter for a brief biographical discussion of Farquhar. He served only a very short time in Prince of Wales Island, before being sent back to India. It therefore seems clear that Farquhar was not seen as a suitable leader at the time. It also seems clear that his plan to encourage the Chinese to continue smuggling themselves out of China could not have done him much good with his London employers, who at the time were not interested in alienating China.

66. See *Ta Tsing Leu Lee*, p. 515ff., for discussions of the ways in which the Chinese attempted to regulate foreign commerce at Canton, where many ships of the East India Company did business. The general laws can be found in ibid., p. 145ff.

Chapter 4

1. Most works that touch on what was being smuggled address the subject briefly, for one particular time and at one particular place. Even so, none of them claims to be objective or exhaustive in its data collection. For one interesting work that attempts to document what was being smuggled in the Port of Mumbai, especially in the years after WWII, see the quirky work by Sripad Gopte, *Thrilling Seizures: Memoirs of a Customs Officer* (Mumbai, 1998). It provides an interesting narrative of how customs collectors operated, and what it was that they seized. Finally, a broad general report on smuggling can be found in *The Parliamentary Register: House of Lords*, vol. xiv (London, 1784), p. 154ff.

2. For a discussion of Columba Bush, please see chapter 3; material in that chapter has also been drawn from Alan L. Karras, "Smuggling and Its Malcontents," in *Interactions: Transregional Perspectives in World History*, ed. Jerry H. Bentley, Renate Bridenthal, and Anand A. Yang (Honolulu, 2005), pp. 135–49. For a discussion of smuggling on England's south coast, see, for example, Mary Waugh, *Smuggling in Kent and Sussex, 1700–1840* (Newbary, 1985). There are many other such works available.

3. For a brief discussion of French products being passed off as British produce, see *The Free Port System in the British West Indies. A Study in Commercial Policy, 1766–1822* (London, 1953), pp. 46–47. For a recent discussion of the role that tobacco smuggling has played in organized crime, see Dale Coker, "Smoking may not only be hazardous to your health, but also to world political stability: The European Union's fight against cigarette smuggling rings that benefit terrorism," *European Journal of Crime, Criminal Law and Criminal Justice* 11, no. 4 (2003): 350–76. For a very readable discussion of the lengths to which the British East India Company went to keep salt from being smuggled into its territories, see Roy Moxham, *The Great Hedge of India* (London, 2001).

4. Though it is not my intention to direct readers to the voluminous literature on the illegal drug trade, the following articles may be of some interest: "US-Jamaica relations tense. Some offended by efforts to crack down on drug trafficking," *The Dallas Morning News*, 16 March 1997; "Navy island base is also drug smugglers' port of call," *Washington Post*, 1 November 1995; "'Crazy medicine' flows out of Burma—U.S. trains Thai unit to block methamphetamine traffic," *Washington Post*, 17 July 2001.

5. For the marijuana market and the debate over decriminalization, see, for example, "High times over for marijuana: Globalization plus U.S. efforts shrinking crop," *Sun-Sentinel* (Florida), 1 March 2001; "2660 pounds of marijuana seized after high seas chase," *Virginian-Pilot* (Norfolk), 27 May 1999.

6. This is, in fact, reminiscent of the argument that utilitarians such as John Stuart Mill made. Individuals believe that they are pursuing their own good in their own way but government action prevents them from continuing to do so.

7. One need only search in Lexis-Nexis to discover thousands of articles on this subject. Recent examples include: "More young, socially vulnerable Lithuanian girls become victims of human smuggling: Experts," *Baltic News Service*, 19 March 2008, or Jorge Barrera, "Human smuggling has self-appointed protectors ready to shut down border," *Toronto Sun*, 5 April 2007.

8. Remittances from expatriates can be done legally, or they can be done off the books, through smuggling currency across borders without declaring it. Failure to report it to legal authorities may not deny the state money, but may allow a state, without its knowledge or consent, actually to finance its own enemies. See, for example, "UN warns Bangladesh of terror financing through remittances," *BBC Monitoring South Asia*, 6 June 2007, and Jerry Seper, "Fed-Mexico plan eases bank transfers: Critics say aliens could abuse it," *Washington Times*, 6 December 2006, p. A1.

9. On slaves who smuggled themselves, see Alan L. Karras, "Caribbean contraband, slave property, and the state, 1767–1792," *Pennsylvania History*, vol. 64, no. 5 (1997): 250–55.

10. Ibid.

11. See David Geggus, "The Haitian Revolution," in *The Modern Caribbean*, ed. Franklin Knight and Colin Palmer (Chapel Hill, 1989), pp. 21–50, for an excellent discussion of the changes that took place during this period. Also see Dale Tomich, *Slavery in the Circuit of Sugar: Martinique and the World Economy, 1830–1848* (Baltimore, 1990), pp. 14–21.

12. See Robert Louis Stein, *The French Sugar Business in the Eighteenth Century: An Old Regime Business* (Madison, 1979), for discussions on smuggling and the end of the slave trade.

13. Oddly enough, Zachary Bayly's father had been a customs collector for Jamaica in the late 1760s; he assumed the position after another customs collector, Mr. Douglas, was removed for corruption. See "Memorial of the Commissioners for Managing and Causing to Be Levied and Collected His Majesty's Customs," 23 July 1771, TNA: PRO, CO 137/66, p. 207.

14. See *Bahama Gazette*, 28–31 August 1792.

15. Ibid.

16. Ibid.

17. Ibid.

18. For examples of coin clipping in the eighteenth-century Caribbean, see John Dalling to Dartmouth, 3 January 1774, TNA: PRO, CO 137/69, p. 55. Also see Johnstone to Portland, 12 February 1799, TNA: PRO, CO 71/31, and a proclamation against it in *Mrs. Brown's Roseau Gazette and Dominica Chronicle*, 2 August 1798, to be found in TNA: PRO, CO 71/31.

19. This is also a topic that Adam McKeown has dealt with in the nineteenth and twentieth centuries in *Melancholy Order: Asian Migration and the Globalization of Borders* (New York, 2008). See, for example, pp. 37, 282–83, and 352.

20. See Karras, "Caribbean Contraband, Slave Property, and the State."

21. Here, the historical record is relatively clear. There were not large numbers of court cases that addressed smuggling, nor were the local papers full of information on the subject. Rather, the odd case that appears in the historical record reveals what happened when one of the unlucky few was actually caught. Such cases ought not to be seen as representative, since representative cases would have evaded the historical record altogether. Also see Eric Tagliacozzo, *Secret Trades, Porous Borders: Smuggling and States along a Southeast Asian Frontier, 1865–1915* (New Haven, 2005), p. 3, and then p. 317ff.

22. This kind of assertion fits nicely with Max Weber's discussion of the ideal type that is associated with bureaucratic behavior. See Weber, "Bureaucracy," in *Max Weber: Essays in Sociology*, ed. Hans Gerth and C. Wright Mills (Oxford, 1946), pp. 204–9. The ideas are discussed in general terms in Martin Slattery, *Key Ideas in Sociology* (Cheltenham, 2003), pp. 27–33. For Weber, the bureaucrat needed to separate his personal interests from that of the bureaucracy that he served. This was, of course, harder to effect in real terms than might otherwise be imagined.

23. The British government effectively made itself the Atlantic World's police force when it began to stop non-British ships for slave trading, even if the country doing the shipping had not yet outlawed slavery. Even with this administrative and enforcement stretch by the British, it does point to a very real position. Britain was determined after ending its own slave trade to prevent smuggled slaves from entering its Caribbean territories.

24. See R. T. Farquhar, "Observations on the Proposed Plan of Introducing Chinese Settlers at Trinidad and the Other West India Islands and Establishing a New Branch of Commerce, By Opening a Direct Intercourse between the East and West Indies," [n.d., 1805] Add. MSS. 13870.

25. For a general discussion of various European states being content with residents of other European states violating their home country's laws, see Alan Karras, "Custom Has the Force of Law: Local Officials and Contraband in the Bahamas and the Floridas, 1748–1779," *Florida Historical Quarterly*, esp. pp. 284–89.

26. Eliga Gould, in "Lines of Plunder or Crucible of Modernity? The Legal Geography of the English-Speaking Atlantic, 1660–1825," in *Seascapes: Maritime Histories, Littoral Cultures, and Transoceanic Exchanges*, ed. Jerry Bentley, Renate Bridenthal, and Kären Wigen (Honolulu, 2007), pp. 105–20, correctly asserts that the "great democratic revolutions tended to obscure the new order's origins in acts of piracy and irregular warfare." I would argue that it also obscured its contraband past. Caribbean colonial consumers were, in many respects, better served than those in the newly formed United States, because they continued to be able to avoid those laws that impeded consumption while those in the United States were increasingly subject to European ideas of law.

27. For the population figure, see William Taggart's Declaration, 21 April 1760, TNA: PRO, CO 152/46, p. 267. Also see Alan L. Karras, "Smuggling and Its Malcontents," in *Interactions: Transregional Perspectives in World History*, ed. Jerry H. Bentley, Renate Bridenthal, and Anand A. Yang (Honolulu, 2005), p. 142.

28. See William Taggart's Declaration, 21 April 1760, p. 267. William Shirley reported a figure of from four hundred to five hundred ships annually. See Shirley to William Pitt, 1 August 1760, TNA: PRO, CO 152/46, p. 265. Also see "Deposition of Martin Garland," 31 May 1787, TNA: PRO, CO 5/1068, p. 18. For a discussion of laws being violated, see Karras, "Custom has the force of law," *Florida Historical Quarterly*.

29. This letter is available in original copied form. See "Copy of the Lieutenant Governor of Monte Christi's Letter to Governor Shirley Dated St. Fernando de Monte Christi, 1 March 1760," TNA: PRO, CO 152/46.

30. Ships that were deemed "enemies," meaning that their countries were at war with each other, could legally be captured. Countries that were at peace with each other should have had no cause to capture each other's shipping. In 1760 Britain and France were at war. Britain and Spain remained at peace.

31. William Shirley to Lt. Governor of Monte Christi, 26 March 1760, TNA: PRO, CO 152/46, f. 261 (verso).

32. It is, however, conceivable that French ships could have stopped them. It bears mentioning that trade with Spanish-licensed ships within French territory would have been forbidden under the French *Exclusif*. This is just one example of how the various European states' economic policies intersected and overlapped in the Caribbean. It is also easy, then, to understand how residents of one state might get permission to violate the laws of another state. See Armytage, *Free Port System*, pp. 32–38; and Jean Tarrade, *Le Commerce Colonial de la France à la Fin de l'Ancien Regime: L'evolution du régime de «l'Exclusif» de 1763 à 1789*, 2 vols. (Paris, 1972), esp. 1:101–12.

33. In fact, such a case did take place—in 1752. I have written about it in "Smuggling and Its Malcontents," p. 144.

34. William Shirley to Lt. Governor of Monte Christi, 26 March 1760, TNA: PRO, CO 152/46, f. 261 (recto).

35. Ibid.

36. Ibid.

37. This sort of trade beyond what had been licensed, of course, also took place in the British world. That being said, there were nevertheless legal ways around the proscription. One could argue extraordinary circumstances: drought or hurricane and/or destruction of the food crops always pointed to the risk for starvation, especially of the slaves. This happened almost yearly in many Caribbean islands in the years after the American Revolution. It had the effect of allowing prohibited articles to continue to enter the market. Consumer propensities once again trumped legal prohibitions.

38. Spanish ships picked up French manufactures in the French ports and then passed them on to visiting British ships from North America and elsewhere in the Caribbean. The Spanish also brought some of these goods to Cuba and Puerto Rico, and brought into the French and Spanish territories North American and British products that had been prohibited. In short, the Spanish at Monte Christi were facilitating contraband trade throughout the hemisphere.

39. William Shirley to Lt. Governor of Monte Christi, 26 March 1760, TNA: PRO, CO 152/46, f. 262 (recto). Had the ships been legally cleared from a Spanish port, there

would have been an indication that duty had been paid upon them to the Spanish government, for either import or export. The cargoes had no such papers, leading Shirley to conclude that they had never been entered into a Spanish port and therefore the king of Spain's revenue had been defrauded. Because they had not been properly cleared into the Spanish ports, the cargoes remained French—and therefore liable to seizure—because, of course, France and Britain were at war with each other.

40. William Shirley to Lt. Governor of Monte Christi, 26 March 1760, TNA: PRO, CO 152/46, f. 263.

41. See also William Shirley to William Pitt, 1 August 1760, TNA: PRO, CO 152/46, p. 265, and for the list of fees and prices current, Shirley to Pitt, 10 April 1760, TNA: PRO, CO 152/46, p. 269.

42. See also Andrew O'Shaughnessy, *An Empire Divided: The American Revolution and the British Caribbean* (Philadelphia, 2000), pp. 61–62.

43. Lauren A. Benton, *Law and Colonial Cultures: Legal Regimes in World History, 1400–1900* (Cambridge, 2002), p. 22. Benton's argument works here when one acknowledges that the "local institutional practice" developed in response to colonial law; it was not an indigenous practice—except insofar as Smith's human propensity to "truck, barter, and exchange" holds true. It may, however, have been an indigenous practice in other parts of the world, such as Southeast Asia, at other times.

44. William Shirley to Lt. Governor of Monte Christi, 26 March 1760, TNA: PRO, CO 152/46, f. 263 (recto).

45. Ibid.

46. "Copy of a Letter Rear Admiral Holmes to John Cleveland, Esq. Secretary of the Admiralty," 23 July 1761, TNA: PRO, CO 137/61, f. 37 (verso).

47. Ibid.

48. Ibid., 38 (verso). The group numbered among its members several of the wealthiest island residents, including Zachary Bayly (the customs collector), Augustin Gwyn, and Simon Taylor.

49. Ibid., ff. 37 (recto) and 39 (recto). If, for example as has been discussed elsewhere, Holmes were removed and a more pliable official put in place, the clandestine commerce might be more easily carried out.

50. Ibid., f. 38 (recto). He also singled out Robert Stirling as someone who was trading illegally with the French. For a discussion of Stirling's career, see Alan L. Karras, *Sojourners in the Sun: Scots Migrants in Jamaica and the Chesapeake, 1740–1820* (Ithaca, 1992), pp. 72–75. Trading in French produce, of course, was illegal at all times, but liable to seizure absent a treaty of peace.

51. Very often "droghing passes" were required for travel between ports on the same island. They too were the subject of fraud and transgression, either through forgery or through bribery, of the sort described above for Monte Christi. The British navy was always on the lookout for those ships who could not produce the appropriate pass or whose passes seemed bogus. An extended discussion of droghing passes, and finding ways to stop their use in smuggling enterprises, can be found in a series of correspondence between James Leith, Captain General, Basse Terre, Guadeloupe, and the Collector and

Comptroller of H.M. Customs, St. John's Antigua, 22 August 1815, TNA: PRO, CUST 34/174. The correspondence goes on several years and results in a requirement that passes be turned in for inspection at every port, and, signed at every port by a customs inspector. Failure to do so would result in legal action. See also "Notice" in *The Weekly Register*, 11 April 1820, TNA: PRO, CUST 34/174.

52. See Benton, *Law and Colonial Cultures*, pp. 204–5. This case differs from Benton's, in Uruguay, in that the plural legal regime in Uruguay was created through negotiations between settlers and indigenous residents. In these smuggling cases the settlers had become the indigenous residents, and the European "enforcers" and officials took on the role of Benton's settlers.

53. Much has already been written about the global opium trade; I do not intend to add to that literature here, nor ought drug smuggling be considered as a principal focus of this book. For a good general discussion of the historical opium trade and some implications of it for the modern drug trade, see Carl A. Trocki, *Opium, Empire, and the Global Political Economy: A Study of the Modern Opium Trade 1750–1950* (London, 1999), esp. pp. 160–73; David Anthony Bello, *Opium and the Limits of Empire: Drug Prohibition in the Chinese Interior, 1729–1850* (Cambridge, MA, 2005), esp. pp. 16–20; and Amar Farooqi, *Smuggling as Subversion: Colonialism, Indian Merchants, and the Politics of Opium* (New Delhi, 1998).

54. For example, West Indian newspapers were regularly filled with declarations that the ports were being opened to foreign commerce in the years after treaties of peace were signed. The argument went that the population needed to replenish itself from supply shortages that resulted from warfare; the problem was that such decrees were often loosely defined attempts to give smuggled products the cover of legal entry. One discussion of this can be found in "Draft Letter to Mr. President Bishop," 29 May 1800, TNA: PRO, CO 28/66. Barbados's Governor Ricketts was in some trouble for opening up ports without demonstrating adequate need. See Portland to Ricketts, November 1800, TNA: PRO, CO 28/65.

55. The archival record is full of just this sort of complaint; for one example see Petition of "Us the Subscribers" to Admiral Rodney, n.d. [1773?], TNA: PRO, CO 5/119 (part 2), pp. 424–25.

56. This is the second Earl of Caledon, Dupré Alexander; Lord Caledon's family was Scots-Irish, from Londonderry, via Stirling, in Scotland. His father had made a fortune in India, so his governorship of the Cape Colony for his son was not especially surprising given the East India Company's mechanisms for making money. He did leave the colony under a cloud; harsh administration seems to blame. (The story described here can be found at: IOR, G/9/2, p. 10ff, BL). Also see Joshua Wilson, *A Biographical Index to the Present House of Lords, Corrected to October 1808* (London, 1808), pp. 103–4.

57. Private traders generally were not allowed to import these goods on their own accounts, and their ships were also to be forfeited if they were found to be doing so. The East India Company had a monopoly on these products. See 33 Geo III, c. 52, sections 129–133, in *A Collection of Statutes Relating to the East India Company* (London, 1810), pp. 319–21.

58. See "Memorial of J. Cowham," 30 December 1809, IOR, G/9/2/, p. 10ff, BL.

59. It would not have been uncommon for a crewmember to have been transacting private business on board the long voyages between Britain and India. They purchased goods themselves, which they hoped then to sell at a profit.

60. See "Memorial of J. Cowham," 30 December 1809, IOR, G/9/2/, p. 10ff, BL.

61. Ibid.

62. The statute, 33 Geo III, c. 52, includes a discussion of all of the duties that might have applied; the list was long, making it easy to imagine why individuals so frequently sought to avoid them. The statute can be found in A *Collection of Statutes*, pp. 283–331. Also see the 1803 list of duties that appears in 43 Geo III, c. 68, pp. 455–557.

63. John Pringle to Henry Alexander, 10 January 1810, IOR G/9/18, p. 131, BL.

64. John Pringle to Capt. Cowham, 11 January 1810, IOR G/9/18, p. 133, BL.

65. When the British took over Cape Town in 1795, there may have been as many 15,000 inhabitants, of whom 10,000 were slaves; there could not have been many more whites when the colony returned to British hands in 1806. See Leonard Thompson, *A History of South Africa* (New Haven, 1995). Also see C. A. Bayly, *Imperial Meridian: The British Empire and the World, 1780–1830* (London, 1989), esp. pp. 202–4. A contemporary estimate and description of Cape Town's population can be found in Robert Percival, *An Account of the Cape of Good Hope* (London, 1804), pp. 273–74.

66. Three-quarters of every British ship's crew needed to be British; a variety of acts required this, though there were wartime exceptions that allowed foreigners to be counted as British, provided that they had worked on a ship of war for three years. Moreover, the number of the crew that started the trip needed to be the number of the crew that finished the trip for the purposes of this calculation. See 34 Geo III, c. 68, A *Collection of Statutes*, pp. 903–5.

67. The Dutch, who controlled Cape Town until 1806, regularly paid for products imported from India with "bread, cattle, wine, and other produce of the Cape." It would therefore appear that the ship's crew really was trying to get provisions in exchange for the imported goods from India; it was the East India Company's policy that made past behavior the subject of criminal prosecution. See Percival, *Account of the Cape of Good Hope*, pp. 323–24.

68. See the earlier discussion of this incident in chapter 3.

69. Jo Becker, "Bush: Wife meant to hide shopping spree from me," *St. Petersburg Times*, 22 June 1999. The law is decidedly *not* irrelevant, unless officials choose to make it so by ignoring it or negotiating with a public that seeks to ignore it. See Karras, "Custom Has the Force of Law," for an extended discussion on this point.

70. See William Mathew to the Lords of Trade, 6 March 1750/1, TNA: PRO, CO 152/41.

71. Extract of "Letter to General Melvill from His Correspondent in Dominica," dated 8 May 1785, TNA: PRO, CO 71/9, p. 357.

72. See "Letter from William Senhouse, Surveyor General of His Majesty's Customs for the Leeward Islands, to Orde," 18 March 1785, TNA: PRO, CO 71/12, for a neighboring island's request that Orde take stronger actions to prevent smuggling. Orde responded

by directing the customs collectors to stop the trade. Also see "Memorial from Orde to Privy Council" [n.d., 1787], TNA: PRO, BT 6/41, p. 213, for a lengthy description of the smuggling process.

73. For additional evidence, see Alexander McAllister to Mr. Greg, 14 May 1785, TNA: PRO, CO 71/9. Orde, once in London, was able to convince the Privy Council that the charges against him were frivolous; he later returned to his naval career. See Denis A. Orde, "Orde, Sir John, first baronet (1751–1824)," *Oxford Dictionary of National Biography*, 2004 (http://www.oxforddnb.com/view/article/20810, accessed 11 November 2008).

74. For a discussion of this case, see "Correspondence Submitted Respecting the Prevalence of Smuggling in the Districts of Malabar and Coimbatore, in Consequence of the Tobacco Monopoly," 1818, IOR, F/4/626/17002, BL. Though both in India, Malabar is in Kerala, and was sometimes known as the Malabar Coast. Coimbatore is to the north and east, in what is now Tamil Nadu. In 1818, tobacco was smuggled from Coimbatore into the East India territory of Malabar; the East India Company therefore saw its monopoly on importation being violated.

75. "Correspondence Submitted Respecting the Prevalence of Smuggling," 1818, IOR, F/4/626/17002, BL.

76. Ibid.

77. Ibid.

78. Ibid.

79. Ibid.

80. The problem is that we do not know what the authorities were doing or saying, as there appears to be no record of the correspondence on the other side. For now, at least, this will need to be treated as simply one of many possibilities.

81. "Mopla" is a term that referred to Muslims from Malabar. See H. Percy Smith, *Glossary of Terms and Phrases* (London, 1883), p. 329. The other unfamiliar names are place names within the districts of Malabar and Coimbatore. They can be seen on two sections of the "Map of South Coimbatoor," surveyed in 1821–1823, IOR X/2332/1–2, BL.

82. Extract Ft. St. George, Judicial Consultations, 25 November 1817, from Acting Magistrate in Zilla of Coimbatore to the Secretary to Government, IOR, F/4/626/17002, BL.

A *talook* was a tax district. Pagodas were gold coins minted by the East India Company during the period of their rule in Southern India. At the time of issue, they were gold coins believed to be worth about eight shillings. See: Colin Bruce II, John S. Deyell, Nicholas Rhodes, and William F. Spengler, *The Standard Guide to South Asian Coins and Paper Money Since 1556 AD* (Iola, WI, 1981).

83. Extract Ft. St. George, Judicial Consultations, 25 November 1817, from Acting Magistrate in Zilla of Coimbatore to the Secretary to Government, ibid.

84. See Telegram, 6 January 1940, INDO/RSTNF//5451, CAOM, and the discussion of this case in chapter 1.

85. Monigars were surveyors for the East India Company, or other administrative employees. In this case, they were then going to attack the customs officer who turned them in.

86. Extract Ft. St. George, Judicial Consultations, 25 November 1817, from Acting Magistrate in Zilla of Coimbatore to the Secretary to Government, IOR, F/4/626/17002, BL.

87. Ibid.

88. Ibid.

89. The public good did not necessarily consist solely of public health issues, though they were certainly part of the equation. In this case, balancing the state's need for revenue against individual consumer demand harkens back to the discussion in the last chapter. Indeed, there were parliamentary debates over increasing alcohol consumption in India, which raised revenue for the government, and the missionary impulse for temperance. See, for example, J. Gelson Gregson, *The Drink Traffic in India: Extracts from the Commission to Enquire into the Excise of Country Spirit in Bengal, 1883–84* (London, 1885).

90. For an extensive discussion of a contemporary argument about banning opium imports into China as well as other places, see Major-General Alexander, *Contraband Opium Traffic: The Disturbing Element in All Our Policy and Diplomatic Intercourse with China* (London, 1857). Also see the series of essays in James H. Mills and Patricia Barton, eds., *Drugs and Empires: Essays in Modern Imperialism and Intoxication, c. 1500–c. 1930* (New York, 2007). Carl Trocki argues that opium is a "true commodity" in *Opium, Empire, and the Global Political Economy*; David Bello argues in *Opium and the Limits of Empire* that it would perhaps better be referred to as an "addictive consumable," which puts it in line with sugar and tea, and connects it to the phenomenon that Sidney Mintz described in *Sweetness and Power* (New York, 1985). Bello discusses the development of Chinese restrictions in chapter 4 (pp. 114ff.).

91. This suggests the traditional narrative that the British desire for profits led to a prolonged period of drug smuggling to China. That narrative has recently come under attack as scholars have begun to examine whether or not the uses of opium actually led to the drug addiction that has been associated with its usage. There can, however, be no doubt that almost all of the opium trade was contraband commerce, and that it resulted in a net outflow of silver from China to opium traders. Various aspects of this are explored in Mills and Barton, eds., *Drugs and Empires*; see especially John F. Richards, "'Cannot We Induce the People of England to Eat Opium?' The Moral Economy of Opium in Colonial India," pp. 73–80, and Amar Farooqui, "Opium and the Trading World of Western India in the Early Nineteenth Century," pp. 83–100. See also Bello, *Opium and the Limits of Empire*, esp. chaps. 1 and 4.

92. G. Rainy, "Report on the Manufacturing and Smuggling of Ganja," ICS, Joint Magistrate on Special Duty, Calcutta, 1904, IOR, V/27/625/5, BL.

93. See also the "Report of the Commission Appointed by the Government of Bengal Excise Commission to Enquire into the Excise of the Country Spirit of Bengal, 1883–84," p. 94, IOR, V/26/323/4, BL, as cited in "Report on the Manufacturing and Smuggling

of Ganja," by G. Rainy, ICS, Joint Magistrate on Special Duty, Calcutta, 1904, IOR, V/27/625/5, BL.

94. Ibid.

95. Ibid.

96. See the "Report of the Commission appointed by the Government of Bengal Excise Commission to Enquire into the Excise of the Country Spirit of Bengal, 1883–84," p. 92, paragraph 93, IOR, V/26/323/4, BL, for a discussion of the published duties on *ganja.*

97. See also the "Report of the Commission appointed by the Government of Bengal Excise Commission to Enquire into the Excise of the Country Spirit of Bengal, 1883–84," p. 94, IOR, V/26/323/4, BL, as cited in "Report on the Manufacturing and Smuggling of Ganja," by G. Rainy, ICS, Joint Magistrate on Special Duty, Calcutta, 1904, IOR, V/27/625/5, BL.

98. Ibid.

99. For a discussion of the British government's view of *ganja,* and its evolution over time, see Martin Booth, *Cannabis: A History* (London, 2005), esp. p. 135ff.

100. "Report on the Manufacturing and Smuggling of Ganja," by G. Rainy, ICS, Joint Magistrate on Special Duty, Calcutta, 1904, p. 22, IOR, V/27/625/5, BL.

101. Ibid., p. 10 (30).

102. Ibid., p. 11 (34).

103. Of course, this raises several issues of political economy: the role of bureaucracy, as well as individuals failing to obey inconvenient laws. This is nothing new, though fear of just such an eventuality is briefly discussed in Booth, *Cannabis.*

104. "Report on the Manufacturing and Smuggling of Ganja," by G. Rainy, ICS, Joint Magistrate on Special Duty, Calcutta, 1904, p. 22, IOR, V/27/625/5, BL.

105. This is, of course, the same argument that those who wanted to raise the judicial establishment's salaries made during the eighteenth century.

106. "Report on the Manufacturing and Smuggling of Ganja," by G. Rainy, ICS, Joint Magistrate on Special Duty, Calcutta, 1904, p. 13 (41), IOR, V/27/625/5, BL. This argument makes sense. Excise officers needed to earn more money than the cost of a bribe and the savings that would arise from evading the early payment of duty.

107. Again, see McKeown's *Melancholy Order.*

108. Ralph Blumenthal, "Three Guardsmen Charged with Human Smuggling," *New York Times,* 12 June 2007, p. A13.

109. Ibid.

110. Ibid.

111. Ralph Blumenthal, "Answers Sought in Smuggling Case," *New York Times,* 13 June 2007.

112. Ibid.

113. The press release can be found here: http://www.ice.gov/pi/news/newsreleases/articles/080218laredo.htm (accessed 1 August 2008). Oddly enough, at this writing, Private Torres remains in jail, unsentenced.

114. *Bahama Gazette,* 11–18 December 1784.

115. The lack of flour is also discussed in Governor Bruce to Dundas, 13 July 1793, TNA: PRO, CO 71/25. Dominica faced a flour shortage as a result of war between Britain and France. He was able to acquire more flour only by buying some illegally from the Americans. He then sought to open up the island over a three-month period for trade in essential foodstuffs, since the war was disturbing the island's usual trade patterns.

116. Ibid.

117. Another example of this kind of behavior—merchants not being able to sell their goods, which were part of a protected trade—is described in Richard Tyrrell to Philip Stephens, 30 June 1764, TNA: PRO, ADM 1/308. In this case, Tyrrell orders his troops ashore to seize the foreign-made goods that the French residents of Dominica were consuming; his actions were a direct result of the English merchants of Dominica complaining.

118. John Pringle, Cape Town, 29 June 1808, to William Ramsay, Secretary [docketed: received 12 December 1808], IOR, G/9/1/ff. 400–401, BL.

119. Cutting from the *Times of India* dated 15 February 1924, p. 6, IOR, R/2/620/83/ item 3, BL.

120. Ibid.

Chapter 5

1. This general point is discussed in Alan Karras, "Custom has the force of law: Local officials and contraband in the Bahamas and the Floridas, 1748–1779," *Florida Historical Quarterly*, esp. pp. 302–11. In the cases described there, the British government officials in the West Florida colony allowed their local populations to break British law with impunity, even as British naval officials off the coast urged greater legal compliance. The issue therefore became one of what action would most satisfy local residents, as opposed to what action would demonstrate the greatest degree of legal compliance.

2. As earlier indicated, there is a paucity of legal cases in the records, perhaps exacerbated by their tendency to be spread out across several archival groups, if records of them survive at all. J. R. McNeill in *Atlantic Empires* (Chapel Hill, 1985), p. 199, counts the number of seizures in Havana, suggesting that a large number of cases must not have been brought, given the small number of cases that he observed. A document that lists seizures in the Bahamas between 1804 and 1805 is buried in TNA: PRO, SC4/1, pp. 120–23 (the vast majority of the cases were condemned as legal prizes of war.) Another legal case that was in the courts is described in "Facts Opposed to Falsehood, in the Prize Cause Clarissa, Supply Simmonds, Master: Taken by the Daphne Letter of Marque, of Aldbrough, Thomas Abbott, Commander" (London, n.d., [1797?]). Finally, an extended case involving a British ship captured by the French is considered in the document group relating to the *Elisa Ann*, which spans the late eighteenth and nineteenth centuries, Fonds Ministériels, Série Géographique, MAR/43, CAOM.

3. Surveys among Britain's colonies were regularly issued and returned, and they can be found in almost every colony's set of colonial papers. For examples, see TNA: PRO,

CO5/1105, f. 278–82 (for New York) and CO 5/762, f. 397ff (for Massachusetts). There are similar claims in the French and Spanish archives that smuggling took place.

4. One could present an extended discourse on political economy here, but it would be easier to say that the idea of governmental sovereignty and legitimacy residing with the people was certainly present in Locke and Smith. For a discussion of evolving ideas of popular sovereignty, see Lee Ward, *Politics of Liberty in England and Revolutionary America* (Cambridge, 2004). For another recent discussion, see John A. Hall, *Coercion and Consent: Studies in the Modern State* (Cambridge, 1994).

5. Adam Smith, in *Theory of Moral Sentiments* (Oxford, 1976), recognizes that virtuous people must sometimes obey laws with which they disagree if the alternative is violence. See VI.ii.2.16–18. Smith seems opposed to those who would be arrogant in asserting that the perfection of policy can be instituted at once. He suggests that further discussion, or negotiation, is necessary for getting public policy right.

6. The American War for Independence brought the theoretical Lockean ideas of government by the consent of the governed and no taxation without representation into existence.

7. See *The Wealth of Nations* (London, 1776), Book V.II (p. 453). Also see, Book IV.III.1, where Smith claims that duties led to the rise of smuggling between France and Britain (p. 303). His correspondence is also concerned with the subject (p. 550).

8. See Jürgen Habermas, *Legitimation Crisis*, trans. Thomas McCarthy (London, 1976), pp. 98–100.

9. The most nuanced work on this subject can be found in Lauren A. Benton, *Law and Colonial Cultures* (Cambridge, 2002). Though the examples that Benton uses to illustrate her argument are not drawn from the same places and times that I have used to draw this argument, the analytical framework that she establishes works very well with the qualitative data that are used here.

10. One example of violence has already been discussed with the customs collector in Dominica being thrown overboard by a ship's crew. It is also possible to consider violence using another North American case, that of a Rhode Island mob's attack on the *Liberty*, a sloop in the service of the British revenue officers; the crowd attacked the property of the customs collectors, because they had thought this crew had gone too far in its efforts to enforce the revenue laws. A brief discussion of this case can be found in the *Records of the Colony of Rhode Island*, ed. John Russell Bartlett (Providence, 1861), v. 6, p. 593.

11. See Adam Smith, *The Wealth of Nations*, Book III. i (esp. pp. 227–30). Also see Hont and Ignatieff, "Needs and Justice in the *Wealth of Nations*," in *Wealth and Virtue: The Shaping of Political Economy in the Scottish Enlightenment*, ed. Istvan Hont and Michael Ignatieff (Cambridge, 1983).

12. Perhaps Dominica's Governor Orde is a good example here; his early and late careers were with the British navy. When he was not in naval service, and was administering the colony of Dominica, he came into conflict with the colonists over their smuggling behavior. When he was in naval service, he was able to dictate policy toward other governors, or at least not aid and abet them when they wanted help in smuggling. The conflict between West Florida's governor Montfort Browne and Admiral Rodney, in

Karras, "Custom Has the Force of Law," also provides an example of how imperial officials could have differing perspectives on the needs for legal enforcement.

13. For an illustration of the civilian and naval officers coming into conflict with each other in Jamaica, see the discussion about Admiral Holmes in chapter 4 of this book. Also see Karras, "Custom Has the Force of Law," pp. 292–98.

14. For an example of such a document, see the film *The Bank Job*, in which a London criminal records police bribes in a ledger. I have found no comparable documents in any of the archives in which I have searched, though these searches were not exhaustive. It remains possible that such a document could still be there.

15. See, for example, "Report to the House of Assembly of Jamaica in June 1766," TNA: PRO, BT 6/76. In this case, a naval officer was accused of receiving "illegal fees from Spaniards importing Bullion into this island [Jamaica]." The officer was accused of demanding such fees for a long period of time.

16. There is a much larger literature on corruption than on smuggling, perhaps because it is much easier to carry out research on corruption than on smuggling. Some examples of the kinds of work that have been done on corruption include: Michael Johnston, *Syndromes of Corruption* (Cambridge, 2005); Jean-Claude Wacquet, *Corruption: Ethics and Power in Florence, 1600–1770*, trans. Linda McCall (University Park, 1991); John Noonan, *Bribes* (Berkeley, 1984); and the annual reports produced by Transparency International. A brief discussion of historical corruption in the customs establishment can be found in G. D. Ramsay, "The Smugglers' Trade: A Neglected Aspect of Commercial Development," in *Transactions of the Royal Historical Society*, 5th series, v. 2 (1952): 131–57.

17. See the "Petition of Daniel and John Jenks, Merchants of Providence, against the Spaniards for the Illegal Capture of Their Vessel and Cargo and Barbarous Treatment of the Crew," transmitted to Lord Shelburne, 13 April 1768, TNA: PRO, CO 5/1299, pp. 33–44.

18. Interestingly enough, it was perfectly legal during the Seven Years' War for the Americans to trade with the Dutch at Suriname, but not with the neighboring French colony of Guyane. Of course, by this time, the war had already ended.

19. "Petition of Daniel and John Jenks," 13 April 1768, p. 32.

20. In this instance, the governor stood doubly to benefit. In the first place, he would get a share as part of the capturing crew (or informers) who brought the *Kinnicut* into port. In the second place, he would get another share of the proceeds as a government official. Therefore, his personal economic interest was in ensuring any conviction and condemnation stuck, rather than adhering to his country's legal requirements of just when and how capturing ships could be considered legal.

21. See the "Petition of Daniel and John Jenks," 13 April 1768, pp. 33–34. The 1763 Treaty of Paris ended the war; Article III required that all captured ships be restored "with all their crews and cargoes." This petition, in addition, cites the 25th article of the "Preliminary Articles of Peace."

22. See the "Petition of Daniel and John Jenks," 13 April 1768, p. 33. The record is generally silent on the remaining thirty-three crewmembers who had been captured.

23. Ibid., p. 34.

24. Note here that this is still from a British perspective. I am unsure if copies survive of the Spanish documents to which the British records refer; they were not enclosed in the British documents, as would normally have been the case. I have not been able to gain access to the Archives of the Indies.

25. "Petition of Daniel and John Jenks," 13 April 1768, p. 38. The case is also mentioned in the governor of Rhode Island's correspondence. See Joseph Sherwood to Governor Hopkins, 31 October 1763, in Rhode Island, *Correspondence of the Governors of Rhode Island, 1723–1775* (Rhode Island, 1903), p. 352.

26. Using a standard conversion rate, the offer appears to be around £75, which would hardly have risen to the claimed value of the contents of over £2,000.

27. "Petition of Daniel and John Jenks," 13 April 1768, p. 42.

28. Gil may have "appeared" to behave virtuously, taking his cue from Machiavelli, rather than from Adam Smith's more contemporary definition of virtue. See Machiavelli, *The Prince*, and Adam Smith, *Theory of Moral Sentiments*. In this he was in line with other Spanish officials in the Americas who responded, "I obey, but I do not comply."

29. There appear to have been around 2,100 whites on the island and about 18,000 slaves on the island by 1800. See http://www.trinidadandtobagonews.com/historical.html (accessed 15 June 2009) for a population estimate.

30. One illustration can be found in James Campbell to Archibald Campbell, 8 April 1784, TNA: PRO, CO 137/49, f. 139–40. An implied accusation can be found in "Extract of Report of Commissioners of West India Revenue Inquiry," 16 February 1815, TNA: PRO, CUST 34/175.

31. Salaries for the Grenada customs establishment can be found in TNA: PRO, CO 101/47, p. 57ff. Salaries were around £50 annually plus fees that were based on the actions taken; those from the Leeward Islands can be found in TNA: PRO, CO 152/94. Both salary and fees were generally lower in these islands.

32. See Nathaniel Weeks's indictment, 3 July 1794, TNA: PRO, CO 260/4, p. 226. It is, moreover, quite possible that this is the same Nathaniel Weeks from Barbados, who just a few years before was trying to get help from William Pitt to get him out of debtor's prison and get him an appointment as Barbados's sole auctioneer, from where he could also gain extra income. Nathaniel Weeks to William Pitt, 5 July 1788, TNA: PRO, CO 30/8/188, f. 20.

33. The salary structure, therefore, provided opportunities for corruption and for colonial officials to evade the law. See Patrick K. O'Brien, "The political economy of British taxation, 1660–1815," *Economic History Review* ser. 2, XLI (Feb. 1988): 1–32. O'Brien noted that "inefficiency and dishonesty created possibilities for fraud."

34. Lord Sydney to the Governors of Jamaica, Bahamas, the Leeward Islands, Bermuda, Barbados, Grenada, St. Vincent, and Dominica, 8 July 1785, TNA: PRO, CO 5/267. Also see R. Tyrrell to Philip Stephens, 30 June 1764, TNA: PRO, ADM 1/308.

35. Lord Sydney to the Governors of Jamaica, 8 July 1785.

36. Governor Hugh Elliott to Earl of Liverpool, 28 February 1810, TNA: PRO, CO 152/95.

37. Notice, dated 27 November 1809, TNA: PRO, CO 152/95.

38. It is perhaps even easier to understand in the case of Spanish army officers who were charged with preventing contraband and were, themselves, involved in a contraband trade within Mexico. See Christon I. Archer, *The Army in Bourbon Mexico, 1760–1810* (Albuquerque, 1977), pp. 219–20. The temptation was simply too great for many of these officials.

39. See Joseph Partridge to Admiral Tyrrell, 24 December 1763, TNA: PRO, CO 101/9, p. 198.

40. Recall that Dominica had changed hands from French to British control during the war; the change was codified in the 1763 Treaty of Paris.

41. See Joseph Partridge to Admiral Tyrrell, 24 December 1763, TNA: PRO, CO 101/9, p. 198.

42. Tyrrell to Partridge, 30 December 1763, TNA: PRO, CO 101/9, p. 200.

43. Ibid.

44. A copy of Admiral R. Tyrrell's Letter to Captain Partridge, 17 December 1763, TNA: PRO, ADM 1/308. Tyrrell cites the 6th Act of George II as he claims that the actions were illegal; he cites other acts—14 Charles II, c. 11 and 7th and 8th King William. Because the crimes took place at Dominica, which did not have an Admiralty Court, Admiral Tyrrell was doubtful that the case could be heard in Antigua, over whose court he had more influence. But he advised Partridge that his "doubt may be kept secret."

45. John Drew to John Laforey, 19 May 1792, TNA: PRO, ADM 1/315.

46. Ibid.

47. Ibid. A very brief general discussion of the Vice-Admiralty Court's not always strictly upholding the law's letter and intent can be found in Armytage, pp. 107–8. Citing chapter and verse was something that naval officers regularly did, and something that rarely impressed Vice-Admiralty Court judges. See, for example, "A Copy of Admiral R. Tyrrell's Letter to Captain Partridge," 17 December 1763, TNA: PRO, ADM 1/308.

48. For a general discussion of how British judges received their appointments in the Vice-Admiralty Courts across the colonies, see Carl Ubbelohde, *The Vice Admiralty Courts and the American Revolution* (Chapel Hill, 1960), pp. 6–12.

49. See "Extract of a Letter from New England," 3 May 1762. [Letter is docketed: Extract of a Letter from New England to Mr. Clarke, Collector of the Customs at Barbados, dated 3 May 1762, relating to the sale of French passports.] TNA: PRO, CO 117/2, p. 8.

50. Ibid.

51. Recall that France and Britain were still at war in May 1762.

52. Another example of the same kind of accusation is discussed in Governor Shirley's Declaration, published in the *Freeman's Journal or Dominica Gazette*, 8–12 November 1777, TNA: PRO, CO 71/7, p. 20.

53. See "Extract of a Letter from New England," 3 May 1762.

54. For another example of the kinds of problems that forged documents created, see Governor Shirley to Count Robert D'Argout (Martinique), 2 February 1777, TNA: PRO, CO 71/6, p. 94. In this instance, British privateers arrested a French ship that claimed to be coming from French territory, St. Pierre and Miquelon, but had actually been trading with

the rebellious colonies in North America. Though the ship was condemned for having a false passport on board, Governor Shirley prevented the crew of the capturing ship from gaining its share of the ship because France and Britain were still at peace in 1777. Indeed, Governor Shirley stopped unlicensed privateering at this stage of the war by refusing to license any privateers at all. See his decree on the subject, 14 March 1777, TNA: PRO, CO 71/6, p. 126.

55. Evan Neason to James Hume, 21 November 1800, Case, TNA: PRO, ADM 1/3868.

56. "Legal Opinion Signed by J. Mitford and W. Grant," 2 December 1800, TNA: PRO, ADM 1/3868.

57. Also see William Scott to Grenville, 23 September 1795, TNA: PRO, FO 95/373, f. 26, for a discussion of false passes, complicity, and when action could be taken against those who issued them. Scott, who was Britain's attorney general at the time, suggested that the false pass had to be knowingly issued, and not mistakenly issued to someone who lied in order to get access to the pass. If that was not the case, it would be more difficult to take any action against the pass holder.

58. The same could be said of R. T. Farquhar, the East India Company employee who earlier contemplated smuggling people out of China, into Prince of Wales Island, and then on to the Caribbean. See the discussion of this in chapter 3.

59. Inclosure in Dispatch Separate of the 16th June [1842], in China Miscellany, IOR, R/10/72, BL.

60. Ibid.

61. Ibid.

62. On the opium trade between India and China, see Carl A. Trocki, *Opium, Empire, and the Global Political Economy: A Study of the Modern Opium Trade 1750–1950* (London, 1999), pp. 49–52. On the growing prohibitions on opium importation and consumption, especially as a response to commercial disadvantage, see David Anthony Bello, *Opium and the Limits of Empire: Drug Prohibition in the Chinese Interior, 1729–1850* (Cambridge, MA, 2005). And, on the way in which Chinese officials engaged local populations and the regional governments, which might sometimes be considered corruption, see Bradly W. Reed, *Talons and Teeth* (Stanford, 2000), pp. 252–66.

63. "Letter from the Board of Directors to the Secret Committee," 19 April 1820, IOR, R/10/64, BL.

64. Ibid.

65. Bello, *Opium and the Limits of Empire*, briefly deals with the corruption in the Chinese enforcement regime, at least in the Han core, pp. 68–73. Subsequent pages deal with the corruption of enforcement officials in other parts of China.

66. Paris, 4 September 1885, Le Ministère to Monsieur Le General Commandant en Chef le corps expéditionnaire du Tonkin, Fonds Ministériels, Série Géographique, */Indo/AF/227, Dossier L22 (3), CAOM, Aix-en-Provence (translation mine).

67. An example of this is considered in chapter 1, when the village of Hoi An's illegal alcohol production was discussed.

68. Paris, 4 September 1885. Le Ministère to Monsieur Le General Commandant en Chef. A brief general discussion of the dialogue between French law and Vietnamese

law in the colonial period can be found in John Gillespie, *Transplanting Commercial Law Reform* (Aldershot, 2006), esp. ch. 2, which deals exclusively with Vietnam. This would have been one of those instances where the French desire for revenue increased their need to interact with the local population, further increasing resentment toward their legal regime.

69. This seems to have been the approach that the French took, at least initially. See Osborne, *The French Presence in Cochinchina and Cambodia: Rule and Response (1859–1905)* (Ithaca, 1969), esp. pp. 84–88. As such, it can be compared to the French legal regime in West Africa, as presented in Benton, *Law and Colonial Cultures*, esp. pp. 161–66 and 261–65.

70. See Eric Tagliacozzo, *Secret Trades, Porous Borders: Smuggling and States along a Southeast Asian Frontier, 1865–1915* (New Haven, 2005).

Conclusion

1. For Smith's discussion of fellow feeling, see chapter 3 as well as *Theory of Moral Sentiments* (Oxford, 1976), Book I, ch. 1.1.4–5, p. 10; this is also related to his extended discussion of virtue in Book VI.

2. Fair trade products are easily available in most urban areas in Europe, Australia, and North America. They are certainly available elsewhere as well, though perhaps not in as great a supply. It would be folly to think that they are not soon coming to the rest of the world; marketers have clearly seen this as a way to increase sales.

3. For one illustration of a historical version of this argument, see Robert Hardy, *Serious Cautions and Advice to All Concerned in Smuggling: Setting Forth the Mischiefs Attendant Upon That Traffic; Together with Some Exhortations to Patience and Contentment under the Difficulties and Trials of Life* (London, 1818).

4. For very brief summaries of such stories, see Pat Wingert, "Nannygate II: A women's backlash?" *Newsweek*, 15 February 1993; "The Zoe Baird solution," *Washington Post*, 4 May 1994, p. A24; and Paul Quinn-Judge, "Inman failed to pay taxes for domestic," *Boston Globe*, 21 December 1993, p. 1.

5. For example, see Spencer S. Hsu, "Immigration raid jars a small town; critics say employers should be targeted," *Washington Post*, 18 May 2008, p. A1. Also see Shmuel Herzfeld, "Dark meat," *New York Times*, 6 August 2008, p. 23. There are a variety of other articles on this story; most debate whether or not the employer can be held responsible for the self-smuggling of the employee, while others focus on whether or not the conditions of employment were ethically unacceptable to consumers of kosher products. As a result, the issues of *fair trade* are raised in a variety of ways within this single story.

6. A statement of this position can be found in Avi Shafran, "A missing ethic," *The Jerusalem Post*, 23 June 2008, p. 14. Shafran warns that until further facts have been gathered, condemnations of the Agriprocessors' employment practices are premature. An all clear, at least several months later, was provided by David Eliezrie, "It's kosher in Iowa," *Jerusalem Post*, 14 August 2008, p. 14.

7. See Thorstein Veblen, *The Portable Veblen*, ed. Max Lerner (New York, 1976), pp. 74–83, 140–51.

8. See, for example, Hardy, *Serious Cautions and Advice*, and John Wesley, *A Word to a Smuggler* (London, 1793). These are merely illustrative; there are many other examples.

9. See http://transcripts.cnn.com/TRANSCRIPTS/0809/18/sitroom.01.html (accessed 27 November 2008).

10. See http://elections.nytimes.com/2008/president/debates/transcripts/vice-presidential-debate.html (accessed 27 November 2008).

11. Thomas L. Friedman, "Palin's kind of patriotism," *New York Times*, 8 October 2008, p. 31. The Holmes quotation is reported as an anecdote in Felix Frankfurter, *Mr. Justice Holmes and the Supreme Court* (Cambridge, MA, 1961), p. 71. Friedman uses the verb "paying," while the reported anecdote reads "to pay."

—∽—

Selected Bibliography

Unpublished Primary Sources

Please note that these are record groups only; more specific references can be found in the notes in the book if quoted or, alternately, in the various finding aids (where they exist) in the relevant archives.

British Library, London

India Office Records
E: East India Company, General Correspondence, 1602–1859.
F: Board of Control Records, 1784–1858.
G: East India Company Factory Records, c. 1595–1858.
H: India Office Home Miscellaneous Series, c. 1600–1900.
I: Records Relating to Other Europeans in India, 1475–1824.
R/2: India: Crown Representative: Indian States Residencies Records c. 1789–1947.
R/10: China: Canton Factory Records 1623–1841.
V: India Office Records Official Publications Series c. 1760–1957.

Manuscripts Department
Add. MSS 13879: Reports on the State of the islands of Grenada, St. Vincents, Dominica, and Guadaloupe, 1763–1765; Papers respecting the plan of introducing Chinese settlers at Trinidad, 1805.
Add. MSS 73524: (A) Report by Thomas Irving, Inspector General of Imports and Exports, to the Commissioners of Customs, relating to complaints by British naval

officers, including Captain Horatio Nelson, concerning illegal trade, particu-larly with the United States, permitted by local officials in the West Indies [1787?].

Add. MSS 74055: Walpole Papers. Vol. cclxxxvi.

Egerton 1793: RELACIONES, etc., tocantes a la isla Española [Hispaniola, Haiti, or San Domingo], consisting of original despatches from the governors to the Kings of Spain and secretaries of state, with numerous other official letters and papers relating to the internal government of the island, its defence against the English, etc.; 1730–1810.

Stowe 865: "A sketch of the presant (sic) state of Smuggling"; circ. 1800. f. 38.

Cambridge University Library, Cambridge
Jardine-Matheson Papers

National Archives (Formerly Public Record Office), London
ADM 1: Admiralty, and Ministry of Defence, Navy Department: Correspondence and Papers.

ADM 7: Admiralty: Miscellanea.

BT 5: Board of Trade: Minutes.

BT 6: Board of Trade: Miscellanea.

CO 5: Board of Trade and Secretaries of State: America and West Indies, Original Correspondence.

CO 7: Colonial Office and Predecessors: Antigua and Montserrat, Original Cor-respondence.

CO 28: Colonial Office and Predecessors: Barbados, Original Correspondence.

CO 71: Colonial Office and Predecessors: Dominica, Original Correspondence.

CO 74: Colonial Office and Predecessors: Dominica, Sessional Papers.

CO 101: Colonial Office and Predecessors: Grenada, Original Correspondence.

CO 111: Colonial Office and Predecessors: British Guiana, formerly Berbice, Dem-erara, and Essequibo, Original Correspondence.

CO 117: Secretary of State: Havana, Original Correspondence.

CO 137: Colonial Office and Predecessors: Jamaica, Original Correspondence.

CO 138: Colonial Office and Predecessors: Jamaica, Entry Books.

CO 152: Colonial Office and Predecessors: Leeward Islands, Original Correspon-dence.

CO 166: Secretary of State for the Colonies and War and Colonial Department: Martinique, Original Correspondence, Entry Books and Shipping Returns.

CO 194: Colonial Office and Predecessors: Newfoundland Original Correspon-dence.

CO 195: Colonial Office and Predecessors: Newfoundland Entry Books.

CO 217: Colonial Office and Predecessors: Nova Scotia and Cape Breton Original Correspondence.

CO 245: War and Colonial Department and Predecessor: Santo Domingo Original Correspondence, etc.

CO 246: Board of Trade: St. Eustatius Original Correspondence.

CO 260: Colonial Office and Predecessors: St. Vincent Original Correspondence.

CO 266: Colonial Office: Seychelles: Acts.

CO 325: Colonial Office and Predecessors: General Miscellanea.

CUST 34: Board of Customs: Papers Relating to Plantations.

CUST 48: Excise Board and Secretariat: Entry Books of Correspondence with Treasury.

FO 95: Foreign Office and Predecessors: Political and Other Departments: Miscellanea, Series I.

PRO 30/29: Leveson-Gower, 1st Earl Granville and Predecessors and Successors: Papers.

SP 42: Secretaries of State: State Papers Naval.

SP 45: State Papers Office and Other Bodies: Various Administrative Records, Precedents and Proclamations.

SP 78: Secretaries of State: State Papers Foreign, France.

T 11: Treasury: Books of Out-letters to Board of Customs and Excise.

T 28: Treasury: Various Out-letter Books.

Centre des Archives d'Outre Mer, Aix-en-Provence

Fonds Ministériels, Série Géographique

Saint Lucia
C/10a/3
C/10c/4

Guadeloupe
*GUA/CORR/40

Indochina (Vietnam)
Indo/NF/856
*/Indo/AF/227
INDO/RSTNF//5451

Martinique
MAR//1
MAR/27
MAR//43
/*MAR/CORR/55

Department of Archives, Nassau, Bahamas
Bahama Gazette

Published Primary Sources

Alexander, Robert (Major-General). *Contraband Opium Traffic: The Disturbing Element in All Our Policy and Diplomatic Intercourse with China.* London, 1857.

Atwood, Thomas. *The History of the Island of Dominica.* London, 1791.

Bengal Excise Commission. *Report of the Commission Appointed by the Governor of Bengal to Enquire into the Excise of Country Spirit in Bengal,* 2 vols. Calcutta, 1883–1884.

"The Citizen's Procession, or the Smuggler's Success and the Patriot's Disappointment: Being an Excellent New Ballad on the Excise Bill." Song published in London, 1733.

Davis, John Francis. *The Chinese: A General Description of the Empire of China and Its Inhabitants.* London, 1836.

Dickinson, Samuel N. *The Pirates Own Book or Authentic Narratives of the Lives, Exploits, and Executions of the Most Celebrated Sea Robbers.* Portland, 1837.

Earnshaw, William. *A Digest of the Laws Relating to Shipping, Navigation, Commerce, and Revenue in the British Colonies.* London, 1818.

East India Company. *A Collection of Statutes Relating to the East India Company.* London, 1810.

East India Company. *An Exposition of the Political and Commercial Relations of the Government of Prince of Wales Island with the States on the East Coast of Sumatra from Diamond Point to Siack.* Prince of Wales Island, 1824.

Exquemelin, Alexander. *Buccaneers of America.* Translated by Alexis Brown. Mineola, NY, 2000.

Gregson, J. Gelson. *The Drink Traffic in India: Extracts from the Commission to Enquire into the Excise of Country Spirit in Bengal, 1883–84.* London, 1885.

Hardy Robert. *Serious Cautions and Advice to All Concerned in Smuggling: Setting Forth the Mischiefs Attendant Upon That Traffic; Together with Some Exhortations to Patience and Contentment under the Difficulties and Trials of Life.* London, 1818.

House of Lords. "First report from the committee appointed to enquire into the illicit practices used in defrauding the revenue." *Parliamentary Register,* vol. xiv. London, 1784.

Howe, John. *The Journal Kept by John Howe While He Was Employed as a British Spy; Also While He Was Engaged in the Smuggling Business.* Concord, NH, 1827.

James, G. P. R. *The Smuggler: A Tale.* Paris, 1845.

Lipscomb, George. *A Journey into Cornwall.* Warwick, 1799.

Mackay, James Aberigh. *From London to Lucknow.* London, 1860.

Madison, James. *An Examination of the British Doctrine Which Subjects to Capture a Neutral Trade Not Open in Time of Peace.* 2nd ed. London: reprinted for J. Johnson, 1806.

Odell, Thomas. *The Smugglers: A Comedy.* Dublin, 1729.

Percival, Robert. *An Account of the Cape of Good Hope.* London, 1804.

Pope, Charles. *A Practical Abridgement of the Customs and Excise Laws, Relative to the Import, Export, and Coasting Trade of Great Britain and Her Dependencies.* London, 1815.

Popham, Home (Sir). *A Description of Prince of Wales Island.* London, 1805.

Rattenbury, John. *Memoirs of a Smuggler, Compiled from His Diary and Journal: Containing the Principal Events in the Life of John Rattenbury, of Beer, Devonshire, Commonly Called the Rob Roy of the West.* London, 1839.

Reeve, John. *A History of Shipping and Navigation.* London, 1792.

Rutter, Owen. *The Pirate Wind: Tales of the Sea Robbers of Malaya.* London, 1930. Republished by Oxford University Press in 1986.

Ta Tsing Leu Lee: Being the Fundamental Laws, and a Selection from the Supplementary Statutes of the Penal Code of China. Translated by Sir George Thomas Staunton. London, 1810.

Wesley, John. *A Word to a Smuggler.* London, 1793.

Young, William (Sir). *The West India Common-Place Book.* London, 1807.

Secondary Sources

Antony, Robert J. *Like Froth Floating on the Sea: The World of Pirates and Seafarers in Late Imperial South China.* Berkeley, 2003.

Archer, Christon I. *The Army in Bourbon Mexico, 1760–1810.* Albuquerque, 1977.

Armytage, Frances. *The Free Port System in the British West Indies. A Study in Commercial Policy, 1766–1822.* London, 1953.

Barker, Rodney. *Political Legitimacy and the State.* Oxford, 1990.

Bayly, C. A. *Imperial Meridian: The British Empire and the World, 1780–1830.* London, 1989.

Beer, George Louis. *British Colonial Policy, 1754–1765.* New York, 1907.

Bello, David Anthony. *Opium and the Limits of Empire: Drug Prohibition in the Chinese Interior, 1729–1850.* Cambridge, MA, 2005.

Benton, Lauren A. *Law and Colonial Cultures: Legal Regimes in World History, 1400–1900.* Cambridge, 2002.

———. "Legal spaces of empire: Piracy and the origins of ocean regionalism." *Comparative Studies in Society and History* 47, no. 4 (2005): 700–24.

Bhagwati, Jagdish, ed. *Illegal Transactions in International Trade: Theory and Measurement*. Amsterdam, 1974.

Booth, Martin. *Cannabis: A History*. London, 2005.

Brewer, John. *The Sinews of Power: War, Money, and the English State, 1688–1783*. New York, 1989.

Bruce II, Colin, John S. Deyell, Nicholas Rhodes, and William F. Spengler. *The Standard Guide to South Asian Coins and Paper Money since 1556 AD*. Krause Publications, 1981.

Cawthorne, Nigel. *A History of Pirates: Blood and Thunder on the High Seas*. London, 2003.

Coker, Dale. "Smoking may not only be hazardous to your health, but also to world political stability: The European Union's fight against cigarette smuggling rings that benefit terrorism." *European Journal of Crime, Criminal Law and Criminal Justice* 11, no. 4 (2003): 350–76.

Cole, W. A. "Trends in eighteenth-century smuggling." *Economic History Review*, series 2, v. 10 (1957–1958): 395–410.

Cordingly, David. *Under the Black Flag: The Romance and the Reality of Life among the Pirates*. New York, 1995.

Daniels, William. "Specious spy: The narrative lives and lies of Mr. John Howe." *Eighteenth Century: Theory and Interpretation* 34, no. 3 (1993): 264–86.

Davis, Ralph. *The Rise of the Atlantic Economies*. Ithaca, 1973.

Dunn, Richard S. *Sugar and Slaves: The Rise of the Planter Class in the English West Indies, 1624–1713*. Chapel Hill, 1972.

Earle, Peter. *The Pirate Wars*. London, 2003.

Elliott, J. H. *Empires of the Atlantic World*. New Haven, 2006.

Farjeon, Joseph Jefferson. *The Compleat Smuggler: A Book about Smuggling in England, America and Elsewhere, Past and Present*. London, 1938.

Farooqi, Amar. *Smuggling as Subversion: Colonialism, Indian Merchants, and the Politics of Opium*. New Delhi, 1998.

Fisher, John R. "Mining and Imperial Trade in Eighteenth-Century Spanish America." In *Global Connections and Monetary History, 1470–1800*, edited by Dennis O. Flynn, Arturo Giráldez, and Richard Von Glahn, 123–32. Aldershot, 2003.

Flynn, Dennis O. *World Silver and Monetary History in the Sixteenth and Seventeenth Centuries*. Aldershot, 1996.

Folmer, Henri. "Contraband trade between Louisiana and New Mexico in the eighteenth century." *New Mexico Historical Review* 16 (1944): 249–73.

Frankfurter, Felix. *Mr. Justice Holmes and the Supreme Court*. Cambridge, MA, 1961.

Friedrichs, David O. "The legitimacy crisis in the United States: A conceptual analysis." *Social Problems* 27, no. 5 (1980): 540–55.

Geggus, David. "The Haitian Revolution." In *The Modern Caribbean*, edited by Franklin Knight and Colin Palmer, 21–50. Chapel Hill, 1989.

Gillespie, John. *Transplanting Commercial Law Reform: Developing a Rule of Law in Vietnam*. Aldershot, 2006.

Girault, Arthur. *Principes de colonization et de legislation coloniale*. Paris, 1929.

Gopte, Sripad. *Thrilling Seizures: Memoirs of a Customs Officer*. Mumbai, 1998.

Gould, Eliga. "Lines of Plunder or Crucible of Modernity? The Legal Geography of the English-Speaking Atlantic, 1660–1825." In *Seascapes: Maritime Histories, Littoral Cultures, and Transoceanic Exchanges*, edited by Jerry H. Bentley, Renate Bridenthal, and Kären Wigen, 105–20. Honolulu, 2007.

Grahn, Lance. *The Political Economy of Smuggling: Regional Informal Economies in Early Bourbon New Granada*. Boulder, 1997.

Greene, Jack P. *Negotiated Authorities: Essays in Colonial Political and Constitutional History*. Charlottesville, 1994.

Habermas, Jürgen. *Legitimation Crisis*. Translated by Thomas McCarthy. London, 1976.

Hall, John A. *Coercion and Consent: Studies in the Modern State*. Cambridge, 1994.

Hall, Neville A. T. *Slave Society in the Danish West Indies: St. Thomas, St. John, St. Croix*. Edited by B. W. Higman. Baltimore, 1992.

Helg, Aline. *Liberty and Equality in Caribbean Colombia, 1770–1835*. Chapel Hill, 2004.

Hont, Istvan, and Michael Ignatieff. "Needs and Justice in the *Wealth of Nations*: An Introductory Essay." In *Wealth and Virtue: The Shaping of Political Economy in the Scottish Enlightenment*, edited by Istvan Hont and Michael Ignatieff, 8–9. Cambridge, 1983.

Hughes, Martin. "Locke on taxation and suffrage." *History of Political Thought* 11 (1990): 423–42.

———. "Locke, taxation, and reform: A reply to Wood." *History of Political Thought* 12 (1992): 691–702.

Israel, Jonathan. *Dutch Primacy in World Trade, 1585–1740*. Oxford, 1989.

Jackson, Dudley. "Thomas Hobbes' Theory of Taxation." *Political Studies* 21, no. 2 (June 1973): 175–82.

Johnson, Derek, Erika Pladdet, and Mark Valencia. "Introduction: Research on Southeast Asian Piracy." In *Piracy in Southeast Asia: Status, Issues, and Responses*, edited by Derek Johnson and Mark Valencia, ix–xx. Singapore, 2005.

Kamen, Henry. *Empire: How Spain Became a World Power*. New York, 2003.

Johnston, Michael. *Syndromes of Corruption*. Cambridge, 2005.

Karras, Alan L. "Caribbean contraband, slave property, and the state, 1767–1792." *Pennsylvania History* 64, no. 5 (1997): 250–69.

———. "'Custom has the force of law': Local officials and contraband in the Bahamas and the Floridas, 1748–1779." *Florida Historical Quarterly* 80, no. 3 (2002): 281–311.

———. "Smuggling and Its Discontents." In *Interactions: Transregional Perspectives on World History*, edited by Jerry Bentley, Renate Bridenthal, and Anand Yang, 206–27. Honolulu, 2005.

———. "Transgressive Exchange: Circumventing Eighteenth-Century Atlantic Commercial Restrictions, or The Discount of Monte Christi." In *Seascapes: Maritime Histories, Littoral Cultures, and Transoceanic Exchanges*, edited by Jerry Bentley, Renate Bridenthal, and Kären Wigen, 121–33. Honolulu, 2007.

Kiple, Kenneth. *The Caribbean Slave: A Biological History*. Cambridge, 1984.

Langewiesche, William. *The Outlaw Sea: Chaos and Crime on the World's Oceans*. New York, 2004.

Lunsford, Virginia West. *Piracy and Privateering in the Golden Age Netherlands*. New York, 2005.

McClellan, William S. *Smuggling in the American Colonies at the Outbreak of the Revolution*. New York, 1912.

McNeill, John Robert. *Atlantic Empires of France and Spain: Louisbourg and Havana, 1700–1763*. Chapel Hill, 1985.

Mayo, John. *Commerce and Contraband on Mexico's West Coast in the Era of Barron, Forbes, and Co., 1821–1859*. New York, 2006.

Mills, James H., and Patricia Barton, eds. *Drugs and Empires: Essays in Modern Imperialism and Intoxication, c. 1500–c.1930*. New York, 2007.

Mintz, Sidney. *Sweetness and Power*. New York, 1985.

Moxham, Roy. *The Great Hedge of India*. New York, 2001.

Newton, Arthur Percival. *The European Nations in the West Indies, 1492–1688*. London, 1933.

Noonan, John. *Bribes*. Berkeley, 1984.

O'Brien, Patrick K. "The political economy of British taxation, 1660–1815." *Economic History Review* ser. 2, XLI (Feb. 1988): 1–32.

Organization for Economic Co-operation and Development. *The Economic Impact of Counterfeiting and Piracy*. OECD, 2008. E-book available online at: http://www.oecdbookshop.org/.

Osborne, Milton E. *The French Presence in Cochinchina and Cambodia: Rule and Response (1859–1905)*. Ithaca, 1969.

O'Shaughnessy, Andrew. *An Empire Divided: The American Revolution and the British Caribbean*. Philadelphia, 2000.

Pennell, C. R., ed. *Bandits at Sea*. New York, 2001.

Pérez-Mallaína, Pablo E. *Spain's Men of the Sea: Daily Life on the Indies Fleets in the Sixteenth Century*. Translated by Carla Rahn Phillips. Baltimore, 1998.

Phillips, Carla Rahn. "Trade in the Iberian Empires." In *The Rise of Merchant Empires: Long-Distance Trade in the Modern World: 1350–1750*, edited by James Tracy. Cambridge, 1990.

Pitts, Jennifer. *A Turn to Empire: The Rise of Imperial Liberalism in Britain and France*. Princeton, 2005.

Ramsay, G. D. "The smugglers' trade: A neglected aspect of commercial development." *Transactions of the Royal Historical Society*, 5th series, v. 2 (1952): 131–57.

Rediker, Marcus. *Between the Devil and the Deep Blue Sea: Merchant Seamen, Pirates, and the Anglo-American Maritime World*. Cambridge, 1987.

———. *Villains of All Nations*. Boston, 2004.

Reed, Bradly W. *Talons and Teeth: County Clerks and Runners in the Qing Dynasty*. Stanford, 2000.

Reid, John Phillip. *The Concept of Liberty in the Age of the American Revolution*. Chicago, 1988.

Ringrose, David. *Spain, Europe, and the Spanish Miracle, 1700–1900*. Cambridge, 1996.

Roberts, M. J. D. "The concept of luxury in British political economy: Adam Smith to Alfred Marshall." *History of the Human Science* 11, no. 1 (1998): 23–47.

Sheridan, Richard. *Doctors and Slaves: A Medical and Demographic History of Slavery in the British West Indies, 1680–1843*. Cambridge, 1985.

Simkin, C. G. F. "Indonesia's Unrecorded Trade." In *Illegal Transactions in International Trade: Theory and Measurement*, edited by Jagdish N. Bhagwati, 157–71. Amsterdam, 1974.

Slattery, Martin. *Key Ideas in Sociology*. Cheltenham, 2003.

Steensgaard, Niels. "The Growth and Composition of the Long-Distance Trade of England and the Dutch Republic before 1750." In *The Rise of Merchant Empires: Long-Distance Trade in the Early Modern World 1350–1750*, edited by James D. Tracy, 102–52. Cambridge, UK, 1993.

Stein, Robert Louis. *The French Sugar Business in the Eighteenth Century: An Old Regime Business*. Madison, 1979.

Tagliacozzo, Eric. *Secret Trades, Porous Borders: Smuggling and States along a Southeast Asian Frontier, 1865–1915*. New Haven, 2005.

Tarrade, Jean. *Le commerce colonial de la France à la fin de l'Ancien Régime. L'évolution du régime de «l'Exclusif» de 1763 à 1789*. Paris, 1972.

Thompson, Leonard. *A History of South Africa*. New Haven, 1995.

Tomich, Dale. *Slavery in the Circuit of Sugar: Martinique and the World Economy, 1830–1848*. Baltimore, 1990.

Towle, Dorothy, ed. *Records of the Vice Admiralty Court of Rhode Island, 1716–1752*. Washington, 1936.

Trocki, Carl. *Opium, Empire, and the Global Political Economy: A Study of the Asian Opium Trade, 1750–1950*. London, 1999.

———. *Prince of Pirates: The Temmengongs and the Development of Johor and Singapore, 1784–1885*. Singapore, 1979.

Turley, Hans. *Rum, Sodomy, and the Lash: Piracy, Sexuality, and Masculine Identity*. New York, 1999.

Tyler, John W. *Smugglers and Patriots*. Boston, 1986.

Ubbelohde, Carl. *The Vice Admiralty Courts and the American Revolution*. Chapel Hill, 1960.

Verril, A. Hyatt. *Smugglers and Smuggling*. New York, 1924.

Wacquet, Jean-Claude. *Corruption: Ethics and Power in Florence, 1600–1770*. Translated by Linda McCall. University Park, 1991.

Ward, Lee. *Politics of Liberty in England and Revolutionary America*. Cambridge, 2004.

Waugh, Mary. *Smuggling in Kent and Sussex, 1700–1840*. Newbary, 1985.

Wood, Ellen Meiksins. "Locke against democracy." *History of Political Thought* 12 (1992): 657–89.

Political Economy Texts

Bentham, Jeremy. "An Introduction to the Principles of Morals and Legislation." In *The Works of Jeremy Bentham*. New York, 1962.

Engels, Friedrich. "1891 Introduction on the 20th Anniversary of the Paris Commune," postscript to Karl Marx, "The Civil War in France." In *The Marx-Engels Reader*, 2nd ed., edited by Robert Tucker, 628. New York, 1978.

Locke, John. *Two Treatises of Government*. London, 1824.

Machiavelli. *The Prince*. Reprint. New York, 1908.

Marx, Karl. "The Communist Manifesto." In *The Marx-Engels Reader*, 2nd ed., edited by Robert Tucker. New York, 1978.

———. "Corruption at Elections," *New York Daily Tribune*, 4 September 1852.

———. "The German Ideology." In *The Marx-Engels Reader*, 2nd ed., edited by Robert Tucker. New York, 1978.

Mill, John Stuart. *Utilitarianism*, new edition. Boston, 1887.

Smith, Adam. *An Inquiry into the Nature and Causes of the Wealth of Nations*. London, 1776.

Raphael, D. D., and A. L. Macfie, eds. *Theory of Moral Sentiments*. Oxford, 1976.

Veblen, Thorstein. *Theory of the Leisure Class: An Economic Study of Institutions*. New York, 1927.

Weber, Max. "Bureaucracy." In *Max Weber: Essays in Sociology*, edited by Hans Gerth and C. Wright Mills, 204–9. Oxford, 1946.

News Sources

Agence France-Presse. "Pirates take crew of Spanish fishing boat to shore: Report," *Agence France-Presse*, 22 April 2008.

Alcoba, Natalie. "Counterfeit DVD lab busted: Four arrested: 20,000 pirated movies seized from two stores," *National Post* (Canada), 29 August 2006.

Associated Press. "Hostages on French ship freed, and six pirates and loot are seized," *New York Times*, 12 April 2008.

Baltic News Service. "More young, socially vulnerable Lithuanian girls become victims of human smuggling: Experts," *Baltic News Service*, 19 March 2008.

Barrera, Jorge. "Human smuggling has self-appointed protectors ready to shut down border," *Toronto Sun*, 5 April 2007.

Batt, Carolyn. "Bargain hunters sustain shady counterfeit world," *West Australian* (Perth), 16 June 2007.

Blumenthal, Ralph. "Answers sought in smuggling case," *New York Times*, 13 June 2007.

British Broadcasting Corporation. "Somali pirates seize French yacht," BBC Online, 4 April 2008. http://news.bbc.co.uk/1/hi/world/africa/7331290.stm.

British Broadcasting Corporation. "UN warns Bangladesh of terror financing through remittances," *BBC Monitoring South Asia*, 6 June 2007.

Burnett, John S. "Captain Kidd, human rights victim," *New York Times*, 20 April 2008.

Chandrasekaran, Rajiv. "'Crazy medicine' flows out of Burma—U.S. trains Thai unit to block methamphetamine traffic," *Washington Post*, 17 July 2001.

Chronicle Herald (Halifax, Canada). "Piracy's new wave: Big ransoms, technology give plunder on high seas new allure," 24 April 2008.

Dallas Morning News. "U.S.-Jamaica relations tense. Some offended by efforts to crack down on drug trafficking," 16 March 1999.

Deutsche Press-Agentur. "Report: Arrested 'Pirates of Ponant' related to Somali president," 5 May 2008.

Kennedy, Elizabeth A. "Two wives, a home, $90,000; they're the perks of being a pirate off Somalia," *Hamilton Spectator*, 24 April 2008.

Korea Times. "Seoul waging war against illegal copying," 6 April 1999.

Lichtblau, Eric. "Mukasey won't pursue charges in hiring inquiry," *New York Times*, 12 August 2008.

Lillkung, Johan, and Xan Rice. "Focus: Ocean Terror: They opened fire with machine guns and rockets," *Observer* (London), 27 April 2008.

Metzler, John J. "Ahoy! Pirates in Somalia's troubled waters," *China Post* (Taiwan), 3 May 2008.

Meyer, Josh. "FBI agent's 'wedding' is a bust for guests," *Los Angeles Times*, 23 August 2005.

Orange County Register. "Smuggled Cuban cigars a hot property," 17 November 1996.

Plain Dealer (Cleveland). "Taking aim at smoking: Singapore is cracking down," 30 July 1995.

Ross, K. "Navy island base is also drug smugglers' port of call," *Washington Post*, 1 November 1995, A3.

Seper, Jerry. "Fed-Mexico plan eases bank transfers; critics say aliens could abuse it," *Washington Times*, 6 December 2006, A1.

Smith, Tony. "Contraband is big business in Paraguay," *New York Times*, 10 June 2003, W1.

Sun-Sentinel (Florida). "High Times over for marijuana; Globalization plus U.S. efforts shrinking crop," 1 March 2001.

Tagliabue, John. "Suspected pirates arrive in Paris," *New York Times*, April 17 2008.

Tampa Tribune. "Smugglers flock to Hong Kong: City is a lucrative crossroads for the merchants of contraband," 9 December 1990.

Virginian-Pilot (Norfolk). "2660 pounds of marijuana seized after high seas chase," 27 May 1999.

Xinhua News Agency (Beijing). "South China police seize 2.6m-dollar worth of counterfeit products," 25 August 2007.

Index

About the Author

Alan L. Karras is senior lecturer in the International and Area Studies Teaching Program at the University of California, Berkeley. His teaching and research interests are in Caribbean, world, and Atlantic history, as well as in the relationship between political economy and international development. The author and editor of books and articles on Atlantic history, he currently serves on the editorial boards of the forthcoming *Cambridge Dictionary of World History*, as well as the multivolume *Cambridge History of the World*. He is also the current chair of the AP World History Test Development Committee.